Anonymous

Remarks on a Tour through the Different Countries of Europe, Asia, and Africa

Vol. II

Anonymous

Remarks on a Tour through the Different Countries of Europe, Asia, and Africa
Vol. II

ISBN/EAN: 9783744757072

Printed in Europe, USA, Canada, Australia, Japan

Cover: Foto ©Andreas Hilbeck / pixelio.de

More available books at **www.hansebooks.com**

The
Robert E. Gross
Collection

A Memorial to the Founder
of the

Lockheed Aircraft
Corporation

Business Administration Library
University of California
Los Angeles

THROUGH THE DIFFERENT COUNTRIES OF

EUROPE, ASIA, AND AFRICA;

GIVING

A particular DESCRIPTION of the CHARACTERS, CUSTOMS, MANNERS and LAWS of each, with their natural and mechanical PRODUCTIONS.

The POLITICAL and COMMERCIAL INTERESTS of the ENGLISH EAST INDIA COMPANY are accurately delineated:

TOGETHER

With a propofed and well digefted SYSTEM, both for the IMPROVEMENT and better GOVERNMENT of THEIR POSSESSIONS in that Quarter.

A Work of this Kind becomes particularly interefting to the Public, at a critical Moment, in which a late Governor of Bengal is called before the great Tribunal of the Britifh Parliament, to anfwer various Charges of Mifconduct, founded in a great Meafure on this authentic and inftructive Narrative.

IN TWO VOLUMES.

VOL. II.

DUBLIN:

PRINTED BY J. JONES, No. 39, COLLEGE-GREEN.

M,DCC,LXXXVI.

CONTENTS

OF THE

SECOND VOLUME.

LETTER XLIII.—Page 9.

THE objects which first strike a stranger on his arrival in India.—Siege of Tannah Fort, in the Island of Salsette.—Ragonaut-Row—Expedition in his favour.—Elephants.—The country of the Marrattas.—Asiatic Fumes and Perfumes.—The different nations in the Presidency of Bombay described.—The natives of the Malabar coast described—Their marriages.—Balladieres.—Parallel between the Peninsula of Hindostan and that of Italy.—Opinion of the Hindoos concerning Europeans.—Different customs, manners, and notions of the Hindoos.—A British officer marries a Gentoo woman of rank.

LETTER XLIV.—p. 50.

The wise policy of treating the natives of India with humanity and justice.—Of the tenure of territorial property in Hindostan.

LETTER XLV.—p. 55.

Various Institutions proposed for the settlement of affairs in British Hindostan.

LETTER XLVI.—p. 65.
A summary of the new Arrangements that are necessary to a wise and political establishment in Hindostan.

LETTER XLVII.—p. 73.
Hints for the improvement of the East India commerce.

LETTER XLVIII.—p. 77.
Improvement proposed in the collection of the company's revenues.—Strictures on the subordinate councils in India—on revenue chiefs and collectors—on contractors—on writers.—A new regulation proposed with regard to writers—and another with respect to keeping records, accounts, and books.—Characters of divers of the company's junior servants.

LETTER XLIX.—p. 83.
Observations on the Indian trade in the Arabian and Persian seas—on the free trade of the East Indies.

LETTER L.—p. 87.
Impolicy of allowing greater privileges to foreigners residing in India, than to British-born Subjects—Treachery and ingratitude of foreigners thus indulged.

LETTER LI.—p. 97.
Depopulation of the Carnatic.—The Nabob cruelly treated by the company's servants—Impolicy of such conduct.—Settlement of succession to the Nabobship.

LET-

CONTENTS.

LETTER LII.—p. 103.

A plan for new modelling the government and town of Calcutta.—Good policy of separating the seats of government from those of trade—Where to fix the seat of the British government in India.

LETTER LIII.—p. 110.

Strictures on the supreme court of judicature in Bengal.—Story of Nundocomar.

LETTER LIV.—p. 118.

The Governor General's favourites and partizans provided for at the expence of the Company.—Iniquitous contracts.—Distress of the Nabob of Oude.

LETTER LV.—p. 126.

A day, as it is commonly spent by an Englishman in Bengal.

LETTER LVI.—p. 129.

Character of Mr. H———gs — of Mr. F———s — of Sir E—e C———e.

LETTER LVII.—p. 136.

Rohilla war.

LETTER LVIII.—p. 150.

The country, government, manners, revenues, and military strength of the Marrattas.—The rise and progress of the Marratta war.

LETTER LIX.—p. 156.

The same subject continued.

CONTENTS.

LETTER LX.—p. 163.
The same subject continued.

LETTER LXI.—p. 170.
Moderation and good sense of the Marratta regency.

LETTER LXII.—p. 176.
March of an army from Bengal across the peninsula of Hindostan—its sufferings.—Negociation with Moodajee Boosla, Rajah of Berar.—Death and character of Mr. El—t. — Colonel Le—ie lingers in the capital of the country of diamonds.

LETTER LXIII.—p. 181.
Colonel L—ie dies, and is succeeded in the command of the army by Colonel G—rd. — Moodajee-Boosla offers his mediation for effecting a reconciliation between his countrymen and the English.

LETTER LXIV.—p. 184.
Progress of the detachment under Colonel G—rd.

LETTER LXV.—p. 187.
Interesting letter from the Rajah of Berar to the Governor General of Bengal.

LETTER LXVI.—p. 202.
Account of the state of English affairs in India in the beginning of 1780.—Predictions.

LETTER LXVII.—p. 207.
Voyage from Bengal to Madras.

LETTER LXVIII.—p. 211.
Arguments by which the native powers of India endeavour to excite a combination against the English.—Probability that such a combination is in fact formed.

LETTER LXIX.—p. 216.
Voyage from Madras to the Cape of Good Hope.

LETTER LXX.—p. 222.
Madagascar.

LETTER LXXI.—p. 229.
St. Helena.

LETTER LXXII.—p. 232.
Voyage from St. Helena to Dublin.—Island of Ascension.—The severities of three winters encountered in one year.—Irish hospitality and patriotism.—The noble prospects of the Irish nation.

APPENDIX [A].—p. 243.
Containing calculations to demonstrate the present declining state of the commerce and power of Holland.

APPENDIX [B].—p. 248.
Containing observations on Mr. Smith's "Nature and causes of the wealth of nations."

APPENDIX [C].—p. 268.
Containing reasonings in the secret department concerning the Governor General's proposition for a reply to a letter from Mr. Purling, Resident at the court of the Nabob of Oude.

EUROPE, ASIA, and AFRICA.

LETTER XLIII.

To J—— M——, Efq. London.

Calcutta, Nov. 10, 1779.

THE enclofed letter, which I have juft received from a gentleman who has been for feveral years in the military fervice of the Company, may perhaps afford you fome entertainment.

Bombay, 7th *October,* 1779.

— I HAD been informed that you were fent back, in a ftate of captivity to France. By what accident or what miracle did you effect your deliverance? Or is it true, that you were in the hands of the French? And if it is, why did you commit yourfelf to their cuftody? Explain, my friend, thefe myfteries. You are defirous to know how it fares with me, but feem to fuppofe that I am indifferent to your fortune. You write a very fhort letter to me, and in return you require " a very long one, containing my hiftory, and obfervations on this

this country and its inhabitants." If I comply with your requeft, remember that it is on condition of your doing me a like favour, by giving me a narrative of your life, from the moment of our feparation in America.

The means by which I obtained a commiffion in the Company's fervice, the obftacles I was forced to encounter before I accomplifhed it, with other circumftances, will furnifh matter for converfation when we meet. I fhall only mention, in general, that the channel through which I obtained my commiffion, was very different from that through which I expected it.—We fee but a fhort way into futurity: we mark out different walks of life in our own imaginations, and enter upon them with alacrity, in hopes of a profperous journey: but before we have advanced far in thefe paths, oppofing mountains obftruct our way, and we are ready to fink down into defpair. But no fooner do we recover from our aftonifhment, and look around us, than hard by the foot of that very mountain which interrupts our progrefs, we difcover fome opening, either to the right or left, through which we may purfue the journey of life, in paths not marked out by our own fancies, but by the hand of nature and Providence.

I landed in Bombay in January 1773. I need not mention to you, that on arriving in any town in India, a ftranger is ftruck with the complexions, drefs, and fubmiffive deportment of the natives. A nod, a hint from a perfon in the fervice of the Company, they confider as equal to the moft pofitive command. As to your fervants, they watch every movement of your body, and penetrate the rifing defires of your heart from your looks and geftures, gestures, ever eager to prevent your wants, and to anticipate your very wishes. The conveniency I derived from all this servile attendance, did not compensate for the uneasiness I felt, when I reflected on the dependent state of the people of Asia.

The circumstances which next drew my attention, was the extreme indolence of the inhabitants of this country. A person of condition is surrounded by multitudes of servants, each of whom has his particular department. He is dressed, carried about, and put to bed, like an infant. It was some time before I could reconcile my mind to the idea of being borne in a palanquin on men's shoulders: for, besides that I thought that an office unworthy the dignity of any human creature, it constantly recalled to my imagination the manner in which the dead are carried in our country. A bookseller, who is a Moor, very politely invited me to lie, whenever I pleased, in his shop, where I might hear all the news, and where there would be always a pillow at my service.

But the operation of climate soon conformed me to the customs of this country, which I found very natural and convenient. I had passed near a year in Bombay, in a manner, I must confess, that did by no means tend to prepare me for the hardships of war, when our company were called, along with others, to the siege of Tannah fort, in the island of Salsette. Our army consisted of seven hundred Europeans, and two thousand sepoys: the whole under the command of Brigadier General Gordon. A battery was opened against the strong fortress of Tannah, which played for some days without any effect. Captain Campbell, with other young officers, in a council of war, recommended an attack on Fort Tannah by storm. General Gordon, who was averse to this measure, and who insisted on first beating down the fort, or at least making a breach in the wall by the artillery, being limited by his instructions, was forced to yield to the importunities of those who advised an assault. Accordingly two hundred heymals † were appointed to fill up a part of the ditch which surrounded the wall of the fortress, with sand-bags; a work in which they were to be assisted by the soldiers; while one hundred and twenty grenadiers were to cover this dangerous operation. The heymals and a company of foot set out with their bags of sand, and presented a fair mark to the guns of the fort, which played on those miserable porters with dreadful success. The heymals, as soon as they heard the balls from the fort singing about their ears, and saw a few of their companions dropping by their sides, threw down their burthens and fled. This had a strange effect on our soldiers, who were stationed at some distance, and who were spectators of this scene; when they saw the poor heymals throwing down their bags and running, they burst into immoderate fits of laughter. The soldiers who were appointed to assist the heymals in carrying sand-bags, persevered in their perilous journey, but were most of them either killed or wounded: a few bags were thrown into the ditch, but they were only a drop in the bucket. As to the grenadiers who covered this manœuvre, out of one hundred and twenty, only fifty six remained fit for duty. Thus ended a scheme, the wildest that could be conceived.—Indeed it was concerted at a late hour, and in circumstances not the most favourable to cool reflection.

† The people who carry burdens.

In order to draw the attention of the fort from the main battery, one hundred Europeans with field pieces, and one hundred sepoys were stationed within three hundred yards of the fort, on the west side. The field-pieces were pointed through a milk-bush hedge. The Marattas made an attempt to attack our troops in flank, during the darkness of the night, but were easily repulsed. On this occasion, two Marattas, intoxicated with bang, (a decoction of seed somewhat like hemp seed) advanced within an hundred yards of our lines, under a heavy fire, brandishing their swords, and making signs, by waving with their hands, for their companions to follow them. They were both killed; and presently some horsemen had the courage to make an effort, but in vain, to carry off their dead bodies. This they think of great importance; for after the body is burned, the devil can have no longer any power over it.—The Maratta warriors wear, all of them, girdles or belts round their waists. The horsemen have a hook, which they instantly dart between those belts and the dead bodies of their friends, with the greatest dexterity, and therewith carry them off from the field of battle. That the two Marattas I have now mentioned were in liquor, was evident from the quantity of bang that flowed from their mouths after they were killed.

The Maratta horse had for some time been in the practice of crossing the channel, which divides the island of Salsette from the continent, and carrying off the treasure from the mint. With a view to check this practice, the general employed captain Ferrers's division, under the direction of engineer Nugent, to erect a one-gun battery near the mint. While the men were at work at this battery, centinels

nels were of course stationed at a certain post near the channel, to watch the motions of the enemy. One evening, about twilight, a buffalo happened to advance towards the centinel's station : the rustling made by the animal moving through shrubs, and the fallen leaves of trees, represented to the affrighted imagination of the centinel, the Marattas approaching in all the terrors of fire and slaughter. He instantly fired his musket, whereby an alarm was communicated to the party that were carrying on the one-gun battery. This party was that evening commanded by lieutenant S――s : on hearing the alarm the coolies† ran, guarding their heads with their baskets. The soldiers followed the example of the coolies, and lieutenant S――s arrived at the camp as soon as any cooly or soldier under his command.—" What!" said captain Ferrers, " Mr. S――s, I am astonished to see you flying."—" I followed," replied the lieutenant, " to bring the men back to their duty." This retreat before the buffalo afforded much pleasantry, and served to keep up the spirits of the men; who, I have observed, in all seasons of danger, are more than ordinarily disposed to what they call fun and laughter; the seriousness and solemnity of their situations, forming a very striking contrast with any ludicrous incident.

At length a mine being sprung under the fort, the walls of which had been shaken by our artillery, it fell with such a dreadful crash as I had never heard, though hundreds of cannon were daily roaring in my ears. It was then unanimously determined to take the fort by storm. The old Keelidaw, or Maratta governor, was instructed by some of

† Labourers who wrought at the battery.

our

our people who had deserted to the enemy, that the English would make their assault by night. And indeed, some of our rash officers advised that measure: but General Gordon set his face with more firmness against that project, than he had shewn in opposing the bags of sand. He determined to storm the fort in open day, when he would not be exposed to unseen dangers. The fort guns being now silenced, a breach was easily made in the wall, and the rubbish served to fill up the ditch. Our troops rushed into the fort, and a dreadful carnage ensued. The Keelidaw, who had commanded fort Tannah for thirty years, and who was resolved to defend it to the last extremity, had seized the person of the young prince, or Rajah of Salsette, a lad about ten years of age, who was inclined to hearken to terms of accommodation with the English, and confined him in the fort during the siege. The Keelidaw fled by the western gate, while the young prince, in the midst of thousands of his soldiers and subjects, attempted in vain to make his escape by that on the east side of the fort. The pressure and confusion of the distracted multitude shut the gate against themselves: and in that critical situation, like a flock of unresisting sheep driven together into a fold, they received the fire and the swords of the furious victors. It was some time before the general's orders to spare all who should throw down their arms, were obeyed: but at length the fury of our soldiers abated. Many of the Marattas were taken prisoners, and among the rest the young prince, and an artillery man of the name of Campbell, who had deserted from our army to the Marattas, and was a principal engineer in their service. This man was tried by a court martial,

martial, and sentenced to death. General Gordon seemed inclined to pardon him. Captain Campbell endeavoured to persuade the unfortunate wretch to say, that his name was Cameron. The man who had betrayed his country, maintained the point of honour when he was tampered with to deny his name:—" Come, life or death," said he, " I scorn to renounce my name—my name is not Cameron; my name, as well as your's, is Campbell."

The siege of Tannah fort was the first time of my being in actual service. When I marched out of Bombay, I felt not the least impression of terror—but fear crept upon me in proportion as I approached Salsette ; and I was struck with a momentary panic, the first time I heard the report of the guns of the fort. The first thing that cured me of my fears, was the power of sleep. By travelling, and above all by watching, I was so overcome by sleep, that within three hundred yards of Fort Tannah, in the midst of the roar of all its guns, and random shot flying around me, I laid me down on the ground and slept, sometimes startled by the noise that too forcibly assailed my ears, and often dreaming of bombs, cannon-balls, &c. In the course of eight days, my apprehensions of danger were considerably overcome. I was never so overpowered by fear, but that I would have obeyed the dictates of duty and honour. The day after Fort Tannah was taken, presented a shocking spectacle of swarms of crows, kites, and vultures, devouring the unburied bodies that lay in heaps towards the eastern gate, and in different places around the walls. In the midst of this scene of horror, the numerous sand bags that strewed the way of the heymals when they fled before the guns of the fort, recalled to

the

the soldiers minds some ludicrous ideas, which they indulged in preference to those sentiments of humanity and compassion which so many objects obtruded on their minds.

Having remained upwards of three years and an half in the island of Salsette, I returned to Bombay in 1777 : Here I saw the infamous Parricide Ragonaut Row, commonly called Ragoba; who, aspiring to the Maratta throne, had imbrued his hands in the blood of his nephe, entrusted to his care by his brother; who had seized at once the person of the young Maratta prince, and the reins of government. This man's name was Nana Row. He exercised the power of the sovereign, or Ram-Rajah, with the title of Paishwa ; and in this office it was the ambition of Ragoba to succeed him. But a general detestation of his crimes exalted a competitor to the regency, and chased the parricide from his country. He sought and found an asylum in Bombay, where his intrigues, and, as is said, the remains of his wealth which he found means to save when he fled from Poonah, gained him not only a favourable reception, but determined the Company's servants to make an effort to place him at the head of the administration of Poonah. This man, on review and field days, used to walk in the front of the lines, on which occasions he received the common military compliments. His person is tall and slender : his countenance rather austere, but expressive, and not without dignity. He is very superstitious.—I have been in company with Ragoba : he is artful, insinuating, and, as has appeared from his conduct, extremely deceitful. His turban and his arms were always loaded with jewels. He had a son with him in the island of

Bombay,

Bombay, a youth of about fourteen years of age, one of the handsomest figures I ever saw in any part of the world. Ragoba is excessively fond of this boy; he has frequently said, that if he could see his son in possession of the regency, to which he made pretensions himself, he would die in peace. Ragoba, besides troops of his own, sepoys, raised, when he was at Bombay, a company of Armenians, Portuguese, Germans, Danes, Dutch, English, &c. these he called his Christian company. He boasted much of their valour and discipline, and placed, or pretended to place, great confidence in their attachment to his person. This prince, or at least this pretender to sovereignty, had an infinite number of attendants. He lived in a magnificent stile, and was very munificent to the officers of his Christian company.

You have doubtless received at Calcutta, particular accounts of the strange and unsuccessful expedition that was undertaken, under the conduct of field deputies and military commanders, to conduct Ragonaut Row to Poonah. It is a strange humour that merchants have, of subjecting their generals to the controul of field-deputies—this is the jealous policy of the Dutch: this is the policy of the English East India Company. I suppose the artful and deceitful spirit of traffickers, is too cunning to entrust the command of their armies solely in the hands of military men. I have nothing to object to the wary policy of merchants; but if they cannot trust to the fidelity of military commanders, they should never intermeddle with military affairs; and instead of fighting for an extension of commerce, endeavour to improve their trade by the excellence and the cheapness of their
commodities.

commodities. Deliberation and execution cannot go hand in hand: the former muft precede the latter. It is abfurd to inveft men who are not foldiers, with powers incompatible with military fervice, and that fubordination and promptitude of action, which alone can infure fuccefs in any warlike enterprife.

We fet out, about four thoufand ftrong, on this expedition towards the end of 1778, with an enormous quantity of cattle and baggage, which was by no means neceffary to our fubfiftence, and which greatly retarded our progrefs. In Ragoba's divifion of the army, which marched in the van, were a number of huge elephants, with their caftles mounted on their backs, for the ufe of his wives and of his officers: on one of the largeft rode Ragoba himfelf. The elephants walk feemingly with a flow pace, but neverthelefs they make great progrefs, making very long fteps. This circumftance of the length of their fteps, accounts for that rolling motion, of which perfons mounted on their backs are fenfible, and which they compare to the motion of a fhip. Thefe animals, for the moft part, outwalked the infantry, and were generally advanced to a confiderable diftance before the reft of the army. Their enormous weight imprinted their footfteps fo deeply in the wet and foft foil, that our foldiers were incommoded by them in a diftreffing manner: for the holes that were made by their feet, being prefently filled up with water or mire, could not be readily diftinguifhed from the furrounding furface; into thefe pits our men frequently plunged, to the entertainment indeed of their companions, but their own fad moleftation. During the whole march, there was a never-ceafing volley

volley of curses poured forth on Ragoba's elephants.

The castles that are fixed on the backs of elephants by a kind of harness under their belly like the girth of a saddle, resemble tents: each of them will contain eight or ten persons. In the time of battle, these tents are thrown open, by pulling aside the curtains, at four different places, whence the people within throw darts, shoot arrows, or use musquetry. In the mean time, the creature that supports them rages with the fury of war, and is impatient to be in the midst of the enemy. If by chance the contending armies should close together, which seldom happens, the elephant, by means of a chain which he wields with his trunk, makes dreadful havock among his enemies with that weapon.—I have been told wonderful stories in this country, of the sagacity of this animal. I shall not take the present occasion of reciting them.—Do you recollect a tale of an elephant at Grand Cairo? A taylor was working on a ground floor with his window open, when an elephant laid his trunk on his board, amidst his work. The taylor pricked the elephant's trunk with his needle, whereupon the indignant animal went away, and swallowed an enormous quantity of water, which, after returning, he disgorged on the poor taylor. I believed this story when I was a boy; I discredited it when I grew older; and now I confess, I think it not in the least incredible. Thus a certain degree of experience leads to scepticism; but a greater disposes the mind to pay a due regard to testimony.—But I return to our expedition in favour of the murderer Ragoba. Our army was surrounded and defeated near Poonah. We were forced to cry out to the generous

generous Marattas, " we are only poor diftreffed merchants, do with us whatever you pleafe."† That nation did not take advantage of our miferable fituation, but only required that we fhould adhere to former treaties.

While we lay encamped on the fields of Tulicanoon, Ragonaut Row, who had a camp of his own feparate from ours, fent notice to Mr. C——c, the grand field deputy who controlled all matters in this glorious expedition, that he had difcovered three men in his camp, who, as he fufpected, had a defign on his life; he defired to know how he might be permitted to difpofe of them? Mr. C——c returned for anfwer, that he was at liberty to difpofe of them as he fhould think proper. Whereupon Ragoba punifhed one of thefe miferable creatures with the lofs of his eyes; another, with that of his tongue; and the third, he deprived of both his legs by amputation. The laft unhappy fufferer foon died through lofs of blood. The tyrant affigned fome fanciful reafons why one of thefe victims fhould be deprived of the power of fpeech; another, of that of walking; and a third, of the fenfe of fight.

I need not inform you, though you have not been a long time in India, that draughts and carriages in this country are performed, for the moft part, by bullocks. In war, the number of bullocks neceffary to an army is incredible. It frequently happened, that the balls of the enemy facrificed a buffalo, or a bullock. Such accidents, which were not unfrequent, were matter of joy to the men, who, while they carried off the carcafes, would ob-

† Mr. Farmer's fpeech to the Maratta chiefs.

ferve,

serve, with great wisdom, that it is a bad wind that blows good to nobody.

I have frequently wondered in what manner the Marattas, who inhabited a mountainous country, came to be such expert horsemen as they were generally allowed to be; and how they ever thought of maintaining such numbers of horse-troops: for, from all that I had read or heard, it was the inhabitants of plains, and not of hills, that brought into the field of battle any considerable number of cavalry. But this matter seemed no longer a mystery, after I became better acquainted with the geography of Hindostan. It is, perhaps, a singular appearance in the natural history of the world, that the vast ridge of mountains, which extending from Cape Comorin to the East India Company's northern Circars, separate the Coromandel coast from that of Malabar, do not gradually culminate, as they recede from the level of the ocean, but rise on either coast abruptly to their greatest height, and form a stupendous basis to a vast plain stretching along their tops. They do not, like all other ranges of hills, resemble the roof of a modern house, but form a terrace undoubtedly the noblest in the world. On this plain the Marattas breed and train up their horses. In the northern countries of Europe, the soil is commonly the more fertile the lower its situation; because in elevated situations, the air becomes too cold for vegetation. But in this climate, elevation of situation is rather favourable to every vegetable production; and the Maratta plains are as fruitful and verdant as any in the kingdom of Bengal.

When I say, that the chain of mountains that divide Hindostan, support an immense plain, I do

not

not mean to speak with geometrical exactness: beautiful eminences every where arise in it, but these bear no proportion to the level space which they diversify. These eminences are covered with mango and other trees, which are green all the year. I have often walked abroad in the morning in a Batta field, after the grain was cut down, in order to enjoy the fragrance of the newly-shorn herbs. The serenity of the sky, the genial warmth of the climate, the spicy odours that were diffused around me, afforded a pleasure unknown in the climates of Europe, and strongly disposed to a species of enjoyment still more voluptuous.

The luxury of fumes and perfumes, is no where cultivated but in Asia. Your smoakers of tobacco in Europe and America, are yet to be taught the art of smoaking. In India, the smoakers, (that is, every human creature) form a pipe of the leaves of a tree that is of an oleaginous and aromatic nature; and having mixed the tobacco with various spices, light this pipe, which burns at the same time with its contents, and contributes its share to give to the spirits the most agreeable and the most gentle elevation, which terminates in that state, which I know not how to describe so well as in the words of Horoce—" Dulci sopore languidæ." Some of those who refine on the art of smoaking, have a cocoa-nut shell placed on a stand or tripod, and half filled with water. At the surface of the water, a hole is bored, in which is inserted the end of a cryftal pipe, which is very long, and wreathed in many folds in the middle. An aperture is made in the upper end of the cocoa nut shell, in which is introduced the end of a funnel, which communicates with, or is rather a prolongation of, a pan or censer,

wherein

wherein the tobacco is burned with various aromatics. The fumes of this compound are cooled, and rendered extremely pleasant, by the water; with which I have been told they also mix some ingredients which I cannot describe.

I know not any place in the world, where there is a greater medley of different nations than there is in the presidency of Bombay; this region being conveniently situated, not only for commerce by sea with all maritime nations, but also for communication by land, with the Persian empire; part of which having been conquered by Timur-Beg, is now a part of the Mogul empire. Here, besides Europeans of all countries, you meet with Turks, Persians, Arabians, Armenians, a mixed race, the vilest of their species, descended from the Portuguese, and the outcasts from the Gentoo religion, &c. The Turks that resort to this place on account of trade, are like the rest of their countrymen, stately, grave, and reserved; and honest in their dealings, though merchants. The Persians are more gay, lively, and conversible: but I would trust less to their honesty in matters of trade, than I would to the saturnine Turks. The Arabians are all life and fire, and when they treat with you on any subject, will make you a fine oration in flowing numbers, and a musical cadence; but they are the most dishonest of all. The Armenians are generally handsome in their features, mild in their tempers, and in their nature kind and beneficent. They are a kind of Christians, and an honour to that sect. The Turks and Persians are, for the most part, stout-bodied men; but the Arabians are of a smaller stature, and slender: yet these last are accounted the best soldiers. I have

been

been a witness to their agility, and I am told their courage is equal to their activity. I saw a kind of war pantomime between three Persians and three Arabs: they naturally fought in pairs. The Persians kept their ground, and warded off the blows that were aimed at them in the best manner they could. The Arabians, on the contrary, when a stroke was aimed at them, sprung up in the air to an incredible height, and instantly made an attack on their antagonists. In the mean time both Persians and Arabs were singing, or rather muttering some sentences, which I did not understand. The Persians, I was told, were singing the exploits of Shah Nadir, and the Arabs were invoking the assistance of their prophet.

There is a race of mortals in this country, that they call Cafres, that are slaves to every other tribe. They have black woolly hair, and came originally from Cafraya, in the south promontory of Africa. I converse sometimes with these poor devils,—for I think that the opinions and sentiments of all men, however abject their state, deserve attention.—They tell me, that the Moor mans are better masters than the Christian mans. They are sensible of their inferiority in education, at least, if not in nature, to Moors, Hindoos, and Christians; and seem contented with their situation. They are so habituated to slavery, that I am persuaded they have lost all desire of freedom; and that they are happier in the service of a good master, who is their protector and their God, than they would be in a state of independence: in the same manner that a dog would leave the greatest abundance of food in a desert, and joyfully perform with his owner, even though he should sometimes beat him, a long and tedious

Vol. II.   C

tedious journey, subjected to the pain of hunger and of thirst.

The natives of this country are more slim, and generally of a shorter stature, than Europeans. It is a curious sight, to see their children running about naked, and speaking by the time they are half a year old. I was astonished to be saluted by these little figures, who, after giving me the salam, putting their hands to their foreheads, and bowing to the very ground, would ask for something: for all the children of the lower casts, are great beggars; and they go stark naked until they are nearly arrived at the age of puberty. Their mental faculties, as well as their bodily powers, arrive much sooner at maturity than those of Europeans do: yet, it is not true, as is commonly believed, that they sooner decay. Eastern luxury, which affects novelty only in the zenana, seeks for new wives, and soon discards the old: but many fine women are deserted in this manner; and in general, the women of thirty or forty in this country, are as well favoured as women of that age are in Europe.— A native of India, who considers a woman merely as an instrument of pleasure, would be infinitely surprised at the condescension of a good hale man of sixty, walking with a wife upwards of fifty, hanging on his arm.

Children are all taught reading and arithmetic in the open air. They learn to distinguish the letters, and the figures they use in their arithmetic (which, I have been told, is a kind of Algebra) by forming them with their own hands, either in the sand or on boards.

Marriages are contracted by boys and girls, and consummated as soon as they arrive at puberty;
that

that is, when the men are thirteen years of age, and the women nine or ten. The marriage ceremony is performed three times; once when the couple are mere infants; a second time, when the gentleman may be about eight or nine years old, and the lady five or six; and the third and laſt time, at the age I have already ſpecified. Between the firſt and ſecond marriage ceremonies, the young couple are allowed to ſee one another: they run about and play together as other children do; and knowing they are deſtined for each other, commonly conceive, even at that early period, a mutual affection. But after the ſecond time of marriage, they are ſeparated from each other; the bride, eſpecially if ſhe be a perſon of condition, being ſhut up in the women's apartment until the happy day of the third and laſt ceremony, when the prieſt ſprinkles on the bride and bridegroom abundance of rice, as an emblem of fruitfulneſs.

Theſe early contracts are undoubtedly well calculated to inſpire the parties with a mutual and laſting affection. The earlieſt part of life is in every country the happieſt; and every object is pleaſing that recalls to the imagination that bleſſed period. The ductile minds of the infant lovers are eaſily twined into one; and the happieſt time of their life is aſſociated with the ſweet remembrance of their early connection. It is not ſo with your brides and bridegrooms of thirty, forty, and fifty: they have had previous attachments; the beſt part of life is paſt before their union, perhaps before they ever ſaw each other.

I had once the honour to be preſent at the wedding of a Perſee of good condition. Of this I ſhall give you a minute deſcription. Important matters you will find in the writings of grave historians; what I shall relate, will be such trifling circumstances as are below the notice of those personages, but which, nevertheless, curiosity might wish to know.

In Hindostan, the expence of cloaths is almost nothing; and that of food, firing, and lodging, to the natives I mean, very trifling. The Hindoos are not addicted to any expensive vices, their passions and desires being gentle and moderate. Yet they are frugal and industrious, and as eager to amass riches as any of the natives of Europe. A Jew, a Dutchman, or a Scotch pedlar, is not more attentive to profit and loss. What is the reason of this? They are lovers of splendor and magnificence in every thing, but particularly in what relates to their women. It is in their harams, but especially on occasion of their marriages, that they pour forth the collected treasures of many industrious years.

The Persee at whose wedding I was a guest, many weeks before hand, sent invitations to his numerous friends and acquaintance, to assemble at the fixed time, at a spacious hall erected for the occasion in a beautiful field. It was the dry season, when the air was constantly mild and serene, and the whole vegetable world breathed a delightful fragrance. The hall was formed by bamboos, connected together, as is usual in that country, and covered with cloth. It was a medium between an house and a tent, being less solid than the former, but more substantial than the latter. Here the company assembled after the heat of the day was over, to the number of several hundred. After a rich repast, which was served with great regularity, we set out to meet the bride, messengers having arrived

rived at the hall, to announce her approach. The young Perfee was mounted on a camel richly caparifoned, himfelf adorned with a multitude of jewels, and highly perfumed. A number of flaves walked by the fide of the camel, holding an umbrella over the head of their mafter, while others fanned his face. The company had, as ufual, their palanquins. In the mean time we were entertained by a band of mufic, confifting of pipers, blowing very loud on the great pipe with their mouths, and playing with their fingers on another; trumpeters, and a kind of drummers, beating on what they call " tam tams." The mufic was dreadfully loud, but to my ear not very pleafant. There was only one tune; nor did I ever hear another during thefe fix years I have been in India. We arrived at a village, where we were met by the bride, attended by an infinite number of female acquaintance, her near male relations, and a crowd of fervants. A gentleman's carriage in the fervice of the Company was borrowed for the bride. It was an open phaeton, drawn in flow proceffion, by four beautiful Arabian horfes.—The practice of borrowing Englifh equipages, on matrimonial occafions, is very common; and they are always lent with great good humour.—As to the reft of the ladies, fome rode on camels, fome in carriages drawn by fpotted buffaloes and bullocks, whofe horns were tipt with filver, and their heads adorned with flowers bound by ribbands†. The bride was a tall and comely young creature; her long black hair falling down over her fhoulders,

---

† This tafte is not peculiar to the Eaft: In the civil wars of France, Cafimir, the prince palatine, carried off to Heidelberg, the plunder he had made in that kingdom, in waggons drawn by oxen, whofe horns were gilt with gold. This train was accompanied by a band of mufic.

and

and then turned up in wreaths, elegantly adorned with embroidered ribbands and precious stones. It was at that moment, when her husband gave her the salam, in a modest and respectful manner, and at a small distance, when she stood up in the phaeton, veiled only by an umbrella, that I (having had the honour of being near the bridegroom) had a full view of his lovely bride.

At the end of the village an accident happened, which interrupted, for a short time, the joy of the day, and filled the minds of hundreds with the most alarming apprehensions, The men, as well as the women, gave a loud shriek, and ran in a distracted manner, not knowing what they did: even the bride was for a moment deserted by those of her own religion and kindred, and left to the care of her European drivers. Some unlucky wag had, on purpose, set some swine adrift, that were kept by Portuguese families; and it was the fear of being touched by these odious and unclean animals, that turned, for a few minutes, a day of joy into a day of lamentation.—It is impossible to describe the horror that both Persees and Gentoos express at the sight of a sow. The very form of that animal is offensive to them, and makes them shudder. It appears as loathsome to them as a toad does to an European: and you may imagine the horror you would feel at the approach of a toad of the size of a sow.

The swine being beat back (in effecting which repulse, I may justly boast that I was myself the principal hero) we proceeded in joyful procession to the hall; which, spacious as it was, was now insufficient to contain our encreased numbers: wherefore, many of the company were seated on the

the graſſy plain, lamps being hung among ſhrubbery on poles of bamboos, fixed without much difficulty in the ſoft and deep ſoil. The hall, illuminated without and within, diſplayed on both ſides, various pictures of elephants and other animals, and alſo of men. The young Perſee's uncle, who ſhewed great attention to myſelf and the other Europeans, informed us, that the portraits we ſaw were Perſian emperors.—There is Koreſh, ſaid he; and after naming a number of other princes, he pointed to Nadir Scha, and Kerim Khan the preſent emperor.—I cannot think that they could, either from tradition, painting, or ſtatuary, have any accurate notion, if any at all, of the particular ſtature, ſhape, and countenance of Cyrus. The artiſt muſt have been guided merely by fancy.

Various kinds of refreſhments having been, after ſhort intervals, preſented to the company, we were at laſt entertained with a ball, which laſted all night. The ladies were placed by themſelves on one ſide of the hall, and the gentlemen by themſelves on the other. The women wore their veils; but theſe were not drawn ſo cloſely over the face, but that we could get a peep at their eyes and noſes. When their veils were drawn back, in order that they might enjoy the refreſhment of being fanned, we could diſcover their necks and their fine hair. Indeed, on occaſion of weddings, the veil, as I have been aſſured, fits more looſely on the ladies than at other times.—There was not the leaſt communication between the men and the women; no not a whiſper. The men converſed among themſelves; and the women obſerved a profound ſilence, looking ſtraight forward, with inexpreſſible ſweetneſs and modeſty.

But

But now appears a spectacle which commands silence among the gentlemen as well as the ladies, and draws the attention of every part of the hall. A company of strolling dancing girls from Surat, appeared on a platform raised about two feet above the floor. Violins were now added to the band of music, and presently the dance began. The balladieres (for that is the name by which the dancing girls are distinguished on this side of Hindostan) are dressed in the gaudiest manner that the luxuriant fancy of the East can conceive. Their long black hair falling over their shoulders in flowing ringlets, or braided and turned up, is loaded with precious stones, and ornamented with flowers. Their necklaces and bracelets are enriched in the same manner; even their nose jewels, which at first sight appear shocking to an European, have something pleasing, after custom has worn off the effect of prejudice, and by a certain symmetry, set off all the other ornaments. Nothing can equal the care they take to preserve their breasts, as the most striking mark of beauty. In order to prevent them from growing large or ill shaped, they enclose them in cases made of exceedingly light wood, which are joined together, and fastened with buckles of jewels behind. These cases are so smooth and pliant, that they give way to the various attitudes of the body without being flattened, and without the smallest injury to the delicacy of the skin. The outside of these cases is covered with a leaf of gold, and studded with diamonds. They take it off and put it on again with singular facility. This covering of the breast conceals not from the amorous eye, palpitations, heavings, various tender emotions, nor aught that can contribute to excite desire: while at

the

the same time it leaves something for the spectator to guess†. The balladieres imagine that they heighten the beauty of their complexion, and the impression of their countenances, by tracing black circles round their eyes, with a hair bodkin dipped in the powder of antimony. On their ankles, besides jewels, they wear bells, which they think have a good effect; but which, I confess, I do not admire.

The balladieres, it must be observed, are not all of the same rank or condition. It is only the higher ranks among them, who, I have been told, are consecrated to the use of the Bramins, the first cast in this superstitious country, that can afford to have a load of diamonds. Nor do the balladieres of this class stroll through the country. But if the common dancing girls are not usually adorned with diamonds, they have other precious stones and ornaments that strike with equal effect. In every other respect, their dress resembles that of the balladieres of the first rank.

When these girls dance, they do not hop, cut, and skip like our actresses in Europe; they never lift their feet high. Their dances would not be suffered, it must be owned, in an assembly of European ladies. They express, by mute action, all the raptures and extravagancies of the passion of love, when in deep retirement, concealed from every prying eye, the happy lovers, throwing aside all restraint, yield to the irresistable impulse of the most ardent desire of nature. Nor is mute action the whole of this scene. The girls accom-

† The D——ss of K——n, then Miss Ch——h, appeared, in the reign of the late king, in a dress which discovered so great a part of her charms, that his M—y said, she left nothing to guess.

pany

pany their wanton attitudes with lascivious songs, until, overcome by the power of imagination, and the strength of perfumes, their voices die away, and they become motionless; which is the conclusion of this opera, shall I call it, or pantomime?—The ball lasted until morning. Refreshments were presented to the company at short intervals during the night. The bride was accompanied to the house of her husband only by her nearest relations. The Hindoo ladies were in like manner taken care of by their husbands or kindred. As to the balladieres, they were escorted home by Europeans.

Moderate in every other respect, the Hindoos love to excess. I was curious to know what were the common topics of conversation among this people; for they are very sociable, meeting together frequently at each other's doors, and smoaking all day long. Upon enquiry, I found they were ever talking about their wives; their age, their qualities, their numbers, and their prospects of getting new ones, &c. &c. The barbarous nations in America talk of hunting and war; in England, the people talk on politics; in Scotland, on religion; in France, of the grand monarque; in Hindostan, the constant theme is love and marriage.—There are several analogies, which occur to my imagination at the moment of writing this, between the peninsula of Hindostan and that of Italy; which I shall commit to paper without examining them: The Hindoos were once a flourishing and powerful people; and their knowledge, religion, and laws, spread over many countries of Asia. In like manner, the knowledge, the religion, the laws of Rome, enlightened and blessed the nations of Europe: But, in process of time, the Roman empire was

was over-run, and broken into many independent ſtates, by irruptions of northern barbarians. Such was alſo the fate of the Hindoo empire, which was conquered and torn in pieces by the Mogul Tartars.—The ſtates of Italy at this day are only nominal ſovereignties, being dependent on the emperor, France, and Spain. In like manner, the princes of Hindoſtan have long depended on the protection of one or other of the powers of Europe.—The Italians of the preſent time, are an unwarlike, effeminate, and indolent people, delighting only in love and muſic. This is alſo exactly the character of the modern Hindoos. Other reſemblances might be traced between theſe nations: but on the ſubject of reſemblances, one is apt to grow fanciful; therefore I proceed not any further on this topic.

I have endeavoured, at various times, to lead the natives of this country into a free converſation on Europeans, and their tyranny; but I found them very reſerved. They often complained of the inſolence of the common ſoldiers. The warrior caſt in Europe, they ſay, muſt be very bad mans.— I once overheard a converſation between a Moor who kept a ſhop in Bombay and one of our corporals. The corporal aſked the price of ſome cheeſe; the Moor demanded a rupee (half a crown) a pound; the corporal, after a torrent of abuſive language mixed with threatenings, ſwore that he could purchaſe better cheeſe in Europe for four pence. "Well, maſter," ſaid the cheeſemonger, "I ſup-
"poſe very few in this country will hinder you
"from going to Europe to buy it."—This was the ſtrongeſt inſinuation of the diſlike in which Europeans are held here, that I ever heard from any of the natives of Hindoſtan.—I overheard at another
time,

time, a converfation between a Moor and one of our men, on the fubject of religion. After a good deal of difputation, in the courfe of which the Chriftian loft his temper, and poured forth the greateft curfes on Mahomet and all his followers; the difciple of the great prophet, with great calmnefs, replied, "Mafter, why do Chriftians curfe Mahomet? we Mahometans never curfe Jefus Chrift." The foldier, provoked beyond meafure at this comparifon, would certainly have knocked the Moor down, if his paffion had not found vent in a very feafonable † volley of imprecations.

In Bombay, where people of fo many different nations are collected together, there is a kind of language, which is compofed of the moft common words of the language of each nation, and of natural figns. Converfation is carried on, in a great meafure, by gefticulation, pointing, and various diftortions of countenance. This affords to a ftranger a ludicrous fpectacle. The Hindoos fpeak in a very loud tone of voice, infomuch that it appeared difagreeable to me, before cuftom, that reconciles us to every thing, rendered it familiar: Yet their voices are not harfh, but naturally fweet and melodious. The men fhave their heads, but all the women wear their hair long. The Jews and Perfees wear long beards: but the Gentoos, whofe religion prefcribes cleanlinefs of perfon, fhave their

---

† Although fwearing he a heinous fin, yet does it fometimes prevent other fins, if not more criminal, yet more grievous in their nature. A choleric gentleman in the north of England, the proprietor of a coal mine, ufed to curfe his colliers on occafions, which afforded him prefent relief from the diftracting fury of anger. But as he was a great ftammerer, he had not curfes always at command, in which cafe he was wont to beat them. Wherefore, when the poor colliers faw him ready to burft with rage and unable to fpeak, they would now and then fay, "O! if your honour could get up an oath or two,—"

heads,

heads, leaving only a small tuft on the crown, their beards, arm pits, &c. &c. The trade of a potter is an excellent one in this country; for the Gentoos never use the same pot or plate twice; that would be pollution; but as to plates, their place is generally supplied by the broad and tough leaves of banian trees; and they use no spoons. Ladles they have, made of the shell of the cocoa-nut, with which they serve up their rice, which is commonly mixed with ghee, (a kind of half-made butter, which they keep fresh in leather bottles for years, without salt) and spices, which make it a very savoury and nourishing food. This they eat, not with knives and forks, but with their fingers. The carnivorous appetites of Europeans shock them; for, the warrior cast excepted, the Gentoos eat no flesh meat. Of the English particularly, they say, shaking their heads, " Ah! Englishmans eat every thing, fight every thing."

Indeed, I must say, I was disgusted myself at the practice, so common among Europeans as well as Moors, of eating snakes and frogs. The frog of this country is as large as a chicken. It makes a loud croaking noise in the tanks and fields in the evenings. This supplies the place of the melody of European birds. The frogs are fed with great care after they are caught. I am told by the frog-eaters, that they are most delicate food. I take their word for it. The late General Wedderburne was so fond of frogs, that he kept a frog-catcher, as gentlemen in Europe keep fowlers.

There is a kind of serpents, capable of being tamed, which become domestics in families, and which undoubtedly have a sensibility to the charms of music; for, at the sound of a violin, they raise
their

their heads, and move their bodies in concord to
the mufical notes. When you ftroke their beautiful backs, they feem fenfible of the carefs, their
necks and heads moving more brifkly to the mufic, and their eyes fparkling with encreafed luftre.
It was, doubtlefs, in allufion to this fpecies of fer-
pents, that Solomon ftigmatized the deaf adder,
that "would not be charmed by the voice of the
charmer, fhould he charm ever fo wifely."

I have never yet, either by reading or converfation, obtained any fatisfactory account of the origin
of thofe ideas of pollution, and fingular antipathies
and abhorrences, which prove fo great torments to
the Hindoos. Different writers have attempted to
trace them back to the arts of priefts and politicians.
But prieftcraft and policy do not infpire mankind
with new defires and averfions. They may fanctify
and confirm prejudices already entertained; they
may improve and heighten them, and ufe them as
engines for their own purpofes; but I apprehend
they feldom ftudy to create them. However the
fuperftructure may be the effect of art, the foundation is laid in nature. It is political wifdom, perhaps †, to punifh unnatural crimes; and in fact
they are punifhed: but does the punifhment of
fuch crimes originate in views of policy? It is a
natural abhorrence that firft impels men to punifh
them, in the fame manner that a fchoolboy is urged by a natural antipathy to kill thofe odious rep-
tiles that offend his eye in his wandering excurfions
in woods and fields.—Europeans are confcious of
many antipathies, which it is impoffible to trace to

---

† The prefident Montefquieu is of opinion, that the punifhment of unnatural crimes is by no means neceffary. Nature will maintain her own rights
without the intervention of the magiftrate.

any

any fource of fuperftition or policy: the Afiatics, in like manner, have theirs; with this difference, that they are at once more violent and more numerous. There feems to be a greater irritability in their nerves; they are more forcibly ftruck by every object.

The manner of drinking among the Gentoos is remarkable. They religioufly avoid touching the veffel that contains the liquor with their lips, and pour it into their mouths, holding the bottle, or other veffel, at leaft at a foot's diftance. Their idea is, that they would be polluted by ftagnating water. They will drink from a pump, or of any running ftream, but not out of a pool.

The Hindoos preferve the Afiatic cuftom, of which we read in the bible, of threfhing out their corn by the treading of oxen. A pole is fixed in the ground, in the upper end of which is fet a pivot, which ferves as an axis for a wheel, or rather a wooden frame, which is turned round by the oxen, and which confines their fteps to the threfhing floor. The grain is fhaken from the hufks and the ftraw by the beating of their feet and legs. A couple of oxen will threfh two or three hundred bufhels of rice a day.—There have been various attempts in Europe to contrive a machine for threfhing corn, the moft laborious and expenfive operation in hufbandry. Might not our farmers for once take a hint from the Afiatics, and try the method of threfhing by means of oxen? The threfhing floor is formed by fpreading on the furface of a fpot of level ground, a pafte compofed of water, earth, and cow-dung. This operation is formed by the women.

There

There is not a more precious substance in the eyes of the Gentoos, than cow-dung. It is not perhaps known in Europe, that cow-dung is an infallible preservative against the destructive effects of all kinds of vermin. It is for this reason, that it is used in forming threshing floors. It is for the same reason, that it is used as plaister to the houses, which are overlaid with this substance, mixed with water and a very little earth, both without and within. A layer of this composition being spread on the walls, and sufficient time being allowed for it to dry, a second stratum is added, for the purpose of filling up any chinks that may be occasioned by excessive drought. A smooth and solid paste being thus formed, it is white-washed with a very fine and white lime made of oyster-shells. These white walls are variegated without as well as within, by the figures of different animals, especially elephants. But I have not yet fully described the great importance of cow-dung†. It is not only a necessary article both in agriculture and architecture, but also in religion. The pollution that is occasionally conveyed to their houses by the contact of Christians, the Gentoos wash away by the precious ointment of cow-dung. The pagodas in the island of Salsette, having been used by our soldiers as lodging-places, during the war with the Marattas, were considered as defiled, and were wholly abandoned until they had undergone a pu-

† When a Parsee prince and a Brahmin were lately in England, Mr. Burke, with his usual generosity and public spirit, recommended to the East India Company to provide a handsome lodging for them somewhere in the parish of St. James's. But had that gentleman been aware of the reverence in which cow-dung is held in India, he would not have fixed upon any part of the parish of St. James as a proper residence for those strangers, but on West-Smithfield.

rification

rification by cow-dung. It is not a little humiliating to a profeſſor of Chriſtianity, that he ſhould be conſidered by the antient and numerous ſect of the Gentoos, as a piece of animated ſubſtance infinitely more loathſome and odious, than the excrement of a buffalo or a bullock.

The Gentoos are undoubtedly groſs idolaters. What are the doctrines of their prieſts, I know not: they worſhip figures of men with elephants heads, and a variety of other images. The human figures which are the objects of their devotion, have many hands, and are enormouſly corpulent. They alſo worſhip different animals: I have ſeen in their temples live bullocks. It occurred to me, that theſe were going to be ſacrificed to their god or gods; but I was ſoon given to underſtand, that they were gods themſelves.

The Perſians of this country, as is generally known, pay divine adoration to fire, but not in a ſenſeleſs and idolatrous manner; for I have been aſſured by very reſpectable characters among the Perſees, that they worſhip fire only as an emblem of the Divinity, and as his chief agent in the ſyſtem of the univerſe.—They never extinguiſh fire. They will ſtand for hours by their lamps, putting up their prayers to God, with folded hands, and their eyes turned towards Heaven with great marks of devotion. They utter ejaculatory prayers all day long, and conſtantly mix buſineſs, and even common converſation with devotion.

They have a ſuperſtitious veneration for cocks and for dogs. They breed great numbers of dogs at their own houſes, and feed them regularly twice every day with rice and ghee. To all dogs, whether their own or not, they are very hoſpitable.

Whenever they see a dog, they presently call him and offer him food. If you walk abroad with a dog in any of the Persee villages, you presently hear "jo! jo!" at every turn; every body striving to be the first to entertain your dog. Dogs are also sacred in all the Turkish dominions†. The dogs on the island of Bombay, a few years ago, were many of them mad: whereupon an order was given by the governor, for killing all dogs without exception. This order being known, the Persees were greatly alarmed, met together, and entered into a solemn league and covenant in defence of their dogs, and threatened to protect their lives at the risque of their own. It was therefore thought prudent, not to insist on the execution of the decree that had been issued against those faithful and affectionate domestics.

How difficult it is to distinguish the sentiments of nature, from the prejudices of education! Most nations with whom we are acquainted, are careful to bury their dead, and consider it as a kind of mis-

† In the year 1743, the dogs at Constantinople had multiplied so exceedingly, that they became an intolerable burthen to the inhabitants, who were obliged to feed them, left being ravenous through hunger, they should attack their cattle or even their children, as has sometimes been the case. This became so serious a matter, that it was taken into consideration by the Divan. That council was in the greatest perplexity, not knowing how to redress the grievances complained of by the Constantinopolitans, consistently with the doctrines of their religion, which expressly prohibits its votaries from taking away the life of a dog. The Divan was at last relieved from their embarrassment by the ingenuity of a Grand Vizir. That minister observed, that though the holy prophet had forbidden all Mussulmen to kill a dog, he had not however forbidden them to transport them from one place to another. He therefore, with the hearty approbation of the Divan, banished the dogs of the Turkish capital to a desert island in the Archipelago. Several ships were loaded with those passengers, who were set on shore in great safety, and who soon died miserably of hunger. The crew of an English ship, that sailed in the night of the second day after the debarkation of the dogs, hard by the isle on which they were landed, were struck with horror at their yelling, the cause of which they learnt when they came to Constantinople.

fortune

fortune to their departed friends, if by any accident their inanimate bodies fhould not be honoured by a decent interment. That very circumftance, however, which, in the opinion of Homer, and thofe to whom he addreffed the Iliad, aggravated the hard fate of thofe heroes who fell, in the Trojan war, whofe unburied limbs were devoured by hungry dogs and ravenous vultures: that very circumftance, fo full of horror to a Grecian mind, would have appeared to a Perfian, matter of the greateft confolation. For the Perfees expofe the bodies of their dead to birds of prey, as the laft good office that friendfhip can perform to the deceafed. They erect for this purpofe fabrics about ten feet high, over the walls of which they fix an iron grate, whereon they place the dead. Thefe buildings are very like kilns, fave that they want roofs. Crows, kites, and vultures, quickly devour the flefh; and the bones, after being bleached for many years, are at laft pulverifed, and drop gradually into the cavity of the building, thus making way for new carcafes.

I prefer to this, the manner in which the Gentoos difpofe of their dead. They burn their bodies with fandal-wood and other aromatics. A very worthy gentleman of my acquaintance, Captain W—ft, is fo much delighted with this practice, that he has given orders, that his body, after he is dead, fhall be burnt after the Gentoo manner, with fandalwood.—The poor Faqueirs, of whom you have heard fo often, bury their dead within their very places of habitation, which are fometimes huts, and fometimes caverns. The felf-denied Faqueirs will lie whole days and nights, covered with duft, under banyan-trees, confeffing their fins, and expiating

piating them by repentance, supported only by a bottle of water and a little gram, or parched corn, not unlike peafe, but sweeter to the taste. This mendicant order of religious, often supply our patty-maurs † with provisions on their journies, when, avoided by the superstitious Gentoos as if they were some noxious animals, they would be in great danger of starving.

It is generally known, that the practice of inoculating for the small-pox is common in all Asiatic countries. But there is an art in Hindostan not yet known in Europe, by which the women effectually prevent any traces of the small-pox on the faces of their little ones. This preservative is composed of a salve made of certain Indian herbs, and a certain kind of oil, which they apply as soon as the pock begins to blacken. I am surprised that none of the Company's surgeons have ever enquired into the nature of this preparation: for, I presume, if they had, they would have discovered it; and the fact, that the Hindoos know how to save their skin from the ravages of the small-pox, is undoubted.

I shall, now I have got on the subject of Hindoo surgery, mention another operation of the chirurgical kind, which I am well assured is attended with the happiest effects. When any person happens to be bruised in any part of his body, by a fall, a blow, or otherwise, those who are nearest to him, presently strip off the greatest part of his cloaths, and with the palms of their hands gently rub the afflicted part, and proceeding from that spot, rub over, with greater force, the whole of the body.

† Messengers or posts.

This good office is generally performed by the women, who are indeed the furgeons and phyficians of this country, and who handle their patient with all the eafy addrefs of the moſt experienced member of the faculty in Europe.

Before the Hindoos rife from their beds, they ſtretch themſelves, darting out their legs and arms with a ſudden motion feveral times. Then they proceed to the doors of their houſes, where they fit in circles, in order to pick and to waſh their teeth. They fill their mouths repeatedly with water, and holding back their heads, make a croaking noiſe, like fo many frogs. Thofe of the Gentoo religion perform divers other ablutions in fecret.

Although the Hindoos are the meekeſt people on earth, yet they ſometimes quarrel with one another. Will you pleafe to attend to fo trifling a defcription as that of an Hindoo fcolding-match? Storms fometimes difplay the nature of the foil in which they fall.—The enraged parties begin with complaining of each other's injuſtice; and retail a great many moral and religious maxims, which, by that injuſtice, have been violated. They enumerate the acts of violence or of fraud, which their antagoniſts have committed againſt others, as well as themſelves. They undervalue each other's families:—" Your fiſter went on a certain day to fetch water from the well, and was embraced by a Chriſtian foldier:—" Your father dying young, your mother did not ſhave her head, but made her clopement with a fepoy:—" From a niggardly difpofition, you violated the laws of our holy religion, by making the fame earthen pot ferve you a whole week:"—And, " You got fo drunk, on one occafion, with brabtree toddy, that you not only touched

ed the veffel with your lips, but bit it with your teeth." In this manner they kept fcolding for fome hours: but now the contention becomes fiercer, and the opprobrious terms of Caffre and Hallachore are retorted with great fury. As the laft poffible infult, they pull off their fhoes, fpit in them, and throw them in each other's faces †. Anon, they proceed to action, tearing each other's hair, and fmiting each other, not with their fifts, but with the palms of their hands, like women or children. After they are fufficiently fatigued by this exercife, they part, each declaring that he would have inflicted on his adverfary more fevere marks of his vengeance, if he did not confider himfelf as much polluted by touching him, as he would be by coming in contact with a fow or a Chriftian.

I never beheld fo ftriking a proof of the influence of food on animal conftitutions, as in the battles of dogs in this country. The dogs of fuch of the natives as feed them only with rice and ghee, are no more a match for the dogs that are bred by the Englifh, though of the fame fpecies, than one of thefe would be a match for a lion. Our foldiers take great delight in promoting fights between their dogs and thofe of the Hindoos, which is very cruel entertainment.

It will not furprife one, who knows the refolution of Hindoo women in burning with their hufbands, to be told, that there is at prefent in Bombay, a woman, a native of Mangalore ‡, who, affuming

---

† It fhould be obferved, that when the Gentoos enter their temples, or the apartments of any great man, they pull off their fhoes, and leave them at the door. As appearing in your prefence without fhoes, is the greateft mark of refpect; fo to throw one's fhoes in his neighbour's face, is the very laft mark of contempt.

‡ Hyder Ally's capital.

the habit of a man, inlifted in a company of fepoys, in order to have a chance of meeting with her fweetheart, who had inlifted in our fervice in the laft war. After having been in one or two engagements, in which fhe difplayed a manly courage, fhe found her lover, to whom fhe made herfelf known, and became his wife. The wives of the heymals, as well as their hufbands, follow the employment of porters, and are kept to their labour as well as the men, by the terror of a fcourge. The conftancy and heroifm of this lady, has been rewarded by an appointment to the office of overfeer of the wives of the coolies. I have feen her with her rattan in her hand, acting in the capacity of a female ferjeant.

There have been frequent inftances of the daughters of Moors and Perfees marrying, with the confent of their parents, European gentlemen; but I do not know, that ever a European married a Gentoo. The ladies, I believe, might fometimes be prevailed on to facrifice religious prejudices to the power of all-conquering love, if they were not reftrained by the authority of their parents.—Lieutenant L—th, happening to walk abroad in the fuburbs of Bombay, perceived a very beautiful lady looking from a window of a houfe, one of the walls of which almoft touched that of the garden in which it was inclofed. He ftopped to contemplate her charms; which the lady perceiving, fhe inftantly withdrew into her apartments. Mr. L—th kept his ground, in hopes that his charmer would appear again at the window: nor were his hopes deceived; for, whether from curiofity, the vanity of being admired, or the dawn of a paffion fimilar to that which began to fire the lieutenant, fhe approached

proached the window again, but without looking out, as she had done before. Her admirer bowed respectfully, and endeavoured, by natural signs, to make her sensible of the tender emotions which she had inspired. How eloquent is nature, even unassisted by the power of speech! The lady seemed to understand his meaning: for after darting a short glance, which did not express either aversion or contempt, she shook her head, and forthwith retired. The lieutenant, who could think on nothing but this scene, repaired to the same spot next day, at the same hour. After waiting for some time, the lady happened again to look out at the window; and the same mute expression was renewed, which had passed the day before, but longer continued.

Although the East India Company make a considerable addition to the pay of such officers in their service as understand the language of the natives, Mr. L——th, who is by no means a lover of money, had never given himself the trouble of acquiring it: but now, to the surprise of all his acquaintance, he became a great student, and his only companion was "Richardson's Persian Dictionary." He soon acquired as much Persian as enabled him to express in words, what he endeavoured to communicate to his angel by the language of nature. In the mean time, his visits were regularly repeated, and the lady did not fail to give him audience. The time of meeting was changed from day to night, whose silent shade is favourable at once to the success of lovers, and the delicacy of their passion. Mr. L——th and his Gentoo fair one, now glowing with a mutual flame, exchanged the sentiments of their hearts, at a distance from
each

each other, like Pyramus and Thisbe, but met with a kinder fate: for the lady, having arrayed herself in her richer robes, adorned with all her jewels, at the hour of midnight threw herself, by means adapted to the delicacy of her frame, into the arms of her lover; thus bidding an eternal adieu to her father's house, her kindred, and religion. The father of this young woman made grievous complaints to the governor of Bombay, of the conduct of Mr. L—th, who, he affirmed, had degraded his daughter below the rank of an Hallachore, and brought an indelible disgrace on his family. In short, he prayed, that, as some reparation to the dignity of his house, lieutenant L—th might be dismissed from the Company's service.

The governor replied, that if Mr. L—th had used either fraud or violence, in order to carry off his daughter, not only would the Company have discarded him from their service, but the British laws would have inflicted severer punishments: but since it appeared, that what had happened was with the lady's consent, it was incompetent to him or the British government, to stigmatize, in any shape, the lieutenant's conduct.—Mrs. L—th has for ever lost the regard of her family; but that circumstance only serves to endear her the more to the heart of an affectionate and generous husband.——

On looking back to the date when I began to write this letter, I find it has furnished employment for my leisure hours for five days.—I might give you a great deal more of this bagatelle, but the pattymaur sets out for Calcutta to-morrow.

I am, &c. &c.

LETTER

LETTER XLIV.

To J—— M——, Efq; London.

Calcutta, Nov. 10, 1779.

IF the British nation would derive all the advantages from the soil of Hindoftan, and the ingenuity of the natives, which they are capable of yielding, they muft refolve to treat the Hindoos, not as flaves or inferior animals, but as fellow-men, entitled to protection, liberty, and juftice. Thefe alone infpire thofe habits of induftry, which are the life of commerce. The mifery and defolation which have been occafioned by tyranny and injuftice, will at laft open the eyes of oppreffors, and expofe to their view the folly as well as the enormity of their crimes. But it is not lefs difgraceful to the Englifh, than it is unfortunate for the Hindoos, that Juftice, if fhe make her appearance at all, will come too late; and that liberty will not be the voluntary offering of generofity, but a tribute to felf-intereft, taught by long experience the pernicious confequences of oppreffion, even to oppreffors.

A people enjoying, like the Englifh, the bleffings of liberty themfelves, fhould be the laft in the world to impofe flavery on others: but the hiftory of the world fufficiently proves, that the freeft governments have been the fevereft mafters to their dependents; fo little influence in public as well as in private conduct, has that juft maxim in morality, " To do unto others whatever, in their fituation, we fhould think reafonable in them to do to us."

But,

But, as in private life, experience evinces, that virtue leads to happiness, and vice to misery; so, it is to be hoped, will the ruinous consequences of oppression, teach the governors of kingdoms the wisdom of political justice. The time, I hope, is not far off, when the natives of India, who have so long languished under slavery, will have reason to assume for their motto,

" Libertas, quæ sera tamen respexit inertem."

The most important point, which the legislature of Britain will have to settle in Hindostan, when they shall come to make new arrangements in that country, will be, the tenure of territorial property.—Give me leave to propose to your consideration, and through you, Sir, to the consideration of such of our friends as are particularly interested in the affairs of India, the following thoughts on this subject.

All nations who acknowledge subjection to a supreme head, whether this submission hath been acquired by conquest, or yielded by compact, have committed a virtual property of the whole soil of the country in reversion, to the sovereign power; to the end, that this ideal vestiture may render the actual possessor amenable to the established laws of the community, and the property itself feudatory, and chargeable with such burdens and taxes, being equitably apportioned, as the public exigencies may require: but in every other view, the real property of the soil is vested in the possessor, according to the particular conditions on which the lands were originally conceded to the individual members of the community, or declared in formal compacts between the state and its subjects. No consideration

tion whatever should be suffered, directly or indirectly, to invade the fundamental laws of the constitution, provided that the preservation of the constitution itself does not render certain alterations in these laws indispensably necessary. I say, directly or indirectly; because innovations acquiesced in, are converted into precedents, and precedents established in laws. The evils arising thence cannot be remedied without violence; and the restoration of good order must necessarily be preceded by anarchy and bloodshed; for the sovereign power gradually assumes greater prerogatives than originally belonged to it, and, its invasions and influence reciprocally stimulating and strengthening each other, tyranny seizes the reins of government, and rules with a rod of iron, until the people, reduced to extremities, are forced, in self-defence, to assert their constitutional and natural rights, thus blended together, which is only to be effected by the death of the tyrant.

The Hindoo constitution, on principles of the soundest policy, continued unaltered even after the Mogul conquest, and during the several successive stages of that government in Hindostan. But the Mogul empire was shaken into pieces by the bold ambition of subordinate princes, who at once departed from their allegiance to the emperor of Delhi, and exercised on their subjects the most wanton cruelties; to which cruelties their own lives, for the most part, fell sacrifices.

Miraculous successes in the field, and the gratitude of the emperor, lavished without bounds or measure, have raised the English East India Company to the dominion of a vast extent of territory, and over twice the number of inhabitants contained

in

in Great Britain, as well as the high prerogative of being arbiters of all Hindoſtan. But inſtead of improving theſe advantages, they have in reality converted them into diſadvantages : for, intoxicated by a flow of proſperity that they neither deſerved nor were able to bear, they abandoned themſelves to the government of paſſion ; ſubverted the original conſtitution of the country ſubjected to their power; and perplexed it with a compoſition of law and form, as little known to the Britiſh conſtitution, as that into which they have violently incorporated it. The immediate effect of ſo fatal an error, was the depopulation of thoſe flouriſhing countries whence they drew their greateſt wealth. Several fertile tracts were laid wholly waſte ; agriculture, manufactures, induſtry of every kind, were every where diſcountenanced ; and oppreſſion, in all its dreadful forms, not only connived at, but encouraged. Inceſſant acts of public injuſtice and private outrage perpetrated with impunity, have excited all the powers of India into a confederacy againſt Engliſh uſurpations, treachery, and breach of public faith ; and taught the natives the art of war; and the uſe of arms.—Arms not inferior to thoſe of Europe, are now manufactured in the very heart of Hindoſtan.

I obſerved, in a former letter, that many of the Hindoo tribes, moſt or all the deſcendants of Moors, and the numerous emigrants from Perſia and its borders, are brave and cool in battle. Having the ſame weapons, and being under equal diſcipline, they may, doubtleſs, become a match for their countrymen, ſerving in the army of the Company. The want of European auſpices may be

compenſated

compensated by numbers, perhaps by the invincible spirit of liberty and genuine patriotism. These are serious objects of consideration. An inattention to these things has already produced the most alarming disadvantages in trade, and disappointments in revenue, and seems, indeed, to threaten the extinction of the present East India Company.

In order to remedy these evils, and avert that danger, justice and sound policy should go hand in hand, to convince the people of India, that however corrupt the practice of British emigrants, the regular administration of justice at home was still maintained in its full vigour;—that however the streams may have contracted pollution in the length of their course, the British fountain was yet pure; and that the abuses in India sprung from the concealed evil measures of the Company's principal servants, an unwarranted misapplication of power, consequent misrepresentations of facts and circumstances, and distance of place, which, until now, had shut up the avenues to truth.

A gentleman of the most distinguished abilities, and a trusty servant to the East India Company, has devoted as much of his time and study, as the avocations of time would allow, to a thorough investigation of Hindostan tenures, and of the most effectual means of restoring to that paradise of nations its former splendor. The result of his honest and diligent researches he communicated to the Court of Directors in that easy, fluent, and convincing strain, which characterises him as a writer as well as a speaker; for which, I have been informed, he received their warmest acknowledgments. It is said, that he modestly reprobated the measures heretofore pursued, in general terms,

some

some of which, however, were pretty pointed; and that his own plans are founded on principles of justice and benevolence towards the natives, whose rights and political constitution he wishes to preserve inviolate, gently tempered with such innovations only as tend to protect liberty and property, and to procure a fixed revenue to the British nation, and a beneficial trade to the India Company. After so able a man has reduced his observations on the present state of India to a system for its future settlement, it may appear presumptuous in one of inferior abilities and less knowledge, to enter upon the same subject. But as the paper which that gentleman submitted to his employers, and through them to government, has not yet transpired, I solicit his permission to make a few short observations on the same matters which he has treated; at the same time that I confess the flattering pleasure I should feel, if my ideas should be found in general to coincide with those of Mr. Francis.—In the mean time, I am, &c.

LETTER XLV.

To J—— M——, Esq; London.

Calcutta, November 21, 1779.

EVEN Mr. Hastings, while his judgment was directed by his innate feelings, and before the noblest passions of the human heart were superseded by principles of a less honourable nature, favoured, in the strongest terms, the idea of indulging the natives of Hindostan in the enjoyment of their original constitution, as essential to the
security

security and prosperity of the Company's possessions and trade. This system he recommended by the most convincing arguments, in a letter to the Court of Directors, dated the 24th of March 1774, accompanying the translation of the two first sections of the Gentoo laws†. If

† Abstract from Mr. Hastings's Letter.

"From the labours of a people, however intelligent, whose studies have been confined to the narrow circle of their own religion, and the decrees founded upon its superstitions; and whose discussions, in the search of truth, have wanted that lively aid, which it can only derive from a free exertion of the understanding, and an opposition of opinions; a perfect system of jurisprudence is not to be expected.

"Yet if it shall be found to contain nothing hurtful to the authority of government, or to the interests of society, and is consonant to the manners, ideas, and inclinations, of the people for whose use it is intended, I presume, that on these grounds, it will be preferable to any which even a superior wisdom could constitute in its room.

"It is from this conviction, and from an apprehension of the effects which a contrary opinion might produce, that I have been so earnest in transmitting these sheets for your information; as they will afford, at least, a proof that the people of this country do not require our aid to furnish them with a rule for their conduct, or a standard for their property.

"I have ventured to say thus much on a subject which may possibly appear to have been irregularly obtruded upon your notice, because reports have a long time prevailed, and been communicated to us by the belt of private authority, of an intention to frame new courts and forms of judicature for the inhabitants of these provinces. Whatever foundation these reports may have in truth, or whatever may be the extent or principles of the jurisdiction herein supposed, I cannot but express my hope, that nothing of this kind may be finally concluded, without an opportunity being given to the members of your administration, to communicate such ideas as their experience may suggest to them; and this I conceive to be my duty, from the consideration of the hurtful effects which an unadvised system might possibly produce, to the quiet of the people, and the security of your revenue."

In the Sections of Gentoo laws referred to by Mr. Hastings, are some passages which do ample justice to the sentiments and opinions which he expressed and recommended.—Under the head of "security for debts," the principles are literally conformable to the common law of England, and strictly consonant to equity in Sect. III. par. 123 and 4.—So par. 5. 6. 7. 8. 9. 10. 11. 13. 14. are novel to the English constitution, but remarkably just and equitable: the 15th par. distinguishes the very wise spirit of their constitutions: viz.

" A man shall not accept for security, a person totally unknown to him;
" his own master; an enemy; a prisoner; a very old man; a partner
" living in the same family; a friend, or a pupil."—

Section IV. On discharging debts to whomsoever due, par. 21. it ordains that,

" If a man dies, having incurred debts by gambling or by drinking spiri-
" tuous liquors, his son shall not discharge them." It goes on, saying—

" This

If this mild and wife fyftem fhall be adopted, it will be neceffary, in the firft place, to fix a conftitutional head or fovereignty over Hindoftan, as I have obferved in a former letter. Without this, no line of polity can be purfued, either with propriety or fecurity.

The feveral branches which compofe the landed revenue, fhould be reduced to a plain fyftem, and made intelligible even to the fimpleft capacity. The Company's Afiatic concerns fhould be freed from that confufion in which they are involved, and comprifed under the feveral heads in'o which the rents of each diftrict are confolidated.—The forms of keeping the accounts, which are unintelligible to any but the natives, fhould be made diftinct and fimple. Much confufion arifes in Hindoftan, from the computation of time from two different æras, each of which is irreconcileable to the Chriftian. One common æra fhould be fixed; and in this matter, the prejudices of the natives fhould be humoured: but it is neceffary that the periods and denominations made ufe of, fhould be fully comprehended by the Englifh, and incorporated, for this purpofe, into the Englifh language. The technical terms, which are ftudioufly preferved in the country language, in all the Englifh writings fhould be changed for words of the fame import, as far as that is poffible, in Englifh. The complex divifion of land, and the intricate modes of

---

" This law is calculated for thofe perfons in whom gaming and the ufe of fpirituous liquors are not accounted a moral offence."—
Doubtlefs, this fhort explanation implies, that there are other more fevere inflictions againft gaming and drinking, on perfons of the Gentoo faith.
Sect on V. On perfons incapable of inheritance.—This whole fection difcovers fuch principles of morality and primitive juftice, and is in many inftances fo conformable to many tenets in the Englifh laws, that it claims the higheft commendation, and is worthy of imitation in all civil focieties.

collecting

collecting the rents, calculated for the purpose of embezzlement, should once for all be eradicated, and a fixed measure established, under a denomination applicable to the quality of the production, and the tenure of each district.

In general, every complication which can possibly have a tendency to oppress the ryots, and the body of the people, or to defraud government, land proprietor, or zemindar, should be abolished.

When a regular system for the settlement of Hindostan is once adopted, in order to give it efficacy and permanence, equal to its importance, the natives should receive the most clear and ample evidence, that an European government at length wisely regards their prosperity and tranquillity as interwoven with its own: the first and most persuasive proof of which, will consist in conveying to individuals, such a property in lands, in fee or copyhold tenure, with such salutary restrictions in favour of sub-tenants, as shall yield reciprocal encouragement both to landlord and tenant to improve their possessions to the best possible advantage, without dread of superseffion.

This security of property to the proprietor or zemindar, and to the industrious ryot, against both dispossession and oppression, will operate as a barrier against treachery in favour of either foreign enemies or domestic insurgents, from whom, if successful in their pretensions to supreme power, such indulgent conditions were not to be expected. And thus, by the fidelity and attachment of a numerous people, attached by gratitude and affection to the existing government, and increasing in population, a stronger bulwark of defence would be raised, without incurring public expences, than by

a host

a host of troops, consuming the major part of the revenues of those territories which they defended. It is imagined, that by this mode of granting a property in actual perpetuity, or on leases renewable, at distant periods, to perpetuity, and a division of the most extensive districts and zemindaries into lesser ones, a very large sum would immediately be raised, a similar sum at the expiration of every eleventh or nineteenth year, and an annual reserved rent, equal, if not greater, than the present clear collection.

Justice concurs with sound policy in recommending preferences to such persons, or their descendants, as have formerly had regular grants; or a series of family succession; or fair purchase in possession: who may have acquired such authority and ascendancy over the minds and affections of the people of the district, as may have a tendency to prevent that most dangerous, and most to be dreaded, of all evils, the desertion (and of course the desolation) of the lands, by the inhabitants flying from oppression to seek refuge under a mild and more equitable government: for thus the lands being laid waste, and the remaining inhabitants impoverished and dispirited, rents must consequently be encreased upon cultivated lands, to make up the stipulated engagement of the temporary zemindar, which forces both the zemindar and ryot to the necessity of devising expedients to procure abatements of rent, or to defraud, until both are forced to abscond, leaving the unwise ministers of government in the unprofitable possession of dreary wastes, to hatch plausible but false pretexts for errors they have committed, and for present and subsequent deficiencies. This fatal truth was severely exemplified in the year of that dreadful famine which sweeped off millions of inhabitants. Although there were irrecoverable arrears to the amount of eighteen lacks, thirty eight thousand six hundred and sixty one Sicca rupees, or twenty one lacks, thirty two thousand eight hundred and forty seven current rupees, of anterior engagement engagement in arrears to government from the farmers, by over-rating the rents of the districts; yet the administrators continued, notwithstanding, to raise those of the ensuing year, by encouraging favoured persons of low condition, without either family or credit, to overbid the original zemindars, into the advance of near eleven lacks on the general rent, which in reality, was cruelly adding above thirty two lacks of current rupees to the measure of oppression. It is only a wonder that upon this, as well as subsequent occasions, the natives did not, either move off in a body, solicit the more lenient supremacy of some other power, or perish in an attempt to recover their rights, and original constitution and government, from savage usurpation. By a continuation of such ill-judged measures, it may confidently be asserted, that, notwithstanding the deep traces of desolation and devastation which appeared upon the face of the country, and which are feelingly described in the public records, the remission by government, and balances which are irrecoverable, since the administration of Mr. Hastings in 1772, will, upon a critical examination, be found to approach nearer to a million and an half sterling than to one million. The mighty object of these oppressive measures, was to serve favoured black dependents,

pendents, who of courfe were lavifh in prefents†, and to acquire temporary applaufe at home.

The enormous weight of debt thus fufpended over a timid and defpairing people, forced them to abandon the fields of their nativity, to which an ancient intimacy and lineal intercourfe had attached their fondeft affections, the trueft fource of fidelity to government, and incitement to induftry. After fuch long and painful miferies, an effectual change in the fyftem of government will reftore a happinefs to the natives, not unlike what the ingenious fancy of ancient poets afcribed to the golden age.— But to effect this; to retrieve the devaftations committed by collectors and their train of harpies; to raife the drooping fpirits of the ryot, from fad defpair to confidence and hope; to re-people and fettle the deferted and uncultivated tracts, and to apply the unfertile foil to fuch ufes as it is qualified to bear, will require fteadinefs, probity, judgment, application, and time.

A power of immediate punifhment, not incompatible with the fecurity of property, muft indifpenfably be vefted fomewhere, not remote from each feveral diftrict; and all reftraints and taxes for the public fervice, be laid with as equal and light a hand as the exigencies of ftate will allow. The people of all degrees and denominations being once fenfible of the effect and ftability of the eftablifhed regulations, numbers from diftant countries will be invited by the alluring temptations thus offered to induftry and ingenuity, and an encreafe of

† The Governor's Banyan Cawntoo-baboo, enjoyed leafes of zemindaries to the amount of thirteen lacks and an half annually; and he had contracts, at the fame time, of the value of fixteen lacks. And it is alledged, that befides jewels, the Ranny of Burdwan alone gave twelve lacks of rupees, in prefents to her patrons.—Admirable partiality!!!

wealth

wealth and population will naturally follow in quick succession.

Among the many advantages that may be expected to flow spontaneously from these institutions, considerable savings in the expenditures of government will be manifested in the charges of collection, because the present mode of constituting provincial councils will of course be abolished; in the charges of, and the batta allowed upon, distant remittances; in the charges of the courts of Adawluts, Phouzdary, and Cutchery; in the charges of supporting the Pool and Dow-bunds; and in the various other chargeable departments, both in the country and at the presidency, which will become totally unnecessary. It will be deemed a low estimate to suppose, that these savings may be computed equal to a quarter, or a third part of the entire revenues.

To apply rules with effect, for establishing manufactures and commerce, should be a leading maxim in the constitution of a colony, holding of, and depending on a maritime and commercial nation. In Europe, the laws concerning these, except in Britain, Holland, and some inconsiderable republics, are yet simple, and sometimes ill-judged; because although rivality in trade be gaining ground fast, the profession of a merchant, and its general utility to the state, have not acquired such an ascendancy in the deliberation of state-cabinets, as to counterbalance that adroitness which is constitutional in the people of Asia, some tribes of whom have equal ambition and avarice with Europeans, but whose other passions are never inflamed by liquors, strong viands, and social debaucheries: an advantage which they understand too well, not

to

to avail themselves of the lucrative opportunities it affords.

Since the English became rulers of extensive dominions and trade in Hindoftan, a new field was opened to a subtle clafs of people, who, until that time, held but a middle rank in the country, Banyans and Circars. Thefe have faftened themfelves so fecurely in the springs of every kind of bufinefs, and gained such unlimited confidence, that the moft trifling, as well as the moft important tranfactions, are not only conducted, but projected by them; and Europeans are, for the moft part, not only at the mercy, but under the infenfible dominion of perfons, whofe art and addrefs introduce, in their deportment, an obfequioufnefs and apparent fubmiffion, expreffive of the duty of a fervant to his mafter.

The complicated connections and fecret intercourfes between Banyans, Circars, Gomaftahs, Pycars, and Dellols, added to deep artifice, and confequent power, maintain their ufurpations on the Europeans, as well as on the manufacturers and ryots; who alfo delegate to the fame agents the power of negociation. Thus they act in the twofold capacity of feller and purchafer, reaping the advantages of commiffion and fraud from both, and defignedly obftructing with peculiar acutenefs, thofe perfonal interviews which would naturally beget confidence, fo effential to the interefts of both parties.

This wifhed-for intercourfe and confidence, which the plan for the reception of crude and manufactured goods into public warehoufes, and inftant payment without the chargeable and fraudulent mediation of brokers, can alone promote and effectuate,

fectuate, will be the happy means also, of restoring to goods their former qualities at the former prices, with out injuring the manufacturer or ryot; as in lieu of the difference in quality and price, they will save a greater difference in the emoluments and advance prices usurped by European agents, in the Nazaranas, brokerage, discount on coins, interest usuriously charged on advances, fines for imaginary breaches of contract, and a list of factitious taxes fraudulently trumped up to impose on the ignorant manufacturers and ryots, whose good faith is thus cruelly abused in clandestine contracts.

Various are the ways which the art and ingenuity of men, aiming at the acquisition of riches, devise and practise to impose upon the mass of the people, who from ignorance, a simplicity of education, and habit, are taught to place implicit faith in those who exercise trade, as Banyans, Shroffs, Circars, Gomastahs, Pycars, and Dellols. These dark impositions are, in their own consequences, peculiarly distressing to the country, having a direct tendency to discourage industry and prevent population. If justice does not animate the members of government, in whom all constitutions have necessarily vested guardian authority to interpose their power; sound policy, and the interest and safety of the state, having a view even to an early futurity, will point to the speedy correction of general abuses, by the seasonable application of such remedies as are most likely to prove efficacious, at a time, when it is hoped and expected that a general reform is agitated.

The complicated qualities of weights and measures in India, are much too intricate and perplexed for the comprehension and comparative estimations of of persons not masters of the science of arithmetic, not to subject them to abuses, as well in the sale of their commodities, as in the purchase of necessaries. Therefore, the reduction of weights and measures to fixed legal standards, throughout, will prove materially useful in the general line of commerce; and particularly to the industrious and laborious classes of people, in a country where the banyans, shroffs, and agents of European merchants, as well as those of the Company, by a continual course of practice, understand the rules of proportion, and the intricacies of business too well, not to apply that knowledge, and the ignorance of others, to their own advantage, in all dealings where perplexity is capable of being perverted to the purposes of fraud; in the same manner as shroffs have applied the variety of coins, and reduction of their values, under the hackneyed term Batta, to their own emolument, insomuch, that this class of Hindoos have acquired an influence, which many have thought dangerous to government, and for that reason, ridiculously forbore to regulate their abuses. I am, &c.

LETTER XLVI.

To J—— M——, Esq. London.

Calcutta, Nov. 24, 1779.

IF the reasoning concerning India affairs, contained in my former letters, be just, the new arrangements necessary to a wise and political establishment in Hindostan, may be reduced to the following heads:

1. The

1. The grand preliminary to give folidity and permanency to the new conftitution, will confift in determining to whom the natives owe allegiance as fovereign lord of the country ;—protection and care, being as juftly the claim of the people, as fubmiffion is due from them to the fovereign.

2. The lands to be granted in fee fimple, or in copyhold tenure, at fixed, eafy, quit-rents ;—a fine payable at entry, and every eleventh or nineteenth year in perpetuity.—The lands (without varying the title, or incurring expences) to defcend to heirs, in lineal or collateral fucceffion.

3. The Hindoos to be the landholders, zemindars, farmers, ryots, and manufacturers; preferences being given firft to the original proprietors, and their defcendents; next to perfons of high caft ; then to perfons of original family and influence ; and laftly, to ftrangers: with a refervation of proper tracts of country, for the introduction and encouragement of other fpecies of cultivation and colonization.—Moormen or Mahomedans to be preferred in the adminiftration of public departments in the revenues and polity of government, being, however, rigidly reftricted in the power of oppreffing, or the commiffion of injuftice.

4. That the natives fhall freely enjoy their own laws, cuftoms, cafts, and religion inviolate, except in inftances where innovations may tend to render liberty and property more fafe from arbitrary invafion.

5. The proprietor or zemindar, as in former times, to be accountable for the internal peace and police of his eftate or zemindary; with power to hold courts of cutcherry, to adjudge fines and forfeitures to the ufe of the fovereign, to recover debts,

debts, and to inflict corporal punishments, not extending to life or limb.—That appeals shall lie from the cutcherry court to the supreme court in Calcutta, or to assizes; on which occasions, men of approved integrity, in independent circumstances, and possessing a clear knowledge of the Gentoo and Mahometan laws, shall associate, as expounders of law, with the British judges. And from the supreme court, the cause may be appealed to the court of chancery, &c. &c.—And that the judges of the supreme court shall make their circuits, and hold assizes, in the capital of each province, twice in every year.

6. The quit rents and rents to be paid in the express terms stipulated in the respective concessions, in current coins, or other signs of value by authority, or in manufactures and country produce, at stated prices and standard qualities; with special covenants to encourage and promote such commodities as are proper for manufactures and exportation; and for the general encouragement of manufactures in the most extensive sense.

7. That one general current coin shall be established, to circulate freely without any allowance for exchange or batta; and that endeavours be used to procure it currency in the dominions of neighbouring princes. That paper, under the denomination of bank notes, be issued, and receive effectual currency, as the means of encouraging agriculture, manufactures, and trade; and as a mode to enable proprietors, zemindars, revenue officers, manufacturers, and traders, to remit their rents and monies to the respective capitals†, where they

† Calcutta, Muxadabad, Patna, Decca, &c.

are

are made payable, without incurring either charges or rifque: a confideration of the firft magnitude, in relieving the ryots from oppreffion, and in exciting a general fpirit of induftry.

8. The Company to receive manufactured commodities and crude productions, proper for exportation, particularly opium, falt-petre, raw filk, filk and cotton cloths of all kinds (of qualities improved to what the natives had formerly been in the practice of making, and at the former prices) into ftated provincial warehoufes; and all the manufactures which are for fale by individuals, to be received into thefe warehoufes, and immediately paid for, according to the regulation, in money and bank notes.

9. The artificial dykes or banks, to keep rivers within their channels (as a fecurity againft violent and unfeafonable inundations) commonly called Pool-bundies, fhall henceforward become, as a public duty, chargeable upon the feveral and refpective diftricts that profit by them, and be kept in conftant repair; fubject to infpection, by proper officers, twice in every year; and a delinquency fhall be punifhed by a heavy penalty on the principal, for the firft and fecond offence, and a forfeiture of property in the lands, without affecting the rights of inheritance, for the third offence committed by the fame principal. The forfeitures fhall be at leaft triple the value of the damages fuftained by ryots, and their loffes fhall be made good out of them.

10. The ryots, during the punctual difcharge of rents, taxes, and ftipulated obligations, incident to their refpective farms, fhall not be fubject to removal, at the caprice or pleafure of the land-holder or zemindar.

zemindar.—Their pofterity fhall continue to enjoy an uninterrupted occupancy of lands, without any alteration in the terms or conditions.—An eftablifhed tenure of fub leafes fhall prevail throughout the country invariably, unlefs the nature or quality of the crude or manufactured commodities produced, or other material circumftances, approved by government, fhall render an alteration neceffary.—And in order to encourage and promote population and induftry at home, when families increafe, and require a greater extent of land to cultivate, or villages to fettle in, every poffible indulgence and preference fhould be devifed and granted, as well by government as by the land-holders, to inculcate a fpirit of induftry, and to infure profperity. And farther, the ryots fhall not be reduced to a ftate of uncertainty, as to the quantity and quality of the rents and fervices to be exacted by their landlords.

11. That the current prices of grains, which are the neceffaries of life, be unalterably fixed; unlefs a deviation from this rule for the purpofe of immediate exportation, or upon any actual emergency, for a limited time, be allowed by fupreme authority.—That if neverthelefs, by any combination or affociation of land-holders and others, the rates of grain, or other neceffaries of life, be collufively enhanced, to the prejudice of manufacturers, labourers, and induftrious poor; government fhall in fuch cafe be warranted to exact additional rents in the fame proportion, during the continuance of the monopoly and fraudulent foreftalling.——This regulation will tend to encourage induftry and manufactures; and yield an encreafe of revenue to government, by the increafed eftimation of the productions in future.

12. That large districts and zemindaries be parcelled into lesser divisions; due regard, for the sake of conveniency and the peace of neighbours, being paid to natural boundaries and original subfarms; in such moderate proportions, that many shall be under one lack, and few or none exceed two lacks in the estimation of quit-rent.——Many good reasons may be adduced to justify the policy and expediency of reducing the larger districts, and dividing the lands (in fee or copyhold tenure) among as large a number of the original chiefs, and their posterity, as circumstances will permit. Fidelity, temperance, and emulation, bear a nearer affinity, and are more intimately associated with mediocrity, than with profuse wealth.—Wealth begets ambition, ambition languishes for power, and power in Asia, suggests ideas of treason.

13. That the average, or mesne rent collected from possessions under actual cultivation and good titles, since 1773 to 1781, both included, be the gross sum to be established as the government claim for quit-rents, on the same lands, in perpetuity; and that the division thereof, by assessment on entire or subdivided districts, be apportioned with all the impartiality and equity which knowledge and experience can ascertain.

14. The numerous jaghires, talook, charity, and religious tenures, which occupy a vast extent of territory in the several provinces under the Company's dominions in Hindostan, having afforded subterfuges to gross misapplications, perversions, usurpations, and chicaneries, call for a strict scrutiny; and the titles, as well as the qualities of lands, should be ascertained, in order that government may be enabled to resume its constitutional rights,

rights, in all cafes where ufurpations and fraudulent abufes have been committed. Claims, under a future prefcriptive tenure, in favour of poffeffors, where ambiguity or cafual circumftances render them indiftinct, fhould be admitted in a liberal manner, and without too fevere a fcrutiny.

15. The wafte and uncultivated lands fhall be refumed by government, as if never under cultivation, and granted to individuals, under the fame tenures as cultivated lands, but without exacting any quit-rent for a certain term; upon a moderate quit-rent for a fecond term; and a perpetual quit-rent thereafter.—And great and flattering indulgence fhall be held out, to encourage ftrangers to become cultivators of the foil, and manufacturers in the new villages.

16. That country produce for immediate confumption, and for the Company's warehoufes, be exempted from river and inland duties. That military bazars, (markets) and all country bazars and gunges, be alfo exempt from duties; except where they are exacted to raife a neceffary fund to maintain the internal police and government of any particular diftrict or town.

17. That a regifter general's office, and provincial offices, be eftablifhed for recording grants, conveyances, deeds, leafes, wills, and other folemn titles and documents, having relation to real eftates, inheritances, or fucceffions. That the provincial offices fhall tranfmit original deeds to the general office in Calcutta, every month; and that a copy from either office, duly authenticated, fhall have equal validity in evidence as the original. That the offices have regular dockets of fees, and other rules, eftablifhed by authority; and that

complete

complete indexes be daily upheld, for the ready infpection of records.

18. That if the Hindoo laws concerning divers kinds of prefcriptions, fhall not be deemed fufficient to anfwer the ends of government, blended with the rights and fecurity of the people, others more competent and effectual fhall be adopted.

19. That falutary refervations and laws be eftablifhed, to guard againft the dreadful calamities which follow fevere droughts in thofe warm regions; and that interceffion be made with the Brahmins, for indulgencies and difpenfations, in times of famine, or extreme calamity, for all caftes to fubfift upon animal food, for the prefervation of life.

20. That weights and meafures be reduced to fixed ftandards by authority—To fuch as know the complicated variety of thefe ufed in India, the expediency of a regulation in favour of ryots and manufacturers, will not appear to need any proof.

21. The Hindoo tax, called najay, was a fine affefled on the whole diftrict, to anfwer the deficiencies of individuals. In fome inftances, fuch a tax is irreconcileable to the maxims of juftice; when it is exacted, for example, merely for the benefit and gratification of government, or the proprietor. But it will be a fecurity againft defertion, the malice of wicked neighbours, negligence, and inactivity; for, by making the ryots anfwerable for each other, it will operate as a falutary check, provided the rents are equally proportioned and levied on each farm in the diftrict, according to extent and quality, and that the tax is not demanded when the deficiency arifes unavoidably, by the hand of Providence, or by any oppreffion or violent act of

the

the proprietor: therefore, this tax fhall, under proper limitations, be revived.

Security to private property, and a free trade, are the greateft encouragements that can be held out to induftry and ingenuity, and cherifh in the human breaft a laudable degree of ambition, and a love of affluence: principles which render the ftates that are inhabited by fuch fubjects as poffefs them, wealthy, independent, and powerful. The limitation of the powers annexed to the magiftracy, in its feveral departments; the fuppreffion of every ufurpation of thefe powers by private authority; and facility of accefs to juftice; are the only means by which this invaluable fecurity is to be obtained: and when obtained, it fhould be preferved with the fame facred and folemn guardian care, which is reprefented to have been of old exercifed over the laws of Minos. I am, &c.

LETTER XLVII.

To J—— M——, Efq; London.

Calcutta, November 27, 1779.

AN independent fovereignty over certain territories in Hindoftan, being ceded by the emperor to the crown of Great Britain, the fole property of the falt-petre, ophium, and various forts of piece goods, commodities, and manufactures, which are peculiar to thofe provinces, might be made to operate as a monopoly, which fhould draw a great balance of trade, with all the eaftern coafts and iflands, as well as to facilitate the inveftments from China.—The produce of the Britifh provinces in India might be bartered for that of China, in the same manner that the Dutch carry on an advantageous trade with that country, by means of the rich aromatic productions of Ceylon and the Molucca islands. The same articles, with other piece goods and provisions, might support a lucrative commerce with the southern and western coasts of the peninsula of Hindostan, and also with the Persian and Arabian seas.

The French African islands of Mauritius and Bourbon being reduced under the power of Great Britain, the former should be made a free port, under easy limitations and the exaction of a moderate duty. Foreign nations would then resort to Mauritius, as to a market where they might purchase their supplies on terms considerably lower than either the Dutch, Danes, or Portuguese can purchase them in Europe; and consequently, these nations must, in their own defence, relinquish establishments which involve them equally in loss and discredit. Foreigners coming to this eastern emporium should be obliged to pay at least one-third of the price of the commodities they purchase, in silver bullion, at a standard and assay value, which the seller should be obliged to transmit to India for the benefit of circulation.—The town and port of Port Lewis in Mauritius being made a free port, would be the great avenue through which India commodities would flow into the markets of Europe. Foreign European nations must of course be precluded from all communication with the native powers of the Indian continent. Hence it will become sound policy, and indeed a measure indispensably necessary, to give every possible encouragement to Indian manufacturers, particularly to

establish

establish a constant and ready market for all sorts of manufactures, even in the greatest quantities†. But, in order to make such merchandize saleable, with reciprocal advantage both to the buyer and seller, all the fraudulent and pernicious restraints and impositions, which of late years have occasioned a debasement in the qualities, and an advancement in the prices of goods, must be effectually abolished. All goods must be restored to their original qualities and textures. Let no chicaning intermediate agent be suffered to pass between the manufacturers and the Company's warehouse-keepers and sorters, except the sworn appreciators and examiners, according to standard samples, secreted from the view, and from every possible communication with the owners. Manufacturers should receive punctual payment of all necessary advances and balances, without any diminution or defalcation, in adequate prices for their labour and ingenuity. Manufactures sold to individuals should be subjected to an inland duty of at least ten per cent. on their standard estimations, and exported under bonds to return certificates: but in cases where the individual purchaser shall, within six months, bring them into the Company's warehouses, three-fourth parts of the duty shall be returned to him. By these means, without operating as a monopoly, the goods will be lodged in the Com-

† This project can never interfere with the Company's sale in Europe, because the exported quantity must follow the Company's annual tonnage; and because as the merchants exporting will expect an advance and interest on their outlays, and to be paid freight and insurance, and the freights and charges from the Island to Europe must be at least equal to what the Company pay, it will follow, that the Company, after clearing more than o ver cent. duty in India, can underfell the goods thus imported into Europe from Mauritius; nor is it to be doubted, that the European, American, and African markets will continue equal to India exports.

pany's warehouses, where merchants or other persons having orders or commissions, or desirous of making remittances, may, in one day, complete an assortment of approved, unexceptionable merchandize, paying the prime cost, with an advance of ten per cent. in lieu of warehouse rent, charges, and risque of transportation, and other petty incidental expences. These goods being sent to Mauritius, should be received only under particular dockets and other clearances; and should there be deposited in the Company's warehouses, paying two and an half per cent. in lieu of warehouse rent, lighterage, cranage, and porterage, upon entry, and five per cent. more by the shipper, in lieu of export duty and charges, upon exportation.

Thus a handsome revenue would arise to the Company on this merchandize of about twenty per cent. while the exporter, by the mode of purchase, without any previous advance, or running the risque of losing part of the sums usually advanced to the manufacturers, or of being defrauded by the gomastahs, dellols†, and other agents, employed near twelve months before an assortment is completed, will lay in the goods subject to these duties, &c. at twenty to thirty per cent. cheaper than he could do now; with this further advantage, that the quality of the goods will ensure them a steady and profitable market, as well in Mauritius as in Europe.

I am, &c.

† A species of country Agents.

LETTER XLVIII.

To J—— M——, Efq; London.

Calcutta, Nov. 30, 1779.

IT is a fact of notoriety, that for every rupee which is accounted for in the receipt of the Company's general treafury, their uncontrouled collectors, and the multitude of deputies, and native harpies dependent on them, who ufe the authority and fanction of their names for the purpofes of extortion, receive at leaft five. If an effectual remedy could be provided for this evil, it would releafe commerce from its fetters, and improve the public revenue, as well as relieve the great body of the people from the moft deftructive rapacity.

To this end, the union of the two departments for collecting the Government's and the Company's duties, as they are emphatically diftinguifhed, would be highly conducive. The cuftom-houfes being united, the conftitution of the fingle office arifing from that union, fhould be at once fimple and fyftematical: fimple, in order to fave expences, and prevent embezzlement and ftudied delay of payment; fyftematical, that it may extend to every branch of revenue, that a due fubordination may be maintained among the revenue officers, and that the income of the public may be fecured by proper checks on its collectors, and particularly by the appointment of a comptroller.

A reform may be made general in every public department, and extend not only to falaries and to numbers, but to duty and the exercife of power. The fubordinate councils under the controul of the feveral prefidencies, are merely iniquitous combinations,

nations, having in reality no other object in contemplation, but first to devise the most effectual means of defrauding their employers, and oppressing the natives, for the purpose of enriching themselves in their turns; and then to devise such specious minutes and letters as are most likely to justify, or at least to draw a decent veil over actions that cannot bear the light.

Revenue chiefs, and collectors of districts and provinces, are, if possible, still greater nuisances, and may as easily be dispensed with, by means of an established general coin and valuable currency, a free internal trade, by granting lands on permanent tenures, and ascertaining the number and nature of those tenures.

Thus will all those rich farms which are, by connivance and chicane, concealed from public knowledge, and which are appropriated to the use of individuals as emoluments of office, be discovered, and brought forth to public account.

Contractors are a species of robbers who have the sanction and protection, because they are generally the partners, of leading members in administration. The judicious and disinterested orders of the court of Directors, with regard to the matters I have touched on in this letter; and indeed with regrad to all others, are either secretly evaded, or, where that is impossible, treated with open contempt. They are considered as the impertinent intrusions of men assuming powers that do not belong to them, and arrogating a knowledge in matters, the conduct of which, custom and possession have placed in more powerful hands. The servants of the Company conceive themselves to be possessed, if not of the most just and legal, yet of a very natural authority;

which

which they well know how to ufe as an engine, not only for procuring the remiflion of offences, but even rank and applaufe. Thus they become proper objects of emulation to others, who treading in the fame fraudulent paths, are folicitous to procure powerful friends, who may connive at and protect their own frauds, and quicken the rapid acquifition of fortunes by feniors, that they may the sooner be placed in fituations for acquiring fortunes themfelves.

These evils are mightly encreafed by that great number of young gentlemen which are fent out every year in the character of writers : one third part of which would be more than fufficient to execute all the bufinefs exacted of the whole; and if these young gentlemen were reftrained from entering on this line of life, before their educations were compleated †, and that they had acquired diftinct ideas of bufinefs, and fome knowledge of the world; were they confirmed in principles of juftice, integrity, and honour; and were their judgments matured by time and experience; the Company and the country would equally be benefited by their abilities and virtue; while they themfelves would rife fafter in the fervice than they do now, and make quicker progrefs in that great work of accumulating independencies with unblemifhed characters and ferene confciences.—If this idea fhould be adopted, the appointments of the Company's writers fhould be made fo abundantly competent to their ftations and profpects, as to place them above the commiffion of mean and difhonourable actions, or of be-

† In order to fecure rank and feniority, writers of the age of fixteen years are admiffible; but they generally advance a year upon their ages, and come out between fifteen and fixteen.

coming.

coming the dupes of underhand agents, and of ufurious Banyans and Circars. It is evident, that the Company's expences would continue the fame, were the prefent entire allowance diftributed among a fmaller number, while their bufinefs would be performed with greater promptitude, and with more accuracy and judgment.

This new regulation would, in all probability, foon introduce another, of great importance to the Company in various refpects; namely, the keeping of all their records, accounts, and books, in the Englifh language†, inftead of that of the country, as has long been, and ftill is the practice even in private families. Any accounts that are kept in Englifh, are merely partial abftracts, and tranflations from the country languages. Thus the Company, as well as individuals, are at the mercy of native fervants, from whom alone their employers receive informations of the ftate of their finances, inveftments, effects, and property of every kind, from time to time: a power which the cool and deep-defigning Hindoos will endeavour by all means to preferve.

I may, perhaps, be thought to bear hard, in fome of the obfervations I have made now, as well as on former occafions, on the fervants of the Company. In truth, the conduct of many, nay of the moft of them, affords not any fubject for panegyric. Neverthelefs, we ought, in candor, to make great allowances to the ftrong temptations that folicit them to grafp at fortune at the expence of integrity. The

† It is aftonifhing, that notwithftanding the length of time which the Englifh have traded to Bengal, and that for the laft fixteen years they have acted as independent fovereigns thereof, there is not a fervant in an Englifh houfe who underftands the Englifh language; and fuch is the police of that country, that every Britifh fubject is indirectly a dependent on his Banyan and Circar, and a flave even to the loweft of his own fervants. It is otherwife at Madras and Bombay.

fame

same circumstances which, in some degree, excuse the weaknesses and vices of the Company's servants, enhance the merit of those who preserve their virtue untainted amidst general corruption. True glory consists in persevering in the paths of virtue, in spite of all the allurements of vice. There are, doubtless, among the Company's servants, several who are well entitled to this praise. Such among them I know, and I have had great satisfaction in their acquaintance. Concerning those in the administration of government, I shall be wholly silent. They have had but too much occasion to display their talents, and their principles, either in supporting or opposing the measures on the Company's records. There are, however, among the Company's servants, men whose junior stations have not yielded opportunities of exhibiting the excellence of their characters in so conspicuous a manner; and I mention their names in particular, without meaning to insinuate an idea to the prejudice of any others. I have often found it convenient to acquire a knowledge of characters; and therefore, my friend, I have chosen to point out a few, who will claim your regard, if ever chance should bring you into their society. The favourable impressions which they have made on my mind, are the result solely of their own capacities and integrity.

Mr. Brodie of Madras, although a young servant, and young in years, by a natural and easy address, sound judgment, manly firmness, polite candour, unwearied diligence, probity, and a liberality of sentiment, seems to have gained the universal confidence and esteem of persons of all ranks, denominations, and countries within that settlement. These talents and virtues, joined to a steady

boldness,

boldness, have often presented him to my mind as a person well qualified, with the assistance of Mooda Kistna as interpreter, to undertake a pacific embassy to Hyder Ally.

I esteem it a peculiar happiness, that I have had an opportunity of knowing, with easy freedom, the honourable principles which adorn and actuate the natural and acquired abilities of Mr. George Bogle, Mr. John Shore, Mr. G. Ducarell, Mr. Claud Alexander, and Mr. David Anderson, of Calcutta. To these may justly be subjoined the names of Mr. Herbert Harris, Mr. Samuel Touchett, and Mr. John Mackenzie.

The embassy of Mr. Bogle to the Lama of Thibet, and his letter of resignation, when he found himself unable to accomplish the purposes of his appointment of commissioner of the Company's lawsuits in the Supreme Court, by reason of the extrajudicial proceedings of the judges, do honour to his moral character; as his clear and precise knowledge of the revenues, laws, and customs of the Company's possessions in Bengal, prove him to be one of their ablest servants. But his connection with Mr. H———s, has impressed his mind with an idea, that pure despotism in the uncontrouled hands of an individual, is the only system whereby to govern India.

Mr. Shore, Mr. Ducarell, and Mr. Anderson, have acquired so accurate a knowledge of the revenues of the provinces of Hindostan, and the dispositions, customs, and manners of the people, that, whatever change may take place in the administration, sound policy and good sense will point out them as necessary members. Mr. Alexander, whose unbiassed integrity, and accurate knowledge
of

of accounst, have juftly raifed him to the important ftation which he now occupies, of commiffary general of the army accounts, is worthy of unlimited confidence, and capable of rendering fignal fervice, particularly in any line that requires controul, and a clear knowledge of accounts. It would be injuftice to the moft approved fidelity, to pafs over the diftinguifhed abilities and unfhaken integrity of Mr. Charles Grant, principal fecretary to the Board of Trade. If this gentleman errs in any thing, it is in the fternnefs of his virtue, and the nice fcrupuloufnefs of his feelings in matters of right and wrong. The only good that has been performed by that Board, has been involuntary on the part of its members, and ftands to the fole credit of the fecretary. I am, &c.

LETTER XLIX.

To J—— M——, Efq. London.

Calcutta, Dec. 3, 1779.

THE Eaft India Company entertained falfe ideas concerning the trade carried on from their fettlements in the eaft with the Arabian and Perfian feas, when they either mifled government, or feduced the minifter at the Ottoman court to obftruct the commerce with the Red Sea, and as much as poffible, that from Baflorah and Bagdat to Aleppo and Smyrna. Doubtlefs, they imagined that fuch commerce would interfere with their fales in Europe, and with the trade of the Levant Company; but never was any apprehenfion more groundlefs. Let the Company's fales in Leadenhall-ftreet and the

Cuftom-

Custom-house entries in London be reviewed, in order to afcertain the quantities and qualities of India goods exported to the Levant and the African side of the Mediterranean; and then compare these with the quantities and qualities of the goods sent from India into the gulphs. This comparison will sufficiently evince the Company's mistake with regard to this subject, and no doubt effectually correct it. France and Denmark, who nearly engross that part of the African trade which lies within the straits of Gibraltar, are capable—the one by proximity, the other by constant intercourse, and both by the unrestrained systems of their imports—of underselling the Levant Company in all India commodities. Therefore, unless the Levant Company have actually occasion to monopolize all the bills of exchange negociated in Marseilles, Villa Franca, Genoa, Leghorn, Venice, and other southern states, upon the northern kingdoms and trading cities of Europe (an idea repugnant to the very institution of that society) it is not probable that the portion of trade which is carried on from India directly with Mocha, Judda, Suez, and Bassorah, can sensible affect either the measure or the profits of the traffic of that Company. The articles of remittance to Britain, for goods exported from India into the Persian and Arabian seas, are bills of exchange, Venetian gold, and Spanish and German crowns: nor is it alledged that returns to India are in any respect offensive. It therefore becomes a political question, whether it will prove advantageous to Britain, that the Levant Company shall enjoy new and exclusive privileges, which, without being of the smallest advantage to the British nation in any respect, embarrass the Indian

dian trade, and one branch of which it tends directly to foreclose?

India has been, till of late, in the uniform practice of sending its productions into the Arabian and Persian seas, to the value of about 350,000 l. annually; the principal returns for which, were gold, silver, and other articles of merchandize, which interfered not in any material instance with the trade of the Company, or with British manufactures. The other returns became remittances of the acquisitions of individuals to Britain, and consequently a real benefit to the nation. The importation of precious metals into India, is evidently essential to its prosperity. Such articles as are wanted for consumption, or are indispensable in the improvement of manufactures, and which must otherwise have been bought from foreigners, and paid for with a liquidation of specie, will operate in the same manner with respect to the country, as if the intire returns, except what is sent to Britain, were made in the precious metals only.

Over and above the advantages accruing from navigation to all commercial countries, and profits upon the returns, the sales up the gulphs may reasonably be computed to yield twenty to twenty-five per cent. net profit, if the India goods are judiciously laid in. Thus an annual market will be furnished for about half a million of pounds sterling, and a real balance of trade in favour of the English Company, from places, all commerce with which has rashly been discountenanced and restrained by public authority.—It is an object of importance to the East India Company, and worthy of the support of government, to revive and re-establish those branches of commerce upon a new and comprehensive five syftem. Such a syftem has, after much enquiry and reflection, been already framed in idea; and it is affirmed with confidence, that it might easily be reduced to practice, that it would promote the interest of the Company, enrich individuals, and, on the whole, add to the prosperity of the British possessions in India.

As the commerce to and from India with all parts eastward of the Cape of Good Hope, is as free to individuals as to the Company; it has been wholly carried on, for a considerable time past, by the Company's servants, individually, or on their account; and by others who stile themselves free merchants and free mariners. The fluctuations and insecurity peculiar to any commerce which is restrained by the arbitrary will of an exclusive Company and despotic government, are too obvious not to damp the ardour of even the hardiest speculators in commerce: nevertheless, free merchants, labouring under manifold inconveniences, adventured in this hazardous trade; and would have succeeded in spite of all obstructions, but those which were thrown in their way by the partiality and injustice of that very country which was ultimately to reap the benefit of their genius and industry.

Every possible encouragement consistent with sound policy, should be freely granted to British subjects trading to the east of the Cape of Good Hope. Free traders should, however, be put under particular restrictions and limitations, as well in certain branches of internal privileges and trade, as in the mode of purchasing country manufactures. This measure is absolutely necessary, in order to prevent those abuses which have been so justly and so loudly complained of; the debasement of the qualities, and at the fame time the encreafe of the prices, of commodities. This reftraint ought not to be murmured at, when it is confidered that free traders are exempted from general taxes, and that the charges of the civil and military government, the benefits of which they enjoy, is borne without their participation. Their navigation efpecially, fhould be laid under ftrict regulations. They fhould never be allowed to trade beyond the limits of the Company's dominions without paffports.

I am, &c.

LETTER L.

To J—— M——, Efq. London.

Calcutta, Dec. 6, 1779.

IT is equally unjuft and impolitic, that foreigners fhould enjoy greater privileges and immunities than the natural fubjects of any country; yet Frenchmen are allowed to trade with the moft unbounded freedom, and to amafs large fortunes in the Englifh Company's dominions in India, even while their nation is at war with Britain, and while they facrifice the temporary allegiance they owe to a government which favours them with fo fingular an indulgence, to the hoftile views of their native country. Swifs, Germans, Portuguefe, Armenians, and others, are exclufively indulged with fuch peculiar advantages in trade, that they quickly acquire fortunes, with which they retire to their own countries: whereas Englifhmen, were they equally favoured, would in like manner fpeedily acquire wealth, and carry it home to enrich Great Britain.

It

It is evidently beneficial to any country, that sojourners as well as its settled inhabitants do live in a plentiful and generous manner; for thus encouragement is afforded, by a free circulation of money, to the industry of the manufacturer, the labourer, and the husbandman. Now the natives of Britain are distinguished for a liberality, and even a profusion in their manner of living, both at home and abroad: whereas foreigners are in general as remarkable in their parsimony and mean penuriousness; so that the people among whom they acquire their fortunes, reap but little benefit from supplying their few wants, and at last, have the mortification of seeing strangers carrying away great sums of hoarded money to be spent in their own countries.

The treachery and ingratitude of foreigners enjoying extraordinary indulgences under the constitution of the English East India Company, are so well known, and have so late been so strikingly exemplified in the conduct of Mr. Bolts, Mr. Chevalier, Mr. Somro, Mr. Pollier, Mr. Moneron, &c. that it ought not to be a matter of surprize, that the most secret proceedings in Calcutta and Madras, previous to the late capture of Chandernagore, and the siege of Pondicherry, were known to the two French governors as quickly as the speed of Harcarahs could convey the information. This dangerous evil is encouraged by the wilful violation of one of the standing orders of the Company, prohibiting the Company's servants in India from marrying women of foreign birth or the Romish faith. Two of the Council of Madras are married to French ladies, near relations of governor Law, and rigid Catholics. A late suspended member of the same board is married to another lady of that family;

mily; and several other gentlemen in the service of that presidency, have entered into similar connections: the governor general, Mr. Haftings, has set an example of the same kind in Bengal; and in order to render the practice general, he contrived to draw two of his family into foreign connections. With great confidence may it be afserted, that all the mischiefs which have attended Mr. H——s's administration in Bengal, are to be ascribed to female connection; that the notice given to Mr. Chevalier, the evening preceding the capture of Chandernagore †; the very dangerous leave given to the same Governor Chevalier, after having been taken prisoner in Catack, to embark for France by the shortest route through the Red Sea‡; and a variety of other misdemeanours, originated in, and were carried through by the same influence. The open conduct of the Portuguese house of De C——o, D——s, and P——n, as the agents of Mr. Bolts, in supplying his Niccabar and other settlements, in defiance of the Company's positive orders, as well

† It has been industriously propagated, that Monsieur Chevalier was in his house at Ghyrotty when Colonel Dow entered it, but that he got away by the management of Madame Chevalier.—Nothing is more false.—Two confidential servants of the Company, and particular favourites of Mr. H——s, were with him upon secret business, until two o'clock that morning; and when Colonel Dow surrounded Ghyrotty house, Monsieur Chevalier was concealed in the house of a trusty servant in the town of Chandernagore, three miles distant, together with such papers as would, probably, if seized by Colonel Dow, have brought fatal conspiracies to light.

‡ Mr. Elliot, though deservedly a favourite with Mr. H—s, and with all who knew his abilities and amiable qualities, was too honourable to have the secret of Monsieur Chevalier's mode of escape divulged to him, else he would not have so boldly hazarded his own safety, and at last sacrificed his life, to the seizing Monsieur Chevalier's person.—He sent him to Calcutta, as an acquisition of the first magnitude to the peace and security of the English Company's possessions in India. But the same motives which wrought his escape from Ghyrotty, and the affected feelings of one lady for another, procured him a speedy and safe conduct to France, through the Red Sea, in a French vessel under Danish colours, loaded for his own and Monsieur Moncron's account, with money and merchandize.

as the share which they have had in embarrassing the Nabob of the Carnatic, are further instances of the bad policy of extending greater privileges to strangers than to British subjects. The prostituted name of Mr. De S—a, which has been so often used for the purpose of defrauding the government of Britain, in matters relating to the king's squadrons in India; the plan concerted between Monsieur Bellecombe, Monsieur Moracin, and Monsieur de Larche, in case of the reduction of Pondicherry, for conveying political intelligence of measures in India; the conveniency which the house of Guinett, a French surgeon, settled in Madras, afforded in communicating the transactions in Fort St. George to Pondicherry; the countenance and inconsiderate indulgence granted to Monsieur Salabert, a French officer, for whom M. de la Brilliane, of Mauritius, procured introductions from lady F——r to her friends in Madras, and sent him, under the sanction of these letters, actually as a spy, in consequence of which, and the easy access he had to the families of those members of council who were married to French ladies, he had the liberty of visiting all the fortifications, and procured introductions, for the like purposes, to Ajengo, Tellicherry, and Bombay†.—These are among the many happy effects of that partial indulgence which is shewn in British Hindostan to foreigners.—Salabert returned to Mahé, and joined M. St. Luben and Hyder Ally. Hence he accompanied Captain Rozell, in disguise, to Negapatnam and Tranquebar, and at length (at the very time it was besieg-

† Where his designs were suspected by the shrewd discernment of the blunt Mr. Hornby, who ordered him to withdraw on a very short notice.

ed)

ed) into Pondicherry, whence he embarked in the Pourvoyeuſe to Mauritius.

The hiſtory and conduct of Monſieur Moneron is very applicable to the preſent ſubject. This gentleman's name has already been mentioned as the aſſociate of M. Chevalier into the Red Sea. He found leſs difficulty in procuring a paſſage, through the intereſt of a refugee houſe of trade in London, than a loyal Britiſh ſubject would in one of the Company's ſhips. The ſame houſe furniſhed him money, merchandize, and credit, for which, it is probable, they are now ſmarting. Being a man of addreſs and abilities, he ſoon became a favourite and confident of Monſieur Chevalier; and the ſame properties, together with a knowledge of the Engliſh language, and other uſeful qualifications, rendered him a welcome and confidential emiſſary in Calcutta. His brother was employed as a neceſſary meſſenger, under the denomination of a ſupercargo, to Pondicherry and Mauritius, in the ſhip le Duc de Vrilliere. He was indulged, in compliment to Monſieur Chevalier, to accompany him on his parole through the Red Sea to France, and thence to ſurrender themſelves priſoners of war in England. He nominally chartered a large ſnow, under Daniſh paſſports and colours, though, in truth, ſhe was his own property; he loaded her with proper goods for the Suez, Judda, and Mocha markets, and with money; and they embarked, provided with the moſt ample paſſports, and letters of ſafe conduct from the governor general †. It is more than probable that he touched at Mangalore,

† This meaſure was ſtrongly oppoſed by Mr. Francis and Mr. Wheler in council.

or Choul, on the Malabar coast, in order to confer with Hyder Ally and the Marrattas, as well as with Monsieur St. Lubin; which may account for the vessel's not getting higher up than Judda, in the Red Sea, before the monsoon set in from the northward. Here the friends parted; M. Chevalier to pursue his India schemes in Versailles; and M. Moneron to return to India, more for the purpose of making new discoveries, and of communicating them, than for that of establishing his family, or disposing of his merchandize. Indeed, he had liquidated most of his India concerns before his departure from that country.

He loaded his snow back, traded at Ceylon and Negapatnam, and, with an effrontery peculiar to his countrymen, boldly entered the Houghley, and landed his cargo, which he sold openly to an English merchant in Calcutta. That he might not hazard his neck in case of a discovery, after taking the oaths of allegiance, &c. he continued to pass and repass freely, throughout the English, Dutch, and Danish settlements in Bengal, without demanding any protection, or qualifying as a prisoner of war. In the mean time he learnt the hostile disposition of all the native states in Hindostan to the English; the very reduced state of the English Company's finances; and on the whole, that the present was a proper period for France to execute her purpose of joining the force which lay in Mauritius to those of Hyder Alley and the Marrattas, in order to regain a greater power and influence in India, than had ever been conceived by the most sanguine hopes of Monsieur Dupleix. An English stranger, unconnected with the Company, had an opportunity of learning, that a ship bought in

the

the name of a Portuguese merchant in Calcutta, then loading with rice and provisions for Tranquebar on the coast of Coromandel, in which Monsieur Moneron and his family were to embark as passengers, was really the property of Monsieur Moneron, as well as her cargo, and was actually destined in a direct course to Mauritius, and took several opportunities, in private conversation, of mentioning it, first to Mr. Hastings's friend, and then to some other members of the supreme board. After the ship had fallen down below Calcutta, in the river, Monsieur Moneron was confined to his house at Chandernagore; but although the ship Swallow, mounting sixteen guns, and navigated with one hundred men, lay at Cadgerry ready to slip at a moment's warning to seize the ship, she was suffered quietly to pass, and to proceed to Mauritius: for upon enquiry, it was found, that she had not touched at Tranquebar, or any other part of that coast.

It should be an invariable maxim with states at war, to treat prisoners, not only with humanity, hospitality, and liberality, but with every possible indulgence, consistent with prudence and policy. In India, this law of humanity, thus guarded and qualified, has, however, been transgressed. The Company's servants have departed from the characteristic of Englishmen, by the exercise of parsimony and unnecessary incivility on some occasions, while in others they have shewn the most imprudent indulgences to the enemies of their country. The very polite mode of accommodating Governor Chevalier, and sending him home by the shortest and safest route, to concert the recovery of India in Versailles, while Madame Chevalier was contented

to

to undergo the perils and fatigues of a long voyage in a Danish ship, by the Cape of Good Hope†, and the last-mentioned indulgence to Monsieur Moneron; the pensions doubled ostentatiously to French pensioners in Chandernagore; in return for which, in less than six months, the pensioners doubled the rents of their houses to such British subjects as were desirous of benefiting by the salubrity of an air and situation, so superior to Calcutta; the unlimited freedom given to Frenchmen, of ingress and egress to all parts indiscriminately, and consequently of communicating, with dangerous circumstances, the state of general and particular affairs in India, through the Danish, Dutch, and Portuguese, to the Marrattas, Hyder Ally, Mauritius, and France; the unhandsome, the indeed unnecessary incivility shewn to General Bellecombe at Madras, when in the state of a prisoner of war; the stop-

† Monsieur Chevalier acquired wealth, and what is of more importance, a knowledge of the politics, customs, dispositions, and languages of Hindostan, acting as a remote country agent, with extraordinary indulgences, for English gentlemen, members of council in Calcutta. He had not been in the service of the French Company, or the crown, from the conquest of Chandernagore by Admiral Watson and Lord Clive; but Governor Law discovered his abilities and knowledge, and with a true spirit of patriotism, discovered also the advantage which France might derive from them; and Monsieur Chevalier profiting of his own wealth, reasonably applied a portion thereof to second the recommendation of Governor Law; in consequence of which, he was quickly taken into the service of the crown, and raised as quickly to the second station in India. An enterprising genius, an ambitious mind, and an ardent desire to fulfil the hopes he had raised, conspired to excite his activity, and to support his perseverance. The capture of Chandernagore, by surprise, and a similar attempt upon the house of Ghyrotty, did not deprive him of the means of preserving the copious materials he had collected. He was faithfully assisted in the mode of securing them and himself; and a man, proverbially distinguished for the want of personal address, and the uniform awkwardness of his person, attitudes, and conversation in public, to the astonishment of India, acquired upon this singular occasion, as if by instinct, the tone and polite civility of a Frenchman. Mr. Hastings condescended to extend and rack his invention, in order to accommodate Monsieur Chevalier, and to forward his and the views of France, against the able and wise remonstrances and protests of his colleagues in council, and unfortunately, as chief, he possessed influence, and two votes.

page

page of the subsistence stipulated by capitulation to some of the civil and pensioned officers in Pondicherry, who could not even be accommodated singly, far less with their wives, children, mothers, and sisters, on board the Luconia snow, and who, upon that account, would not leave them behind in misery, but, following the feelings and dictates of nature, declined that occasion of going to Mauritius:—these and other circumstances, sufficiently prove the deficiency of their hospitality in some instances, and its excess in others. But the military manœuvre of Sir Eyre Coote, and the acquiescence of the council of Madras, in inlisting prisoners of war, then under articles of capitulation, who were natural-born subjects of France, into the Company's service, was a measure which condemns the military knowledge of the one, and the political knowledge of the other.

Monsieur Bellecombe, intending to procure favourable conditions, lengthened his requisitions to about forty seven articles, which, with equal efficacy, might have been comprised in a fourth part of that number. Among other superfluous articles, he stipulated, that the prisoners of war should not be tampered with, or inveigled to inlist in the English Company's service. Doubtless, this precaution could only have had allusion to Germans, Swiss, Brabanters, and others, not natural-born subjects of France: it never could have been understood to extend to capitulant subjects, natives of France. The former were certainly free to inlist, because the act of surrender absolved them from the temporary allegiance they owed to France. The latter could not inlist in a British army, being bound by a natural and indefeasible allegiance to the

the king of France. But in the conduct of General Bellecombe on this occasion, we have a striking proof that an unnecessary multiplication of laws defeats its own object. It was thought necessary by Monsieur Bellecombe, to restrain the British from inveigling the prisoners to inlist in their service, by an express stipulation. The British general did not break through this engagement, when he enlisted such of the prisoners as had not been tampered with and inveigled; but who offered themselves as recruits of their own accord. But still, by enlisting French prisoners, he violated the laws of nations; and at the same time committed an act of deadly inhumanity, in placing those ignorant, deluded people in the situation of deserters and traitors, by which they forfeit their lives, or are subjected to perpetual banishment from their country, friends, and families.

The preference granted to the traitors, after their arrival at Calcutta, over regular European troops, as a bribe to secure their attachment, implied a strong distrust of their fidelity to their new masters and commanders. For that distrust, I confess, I think there was great room. I venture to predict, that the precedence given to the traitors will not be sufficient to restrain them from committing, on any favourable occasion, a second act of treachery. Perhaps their enlisting in our service, was a political manœuvre of France: nor was it bad policy to procure such accession of strength and intelligence in the heart of Hindostan. I suspect you will think this conjecture rather fanciful. I allow, that political refinement is frequently a source of error. But the political schemes of France being laid deep, it is necessary, if we speculate concerning them at all, to speculate

speculate profoundly. However chimerical the suspicions I have just now hinted may appear to some; to those well acquainted with the French nation, they will seem very natural. Even French officers would willingly enlist in our army as privates, and serve in that character for years, if by that zeal, they could hope to recommend themselves, by the communication of important intelligence, or otherwise, to the attention of the grand monarque, or to the favour of any of his ministers.

I am, &c.

LETTER LI.

To J——M——, Esq; London.

Calcutta, Dec. 9, 1779.

THE Carnatic, merely by acts of oppression, has decreased in population in a greater proportion than its revenues have diminished. The gross revenues of the Nabob, comprehending the Marrawah conquest, and all other tributary claims appertaining to the nabobship, which even in his time were not much short of forty-eight to fifty lacks of pagodas, or about 2,000,000l. sterling, are at this time computed communibus annis, to run only from thirty to thirty-two lacks; or about 1,200,000l. Some pretend to compute them under twenty lacks of pagodas. These are melancholy reflections, the distress of which is heightened by a clear knowledge that the depopulation of the Carnatic, and the poverty of the prince, have enriched the dominions of an inveterate enemy †, and recruited his army with troops, regularly trained to the use

† Hyder Ally Cawn.

of arms under British officers in the Nabob's service.

The Rajaship of Tanjore, which is incomparably the richest spot between the Kistna and Cape Comorin, and may, in other respects, be called the key, as well as the support of all that extensive tract of country, yielded, before the late unjust revolution and violation of public faith, an annual revenue of from seventeen to twenty lacks of pagodas; but it has been with difficulty, that ten or twelve lacks have been collected since the surrender thereof to the Rajah.

By restoring these rich countries to their original splendour, and especially by bringing them to that happy degree of perfection, which nature in its bounty hath rendered them capable of attaining, what a vast addition will not be made to the trade and security, as well as to the reputation of the British nation?

There is scarcely a character in India so uncandidly exhibited by partisans and adversaries, or a person whose conduct has been so unfairly stated, as that of the Nabob of the Carnatic. That prince owes his greatness, and the very existence of his family, to the British nation. Of this he has ever shewed himself sensible; and has given the most ample proofs of his gratitude, not only to the English East India Company, but to individuals of the English nation.

On the other hand, it is not less true, that the English Company owe their grandeur and success in a great measure to the uniform attachment, fidelity, and friendship of the Nabob; to his treasures, to the pledged credit of his dominions in the days of their insignificancy and distress, and to his judicious counsels and influence, when their own local and

political

political knowledge of India was obscure and superficial.—The Company have constantly done justice to the merit of the Nabob, by the letter and spirit of every paper issuing from Leadenhall street, wherein they were not misled by partial misrepresentations. But, removed far from the field of action, and misguided by the interested, but specious representations of their principal servants abroad, the Directors condescended to become accessaries in scenes of iniquity and guilt, at which their minds would have revolted.

At some times deceived, defrauded, dishonoured, and insulted; and at others amused, flattered, indulged, and exalted; it is not a matter of wonder if the Nabob became suspicious, timid, wavering, and cunning.—The moral characters of men are not so much impressed on them by the original hand of nature, as they are formed by circumstances and situations.—The Nabob of the Carnatic was naturally affable, humane, just, generous, and steady. But this excellent disposition has been changed by necessity, and a regard to self preservation. It is only astonishing, that at an age nearer to seventy than sixty-five years, he should continue to possess such undaunted virtue as enables him to avert those dangers which are hourly hovering over his head, and at the same time preserve all the elegance of princely manners and address, with a countenance the most manly and graceful that the fancy of a painter can conceive.

This prince, in the vain hope of gratifying the insatiable and importunate avarice of the servants of the English East India Company, oppressed his people to such a degree, that his country became nearly depopulated. In such circumstances, a regard to his own safety co-operating with an ambition natural to Moorish princes, he readily yielded to the gilded bait which the rapacity of British subjects held up to his view, when they persuaded him to seize upon the country of Tanjore; on pretences as foreign to justice, as they were dishonourable to the English Company, who were guarantees of the treaty of 1762, and the friends and allies of both. Hence the Nabob's misfortunes—hence he was involved in a debt of near fifty lacks of pagodas†, although he never received a just or valuable confideration for twenty. This enormous debt has accumulated, notwithstanding that by the unnatural plunder of Tanjore, as is supposed, he had enriched his treasures to the value of near as much more. Thus embarrassed, continually beset with duns and harpies, and threatened with the scourge of borrowed power; his taskmasters and plunderers continually changing, and continually extorting the unconscientious price of their assumed protection and support; a state prisoner within his own palace, and restrained from receiving the compliments and visits of persons not intimately connected with the temporary protector, unless by stealth; why should it appear surprising that he, as well as his oppressors should act the politician, and use against them their own deceitful weapons;—Such is his situation, that if he had it in his power, he dares not to pay his just debts; because he dares not to separate the real from the imaginary claims upon him; and he is totally incapable of paying the whole.

These very impolitic measures on the part of the Company's servants, have also wrought upon his mind to be unjust to his own family: an effect

† 2,000,000 l.

which in its confequences may prove highly prejudicial to the Company's intereft. He has two fons arrived at years of maturity. The eldeft is of a mild difpofition, fenfible, a lover of juftice, ftudious, and as candid and fincere as we can expect him to be, if we confider his parentage and oriental education; but too great an attachment to his haram, has rendered him indolent, and unacquainted with bufinefs. The fecond is by nature artful, deceitful, infinuating, and treacherous; but able, active, and perfevering in bufinefs and intrigue. The Nabob, whether through the artful infinuations of the younger, or a diftruft of the paffivenefs of the elder, or from whatever other private caufe, has apparently withdrawn his countenance and protection from the eldeft fon, and is wholly guided by the younger, whom he has made Generaliffimo of his army, and to whom he wifhes and intends to leave the fucceffion of the Carnatic. This influence of the fecond fon, has feduced the Nabob's heart from the Englifh Company: he is, however, divefted of the power of either good or evil; unlefs by fecretly intriguing at the court of Poonah and its vicinity, and by corrupting the morals and fidelity of the Company's fervants.

In the prefent ftate of India, and of the Nabob's age, the intereft of the Company requires an immediate fettlement of the fucceffion to the nabobfhip: becaufe if fuch a fettlement be not made before the old prince dies, the fucceffion will become a fubject of contention between the eftablifhed claim of the eldeft and the hoarded treafure of the younger fon; and the fucceffor, whichfoever of the two he be, muft give or promife crores of rupees to conciliate the countenance and protection of the Company's
fervants.

servants. Four things are therefore necessary to be done, without loss of time, by the East India Company.

First, to appoint commissioners to liquidate all British claims upon the Nabob, by a thorough investigation of his debts, and by appropriating a specific fund for the payment of such capital sums, and legal accumulations of interest, as ought in justice and equity to be paid; and also, with the assistance of agents from the Nabob and Rajah, to liquidate all money transactions depending between these princes, fixing at the same time the conditional rights of each to their possessions, and their relations to each other.

Secondly, to fix the lineal succession to the nabobship in the eldest son, agreeably to the royal Firmaund, and the renunciation of the Soubah†; with a respectable jaghire (a pension chargeable on lands) to the second son, and the rest of the children: and to limit the succession of Tanjore, after the demise of the present possessor, and his direct lineal descendants.

Thirdly, to establish a king's resident upon the coast (unless, upon a new system, the sovereignty shall be assumed by the crown of Britain, and a governor appointed to act under a double commission

---

† By the Mogul Firmaund, bearing date the 26th August, 1765, to the Nabob, "constituting him Governor and Nabob of the Carnatic, and the countries dependent thereon, the reversion and perpetuity thereof is unalienably granted, and specifically confirmed in the Nabob's eldest son Meyonul-muluck, Omdat-ul-Omrah, and their heirs for ever." Which Firmaund was ratified by the Soubah of the Decan, and his claims to the Carnatic for ever, renounced, in a solemn deed or treaty, bearing date the 23d February, 1768, containing the same express limitations on the Nabob's eldest son, the Omdat-ul-Omrah. Thus any act of the Nabob to alter the succession, will operate as a direct breach and forfeiture of the royal Firmaund, and of the Warrantee of the English Company to the Soubah, in the last-mentioned treaty.

from

from the crown and Company) to be a check upon
the rapacity of the Company's government in matters immediately relating to country princes; but
on no pretext to exercise any power which might
in the least interfere with the Company's trade or
revenues.

And fourthly, to secure to the Nabob every prerogative that belongs to his rank and title, and external respect from the natives who occupy the
Company's jaghire lands: but to disqualify him,
or any other person acting for him, or under his
controul, from renting the jaghire lands, or any of
the Circar lands, ceded to the Company by the
royal Firmaund in 1765.

I am, &c.

LETTER LII.

To J—— M——, Esq. London.

Calcutta, Dec. 13, 1779.

I HAVE long flattered myself in vain, with the hopes of a journey to Europe over land. I find
that I must once more commit myself to the watery
element, though my health is but little suited to
confinement on board a ship.—But I am pretty well
inured to disappointments.

I have a few more observations to make on the
Company's affairs in this country. If I find an opportunity of transmitting them to you before I set
sail myself, which I have some reason to expect, I
will embrace it. If not, I shall carry home my
own letters, as testimonies that the distance of an
hemisphere

hemisphere has not rendered me forgetful of my friends, or unmindful of my engagements.

There are few circumstances of a public nature that are more disreputable to the conduct of the English in India, than the plan and general government of the town of Calcutta in Bengal. There is not in the world a country, except the United Provinces, so eminently distinguished for the neatness, regularity, uniformity, and cleanliness in its cities, towns, houses, and inclosures, as England. It is nevertheless a truth, that from the western extremity of California in America to the eastern coast of Japan, there is not a spot where judgment, taste, decency, and conveniency, are so grossly insulted as in that scattered and confused chaos of houses, huts, sheds, streets, lanes, alleys, windings, gutters, sinks, and tanks, which, jumbled into an undistinguished mass of filth and corruption, equally offensive to human sense and health, compose the capital of the English Company's government in India. The very small portion of cleanliness which it enjoys, is owing to the familiar intercourse of hungry jackalls by night, and ravenous vultures, kites, and crows by day. In like manner it is indebted to the smoke raised in public streets, in temporary huts and sheds, for any respite it enjoys from musquetoes, the natural production of stagnated and putrid waters. But while the smoke, issuing from numberless places, saves the inhabitants of Calcutta from one evil, it subjects them to another; for by endeavouring to shut it out at windows and doors, they are forced also to shut out pure air at the hours of retirement, when its use is most essential to respiration and health.

Assuredly,

Assuredly, no people upon earth have so much reason to be grateful to Providence, as those of Calcutta, for having so long miraculously preserved themselves and their properties from those dreadful devastations which naturally arise from a total neglect and abuse of fire. Every house and office seems to be propped by huts (which in the language of the country are called choppers) composed of bamboos; their sides, tops, and floors being covered with mats, straw, or long grass. In these huts, formed of such inflammable materials, as well as in the public streets and vacant spaces, fires are preserved, as they were of old by vestals in heathen temples. These choppers are the habitations of careless servants, palanquin bearers, coolies, and horses. They are also used for the purpose of sheltering carriages. To these choppers, or to a more suspicious cause, is the loss of more than twenty two lacks of rupees, consumed in one of the Company's warehouses on the memorable fifth of November last, confidently attributed.—The public bear these nuisances with wonderful patience, although they are taxed to the extent of about eighty thousand rupees annually, for the express purpose of establishing a police in Calcutta. This heavy tax is applied, in conformity with the general maxims that direct the conduct of the Company's principal servants, to the purpose of enriching some favoured tool, under the unmeaning denomination of Jemmadar, and the appointment of several hundreds of inferior tyrants, oppressors, and tax-gatherers. Of the tax thus levied by authority, it is said, that a quarter part is distributed amongst inferiors, and the remaining three parts become the plunder of the chief, who openly licenses nuisances as the valuable confideration for pecuniary gratifications, formally ftipulated and regularly paid. As to the under-officers of the police, they are by no means deficient in following the honourable example of the Jemmadar, by the connivance, or actual commiffion of thefts, robberies, and abufes of various kinds.

The difeafe is too far advanced to be fpeedily remedied by the application of any medicine, however powerful its general efficacy. The property of individuals is too facred to be violated, and too confiderable to be purchafed; and the various prejudices, paffions, and opinions of men, will never freely concur in any meafure, however obvious its utility to the public. If ever the police of Calcutta be put on a proper footing, it will neither be owing to the wifdom or virtue of the Company's fervants in India: The reform muft originate in Leadenhall-ftreet, and be authorifed by the Britifh parliament.

Whatever plan fhall be adopted for eftablifhing a proper police in Calcutta, may be carried into execution by a conftitutional body, confifting of the governor general, the fupreme council of the Indies, and a certain limited number of perfons, properly qualified, and elected by the free and copyholders of Calcutta, to reprefent them for thefe fpecial purpofes in general affembly. Thefe three eftates fhould be invefted with legiflative powers, fufficient for enacting laws for refuming, felling, throwing down, re-building, repairing, lengthening, widening, cleanfing, draining, and doing every thing confiftent with juftice to individuals, that may be neceffary for building houfes, of making ftreets, fquares, tanks, drains, and eftablifhing

blifhing a regular police within the city and precincts of Calcutta; and alfo for affefling and levying taxes, duties, and impofts on the inhabitants thereof, for thefe purpofes.

As luxury is a conftant attendant in all courts, fo the vices that arife from luxury are enemies to commerce, manufactures, and every fpecies of induftry. It fhould therefore become an invariable maxim in all commercial ftates, to feparate the feats of government from thofe of trade. Eaftern cuftoms have conftituted pomp, parade, and courtly ftate, an effential principle of government. Luxury therefore, in the political conftitutions of India, forms a part of their nature, or as Montefquieu would have faid, of their fpirit. It is abfolutely neceffary, to fecure obedience, and a regular fubordination of rank, from the prince on the throne, down to the loweft of above twenty feven claffes of people. It will be proper to continue, for fome time, the appearance of a practice fo conformable to thofe ideas of fuperiority and power which prevail in the Eaft, and which are therefore material to good government.

But there is not any reafon why trade fhould imitate an example of luxury, which would not only embarrafs it with intolerable charges, but which, by corrupting their minds, and enervating their conftitutions, would render traders and manufacturers debauched, flothful, rapacious, and unjuft.

Perhaps it would favour both the advancement of commerce, and the fcheme of re-building, and reforming the police of Calcutta, that fome other place than that town fhould be allotted for the chief feat of government. The only part of the present city worth preserving, is upon or near the Esplanade, which is principally occupied by the immediate members of government, and courts of justice: the remaining parts of the town are composed of such base materials, that they will be demolished in a few years by the weather. The houses upon and near the esplanade and grand tank, are capable of accommodating such a number of those who now reside in the noxious part of the town, as to enable the commissioners, after an accurate survey, and a judicious attention to particular good houses and streets, to commence in a short time the new modelling thereof, without subjecting the inhabitants to any serious inconveniences. It is notorious, that the waters which settle in Calcutta, although lower than the river when the tide is up, may be conveyed, at a small expence, to the canals, or nullas which communicate with the salt lake.

The next object of consideration should be, where to fix the seat of government. Doubtless, the wealth and superior importance of Bengal, Bahar, and Orissa, as well as many other advantages which they possess, without reckoning up the army which is entertained and stationed in them, and the superb fortress of Fort William, are motives abundantly sufficient to cast the scale in their favour, if it could be supposed to remain for a moment in suspence. It is of no importance, in the choice of the seat of government, which of these is the most centrical to the British dominions in India, as wheresoever it is, it will become the general resort, especially in a country where such respect is paid to civil power, and where the principles of personal address and politeness are better understood

understood and practised, than in any other upon earth. Justice and sound policy conspire to point out the propriety of accommodating the remote provinces with assizes and inferior courts of justice, to relieve the people from the grievous charges and personal inconveniences with which justice has of late years been purchased in Calcutta.

In the choice of the object in question, strict regard should be had to situation, water communication, elevation, and air. Upon the banks of the Houghly, from Cadgeree to Cossimbazar, there is not so eligible a spot as that pitched upon by the representatives of the late French East India Company at Chandernagore. The elevation of that town is such, that all the rain which falls in and around it, will nearly convey itself, at all seasons of the year and tides, without obstruction, into the river. Its situation is even, its air clear, dry, and salubrious. Its soil contains such a proportion of sand, as to render it fertile by instantly absorbing the rain. The river Houghly is navigable to Chandernagore by a third rate man of war, as the late gallant Admiral Watson proved in the Kent of 74 guns; but it is not navigable for a ship of any considerable burthen half a league higher up: a circumstance, by the way, which may give rise to an idea of facilitating the communication between Calcutta and Chandernagore†, by a stone or wooden bridge over the river, below Chinsura. Various advantages in point of security, revenue, and conveniency, might arise from this communication, in which a draw-bridge should be made over one of the arches at each side, for the passage of large

---

† They are situated on opposite sides of the Houghly.

or masted vessels, as well as for occasional defence.

The intimate connection between the trade of Calcutta and the navigation of the river Houghly, and its communication with the several rivers which are navigable into the Marratta territories, and to the northern and eastern extremities of Hindoftan, will naturally claim all possible attention from the inhabitants of Calcutta. Wherefore, it may be thought adviseable to commit to the legiflature of that city, the guardianship of these navigations, as far as the British domain doth extend. Nor is it to be doubted, when our people shall have once heartily engaged in the improvement of these navigations, that the force of example, manifeft advantage, and British influence, will induce the neighbouring princes to purfue, throughout their dominions, the fame plans for the general benefit. The difficulties which the Company's administration allege, in excufe for their own negligence of fo important an object as the improvement of the navigation of the Houghly, would doubtlefs excite the indignation of every Englishman, if they were not fo much calculated to move his ridicule. The means of overcoming these difficulties are assuredly very eafy and fimple. I am, &c.

LETTER LIII.

To J—— M——, Efq. London.

Calcutta, Dec. 3, 1779.

THE prefent mode of adminiftering juftice, under the fanction of a British act of parliament, in Bengal, is a subject which calls aloud for public

public attention and speedy relief. This dreadful evil threatens the extinction of the British power and property in India. Corruption hath usurped the sacred seat of justice, and, shielded by the power of a venal government, hath held quiet possession of this station for six lingering years, without even the veil of hypocrisy to shade the horrors of oppression and savage violence. Here, however, I might joyfully remark a single exception, in the soul of Sir R———t Ch————rs, had Nature, extending to this amiable person her kind liberality, fortified his virtue with resolution to withstand magisterial frowns and supercilious arrogance. The mind, overwhelmed with a confusion of cruel, iniquitous, and violent decisions and executions, is incapable of arranging the various ideas that occur upon this subject of horror. On this account, however, there is the less cause of regret, that the united voice of the whole people has accompanied an humble addrefs to parliament, with an authentic state of facts, which sufficiently paint their deplorable situations. What must be the tormenting feelings of those persons, who recommended to their sovereign, to invest such men with the most sacred and important of his own prerogatives, when they come to discover, that the people who were intended to be made happy under a mild and steady administration of impartial justice, are labouring under the unrelenting scourge of judicial tyrants?

Let the protectors of such men demonstrate their disappointment and concern at their conduct, by yielding them up as sacrifices to that justice which they have so heinously offended. This is the only atonement in their power to make to an injured people:

people: it will suffice, and the example will deter others from treading in their abominable paths.

The memorial and state of facts to which I allude, are said to disclose a scene of proceedings which, by being irrefutable, cannot fail to be redressed, even without their being carried before parliament; unless the neglect of not communicating their contents to the parties complained of, before they were transmitted to Europe, should render it necessary to hear the accused in their own defence, left an ex parté decision, however strong, credible, and authentic the accompanying testimonies, should establish a precedent which might justify their own measures; or unless his Majesty, in compassion to the sufferings of five thousand British subjects, and twelve millions of Indians, should be graciously pleased to order the accused home, to answer for themselves in Westminster-hall.

But the condemnation and execution of Nundocomar; the violent imprisonment and deaths of the native judges, in the cause of the Begum of Patna; the impolitic outrage on the person, zenana, household gods, and property, of the Rajah of Cossijurah; and many other acts of notorious injustice, cry aloud for examples of just vengeance upon the spot where the abominable deeds were perpetrated; in order to convince all Asia, that they had neither the authority nor sanction of the British government, and that, however the stream may be polluted, the fountain of British justice is yet uncorrupted.

The mention of one circumstance may alone suffice, to give an idea of the rapacity of the supreme court of judicature in Bengal, and of the deplorable state of that country, over which it extends its iniquitous jurisdiction.—On a medium computation,

it

it has been found, that the fees of proceſſes and writs iſſuing from the ſupreme court, have amounted annually to the enormous ſum of four hundred and twenty-ſix thouſand pounds ſterling. What muſt be the entire ſum which, according to this ſpecimen, is exacted by the ſeveral members of this arbitrary and oppreſſive court?

The ſtory of Nundocomar, to which I have alluded, is briefly as follows:

Maha Rajah Nundocomar was a prieſt of the higheſt order in the Bramin caſt, and a prince. His family and caſt ſerved only as leading ſteps to the ranks which he had long occupied in the adminiſtration of government in the ſubahſhip of Bengal, Bahar, and Oriſſa; his diſtinguiſhed abilities, addreſs, and knowledge, procured him the unbounded confidence and direction of Muxhadabad Durbar. —His character for intrigue, and in private life, made him obnoxious to many; and his power naturally created jealouſy and rivality.—What in any country, and eſpecially in Europe, would have been diſtinguiſhed and applauded as virtue and pure patriotic zeal, was held criminal by the Company's ſervants, and their native adherents.—He beheld, with jealouſy and anguiſh, the growing dominion of Europeans and Chriſtians in Hindoſtan, and the conſequent decay of native government, influence, and freedom. He ſaw his prince bearing a ſhadow of power, ſupporting a ſham-court, and every day retrenching his rights and affected prerogatives.—His own intereſt, doubtleſs, led the Bramin to view theſe innovations with concern and diſcontent, and the ſame motive might have ſtimulated his deſires to diſconcert them —Whether theſe were the real cauſes of ſuſpicion in the

preſidency

presidency of Fort William, or whether the minister of the present Nabob Mabaruk-ul-Dowla, was not so lavish of his minor master's lacks as was expected; it was their will and pleasure to seize the person of the minister of Nundocomar, to conduct him to Calcutta, and to detain him a prisoner, under a military guard, until the arrival of the supreme council, in October, 1774.

After having borne marks of European despotism, in being punished for imaginary delinquencies, it was imagined, that his nature thenceforward would be pliant and condescending.—His capacity and intrigue were thought useful qualifications to work up General Clavering, in the capacity of banyan to the second in council and military commander in chief, and to second the views of the governor general, whom he was to serve, all the while, in the character of a spy, and as a pensioner. The plan was laid, and the Maha Rajah was willing to undertake the two-fold office of banyan and spy. But the general had had a previous recommendation, and his promise was inviolable.

The civil chief disappointed, renounced the Bramin; who, on his part (not unmindful of past sufferings, and dreading more) finding that the ministry of the Nabob of Bengal, and the distribution of money, became subjects of investigation by the superior board, exhibited to that board, a state of some pecuniary applications, amounting to such direct charges against the governor general, as would have involved forfeitures of place and money.

To

To prevent the operation of the immediate charge by Nundocomar, and to prevent similar acts by other natives, became the neceſſary ſubject of ſecret deliberation. It was diſcovered, that about nine years before the paſſing of the Britiſh ſtatute law, to conſtitute a court of judicature, and to eſtabliſh laws within the town of Calcutta, and the limited precincts of the ſubordinate factories, extending only to natives in the ſervice of the Company, or who voluntarily choſe to ſubmit any deciſion to that juriſdiction, Nundocomar was ſuſpected of having, in the adjuſtment of ſome executorſhip committed to him by a deceaſed friend of his own country and kindred, forged a name to a receipt for money.—Upon this charge a warrant was iſſued out againſt him, though detained by force in Calcutta; and he was committed to cloſe priſon.

It is neceſſary to make you acquainted with ſuch of the Gentoo tenets and the Hindoo laws, as relate to the preſent cauſe. The Gentoo religion injoins ablution, by daily waſhing the whole body, and waſhing of hands before and after every meal; that perſons of different caſts ſhall not eat together; that the food of one caſt ſhall not be dreſſed in the ſame veſſel that the food of another caſt has been dreſſed in, nor be dreſſed by any other caſt; that it ſhall be dreſſed upon the earth; and that theſe ablutions and refreſhments ſhall be performed out of the view of others, or in private. By the Hindoo laws and cuſtoms, and particularly by reaſon of theſe religious principles, perſons are never confined in priſon for crimes or for debts: a guard is placed over their own houſes, or over others houſes where the perſons confined can exerciſe the rites,

rites, &c. injoined by religion.—Forgery is only denominated a fraud in any perfon, and punifhed by mulcts; but no offence whatever is capitally criminal in a Bramin, except ftate crimes, heinous murders, and facrilege; nor is it allowed by their laws to execute the fentence of death, but by fpilling the blood with the edge of a fword.—Strangling is difallowed particularly; becaufe in the fpilling of blood, they conceive that crimes are expiated.—Thefe being their principles of religious faith, confinements and executions which violate them, operate as a double punifhment, and aggravate the public injury.—The laws of his country were not obferved towards Nundocomar; the pretended forgery was committed nine years before the Britifh law was enacted, and the law itfelf exprefsly ftipulated the fubfequent period at which the penal claufes were to have effect, viz. the firft of Auguft, 1774.

When the forgery was faid to have been committed, the civil government was conducted by the Nabob, and the Hindoo laws adminiftered by his judges, and in his courts.—The author of this forgery was the Nabob's prime minifter, and the perfon aggrieved was his fubject; neither of them were in the fervice of the Company, or fubject in any ways to their jurifdiction.—Nundocomar, after having exhibited charges in the fupreme council againft the governor general, and prepared to prove them, was feized for this forgery, and thrown into the common prifon with felons and debtors, whofe company to a Gentoo was pollution; he wanted the means of performing the ablutions and indifpenfable rites of his religious faith and his caft, and of obferving the neceffary rules

of

of preserving life, in the mode of dressing and eating his food.

The governor general refused the competency of the supreme council to take cognizance of any charges against, or crimes imputed to him; but it was necessary to remove the bold testimony of Nundocomar, and by his example to deter others in future. His own, and the supplications of others, to the judges, in behalf of the Bramin, for such indulgences as were consonant to his religion, cast, and civil station, were disregarded. It is confidently alledged, that both witnesses and lawyers were brow-beat at the bar of this tribunal. Mr. M. W— and Mr. J. L—, two gentlemen of the most unblemished characters, and of unshaken integrity, incapable of being influenced, were thought improper persons to remain upon the corrected venire of the sheriff, when the trial came on.—Every plea against the application of the late act of parliament, upon ex post facto principles, and various other matters, were urged in vain. All the bench, except Sir Robert Chambers, declared, that he was amenable to that law. He was found guilty; condemned to be hanged; and was publicly executed within a few paces of Fort William, to the utter astonishment and terror of all Hindostan.—This answered all the purposes of the conspirators; the charge against the governor general dropt, and no native of India has dared to hint a censure against an European member of government in Hindostan ever since. The trial published in England, is universally declared, on this side, to be spurious and false. A narrative of the proceedings in council at that time, printed

by

by order of the Court of Directors, contains many of the atrocious abuses committed on this unhappy Prince and Bramin.

I am, &c.

LETTER LIV.

To J—— M——, Esq; London.

Calcutta, Dec. 21, 1779.

THE avowed system of the present governor general, is to support his own power by providing for his partizans and favourites, in defiance of the Company's orders, and at their expence. By various contracts which he has made, in the name of the Company, with individuals, during the current year, his constituents are injured at least one million sterling. The most important articles in the statement of facts which are the foundation of this heavy charge, will appear upon the Company's records. You would, doubtless, be but little entertained with a minute review of the bullock contract; the contract for victualling the army; that for victualling Fort William; the Budge-row and Pool-bundy contracts; contracts with Mr. A——ms; with Mr. S———n; with Dr. C————ll; with Captain F—d; with Colonel P——r; with Monsieur V——r H——n, &c. &c. But among the various abuses committed under the reign of the present ruler of Bengal, there are some that may not, perhaps, be thought wholly unentertaining. Mr. T———r, who had amassed a capital fortune by contracting with the Company for elephants, was willing to treat, this year,

year, with the supreme council, on the same terms on which he had contracted with them formerly; but the governor general insisted that his demand was not high enough.—The salary of the a——te g——l in the supreme court, was advanced, as an inducement not to do the express duty of his nomination, and to decline the defence of the Company's rights and property. An ambassador was appointed to the Lama or Thibet, at a heavy monthly charge, but never sent.—Captain P——r, the governor's military secretary, at an enormous monthly charge, was sent as an ambassador to the poor distressed Rana of Gohud, to witness the execution of a sham-treaty, which had already had all the authenticity which the custom of the East required.

The post of president at the court of Asoph-ul-Dowla, the Nabob of Oude, is one of those appointments, which, the annual distribution of about a million sterling, renders an object worthy of the acceptance of the first blood royal in Europe. Mr. N——l M——n having executed this trust to the entire satisfaction of his friends, and the impoverishment of the country, it was thought a compliment due to the new associate of the governor, the ribboned knight, to bestow it on one of his friends. He named Mr. H——a; who, on his part, unwilling to trust to events, and the caprice of human nature, posted away with the greatest expedition, to seize the golden fleece, expecting his credentials to follow him. Unfortunately, he reckoned without his host: his departure was premature, for he had not settled preliminaries; his

conduct

conduct was refented; and Mr. C———s H———n P———g, a kinfman of lady C———'s was appointed to the prefidentfhip,

Mr. P———g moved acrofs from his ftation at Rungpore, to take charge of the Vizier's country and treafures in Lucknow, and to procure a proper reception for his benefactor, who followed him in great ftate and pomp to review the army at their feveral cantonments. But alas! the fleece was already clofely fhorn. Empty cafkets, exhaufted treafures, a depopulated and uncultivated country, expofed to the melancholy eye dreary waftes, and blafted hopes to the afflicted mind. Even the preconcerted appearance and pomp of Saudit Ally, the ambitious brother, and rancorous enemy of the Nabob, who accompanied the general from an exile in Calcutta, as an engine of terror, the common inftrument of extortion in Hindoftan, could not, on this occafion, perform miracles, and produce precious metals, and ftones out of affignments on zemindaries that were abandoned.—When we attend to the difappointment of the eager Mr. Hofea, and of the pompous military commander, we are moved with laughter; but we feel emotions of another kind, when we reflect on the miferable ftate to which the princes of Hindoftan are reduced by European tyranny. The country of the Nabob is every where laid wafte; manufactures are extirpated; all avenues to the Perfian and inland trade are obftructed; and the body of the people have fled for fuccour, and the very means of exiftence, to their late avowed and inveterate enemies, the Marrattas and the Jauts. It is confidently alledged, that, were the Company to remove the brigade

which

which is stationed in the province of Oude, out of it, the Nabob, with his whole court and dependents, would be cut to pieces by his own enraged and oppressed subjects.—But the distress of this prince will best appear from the inclosed extract of a letter of Mr. Purling's, the resident at the Nabob's court, dated at Lucknow, Nov. 19, 1779, and from the translation, which I herewith send you, of a letter from the Nabob to the resident†.

Mr.

† I have in vain laid before him (the Vizier and Nabob of Oude) the ruinous consequences of a dismission of any part of the troops which are now employed under the command of British officers, the certain deficiency in the collections, and the laying his country open to foreign invaders. I have in vain urged him, on the glaring impropriety of refusing Tuncaws upon the same districts as last year, and giving them to his own troops without discipline, to support his government; and always ready to plunder every country to which they have been sent.—His answer has been invariable, that while he had the means of providing for the demands of the Company, he had never refused it, but he is now deprived of that ability by the drought, which has obliged him to give deductions to the amount of twenty five lacks of rupees; and even now, the Aumils are desirous of being released from their engagements, upon the plea of inability to comply with them: his family, and that of his father and grand-father, after repeated promises made to them, and broken, are still unprovided for: that he did not believe the council, meant to seize the expences of his table and houshold, which was all that was now left him. When I quitted him, I declared, that I did not imagine the governor and council would ever consent to the reform of the new brigade, and the other present establishments for his collections; that if they were not dismissed they must be paid, and from the sources of that country for the protection of which they were raised; that I would have him for the present to consider the means of granting the supplies, in the hopes of an answer, more likely to be pleasing to our government. A day or two afterwards I received a letter from him, a translate of which (No. 3.) I think it necessary to lay before you. As I have never been able to induce his excellency to adopt any other sentiments than those he first declared; and have received another letter from him, expressing much dissatisfaction at my urgency, on a point he had determined on, and would not give up, unless he should be compelled by the governor and council; I have thought it needless to press him farther at present; but at his request have transmitted a letter from him to the governor general, setting forth his distress.

In this situation, it only remains for me to lay before you the following extract of Mr. Nathaniel Middleton's letter of the 5th instant, the day on which the charge was delivered to me.

" When I have of late pressed his excellency for further assignments, he has pleaded inability to answer the very heavy demands which will this year fall upon him, on account of the drought which has unfortunately happened,

to

Mr. Purling's and the Vizier's letters being read at a confultation in the fecret department the 13th inftant,

to the almoſt deſtruction of the Khurriff harveſt, and the confequent diminution of his revenue. I am concerned to confefs, there are but too good grounds for this plea. The misfortune has been throughout the whole of the Vizier's dominions, obvious to every body; and fo very fatal have been its conſequences, that no perſon of either credit or character, would enter into engagements with government to farm the country, without a very heavy deduction in the laſt year's jumma; which his excellency has been compelled to allow to all who have been appointed to farms; and fome who have engaged under thefe circumſtances, have, to my knowledge, made moſt urgent applications to the Nabob and his miniſters, to be releaſed from their obligations, and allowed to relinquiſh their farms, which they found they could not hold but at a certain lofs to themfelves.

" You will foon be convinced, by undoubted teſtimony and loud complaints from every quarter, of the reality of this miſfortune, which has neceſſarily been the means of delaying the general fettlement of the country, and of preventing my hitherto getting affignments for more than rupees 68,82,000 —but how far its operation and effects preclude the Nabob from anſwering the demands upon him on public account, you will be the beſt able to judge from the ſtatements you will obtain of his eſtimated revenue."

As it appears from the whole of this extract, that Mr. Middleton had met with obſtacles, from a reaſon affigned, which no human foreſight could prevent, I hope your honourable board will not imagine I have been remiſs or inattentive. Nothing but a compulſive order from you, upon an undefined right, could obtain the collection of a rupee more than I have Tuncaws for; and nothing but a deciſive and ſpeedy inſtruction from you, when the time lapſed may not occaſion a material loſs in the revenue, can poſſibly procure the grants neceſſary for the current diſburſements from my treaſury.

Upon this principle it is needleſs to add, that no bill from the preſidency can poſſibly be anſwered, ſince the demands on the treaſury upon the preſent eſtabliſhment, exceed the expected income; and the laſt drafts of the honourable board, and their orders for the payment of two lacks of rupees to Captain Popham, which has been complied with, have fo effectually drained the treaſury, that I have not yet been able to pay the firſt brigade for October.

Tranſlation of a letter from the Vizier to the Reſident at his Court.

The friendſhip between the honourable Company, Mr. Haſtings, governor general, fupreme council, and myſelf, has not the leaſt ſhadow of diſunion. Dominion, property, and honour, are but one and the fame to us.

The ſituation of my affairs reſpecting the preſent time, I informed Mr. Middleton of, both by writing and converſation; and I now proceed to lay the whole before you.

During theſe three years paſt, the expence occaſioned by the troops in brigade, and others commanded by European officers, has much diſtreſſed the ſupport of my houſehold, inſomuch that the allowance made to the feraglio and children of the deceaſed Nabob, has been reduced to one fourth part of what it was; upon which they have ſubſiſted in a very diſtreſſed manner for

theſe

inftant, the governor general recommended the following draught of a letter to be writen to Mr. Purling, which, if agreed to, might ferve as the fubftance of one to be written on the fame fubject to the Nabob.

To Mr. Charles Purling, Refident at the Vizier's Court.

SIR,

"We have received your letter of the 19th November, ftating the objections of the Nabob hefe two years paft. The attendants, writers, fervants, &c. of my court, ave received no pay for thefe two years; and there is at prefent no part of he country that can be allotted to the payment of my father's private credirs, whofe applications are daily preffing upon me.—All thefe difficulties I ave for thefe three years paft ftruggled through, and found this confolation herein, that it was complying with the pleafure of the honourable Company. nd in the hope that the fupreme council would make enquiry from impartial erfons, into my diftreffed fituation. But I am now forced into a reprefentation. 'rom the great increafe of expence, the revenues were neceffarily farmed at high rate; and deficiencies followed yearly. The country and cultivation re abandoned; and this year in particular, from the exceffive drought of the :afon, deductions of many lacks have been allowed the farmers, who are ill left unfatisfied; and I have received but juft fufficient to fupport my abfoute neceffities; and for this reafon, many of the old Chieftains, with their roops and ufeful attendants of the court, were forced to leave it, and now here is left only a few foot and horfe for the collection of the revenues; and hould the zemindars be refractory, there is not a fufficient number to reuce them to the obedience of my collectors.

The late raifed brigade at Futtygur, is not only quite ufelefs to my government, but is moreover the caufe of much lofs both in the revenues and uftoms; the detached body of troops under other European officers, bring othing but confufion to the affairs of government, and are entirely their wn mafters.

In this diftreffed ftate of my affairs, it is juft and requifite, that Mr. Haftigs, General Sir Eyre Coote, and the fupreme council, fhould give me elief.—This year I cannot poffibly provide for the new brigade at Futtygur, he corps of horfe, and other detached bodies of troops in my country. I hope ou will confider well thefe reprefentations, and explain them in a manner ou may judge proper to the governor general and fupreme council.—On my art, country, property, and life, are devoted to the will of the honourable Company, and I hope they will therefore do juftice to thefe my complaints, nd prevent my falling into diftrefs, by not having wherewith to fupport the eceffary expences of my houfehold. For the expence of the brigade at :awn Pore, and other difburfements, I have given Tuncaws and orders upon ny country; the remainder of my revenue, on account of the drought, has allen fo fhort as not to be fufficient for my neceffary expences, being deficint to the amount of fifteen lacks, and the above provifion will bring upon me this year very great diftrefs.—What can I fay more?

to the immediate discharge of the sums due from his government, for the expences of the current year. The principle on which these objections are made, appears to us so repugnant to the Nabob's engagements with the Company, and with the intimate connection of his interests and theirs, that we cannot hesitate a moment to declare them totally inadmissible; and as we have no doubt of the Nabob's ability to furnish the sums absolutely necessary for the service of the year, we require you to repeat the demand in writing, to give weight and efficacy to your requisition. We have judged it expedient to advise him formally by letter, of your being authorised to make it, and that we expect his ready and chearful acquiescence in it. In the present circumstances of his government, and of ours, to disband any part of the troops that we maintain for his service, is a measure no less improper for him to suggest, than it would be for us to adopt. He stands engaged to our government to maintain the English armies, which at his own request have been formed for the protection of his dominions; and it is our part, not his, to judge and to determine in what manner, and at what time, these shall be reduced or withdrawn: but were it otherwise, this is not the time to propose it, when we are threatened with external dangers, common to both, which require rather an augmentation than a diminution of the means which we possess for repelling them. That this gives us cause for the most alarming suspicions, since he cannot be ignorant of the Marrattas, our enemies, and the ancient enemies of his government and family, are in arms, and a war unavoidable. That at such a juncture, a proposition for discharging any

part

part of his forces, cannot fail to encourage them to attack his dominions. That the advice of his ministers, who have instigated him to make it, will, we persuade ourselves, appear to him as insidious as it is dangerous; and that we hope he will dismiss them from his service and confidence, as unworthy of both.

We are, &c.

This letter having been read, the governor general said—I would further propose, that a copy of this letter, or such other as it shall be agreed to write upon this occasion, be transmitted to the commander in chief; and that he be requested to assist with his personal influence and application to the Nabob, to give it effect.

It was agreed—That this subject should lie for consideration.

This important subject was resumed by the governor and council on Wednesday the 15th. I send you a copy of their reasonings on this interesting occasion†, which will serve to give you a just idea of the opposite principles that divide the supreme council. On the argument of Mr. Hastings, and Mr. Francis, I shall make no comment; both these gentlemen possess the most happy talents for writing; and if Mr. Francis ever become a member of the House of Commons, I will venture to predict, that he will soon be ranked among the very first speakers.

I am, &c.

† See Appendix C.

LETTER LV.

To J—— M——, Esq. London.

Calcutta, Dec. 23, 1779.

I AM now to fulfil my promise, to give you a particular account of the day, as it is commonly spent by an Englishman in Bengal.

About the hour of seven in the morning, his durvan (porter or door-keeper) opens the gate, and the viranda (gallery) is free to his circars, peons (footmen) harcarrahs (messengers or spies) chubdars (a kind of constables) huccabadars and consumas (or stewards and butlers) writers and solicitors. The head-bearers and jemmadar enter the hall, and his bed room at eight o'clock. A lady quits his side, and is conducted by a private staircase, either to her own apartment, or out of the yard. The moment the master throws his legs out of bed, the whole posse in waiting rush into his room, each making three salams, by bending the body and head very low, and touching the forehead with the inside of the fingers, and the floor with the back part. He condescends, perhaps, to nod or cast an eye towards the solicitors of his favour or protection. In about half an hour after undoing and taking off his long drawers, a clean shirt, breeches, stockings, and slippers, are put upon his body, thighs, legs, and feet, without any greater exertion on his own part, than if he was a statue. The barber enters, shaves him, cuts his nails, and cleans his ears. The chillumjee and ewer are brought by a servant, whose duty it is, who pours water upon his

his hands, to wash his hands and face, and present a towel.—The superior then walks in state to his breakfasting parlour in his waistcoat; is seated; the consumah makes and pours out his tea, and presents him with a plate of bread or toast. The hair-dresser comes behind, and begins his operation, while the huccabadar softly slips the upper end of the snake or tube of the houcca† into his hand. While the hair-dresser is doing his duty, the gentleman is eating, sipping, and smoaking by turns. By and bye, his banian presents himself with humble salams, and advances somewhat more forward than the other attendants. If any of the solicitors are of eminence, they are honoured with chairs.—These ceremonies are continued perhaps till ten o'clock; when, attended by his cavalcade, he is conducted to his palanquin, and preceded by eight to twelve chubdars, harcarrahs, and peons, with the insignia of their professions, and their livery distinguished by the colour of their turbans and cumberbands (a long muslin belt wrapt round the waist;) they move off at a quick amble; the set of bearers, consisting of eight generally, relieve each other with alertness, and without incommoding the master. If he has visits to make, his peons lead and direct the bearers; and if business renders his presence only necessary, he shews himself, and pursues his other engagements until two o'clock;

† The houcca is the machine from which the smoke of tobacco and aromatics are inhaled, through a tube of several feet, or even yards in length, which is called a snake. To shew the deference or indulgence shewn by ladies to the practice of smoaking, I need but transcribe a card for the governor general and his lady's concert and supper.

Mr. and Mrs. H———s present their compliments to Mr. ———, and request the favour of his company to a concert and supper on Thursday next, at Mrs. H———s's house in town.

1st October, 1779.

Mr. ——— is requested to bring no servants except his huccabadar.

when he and his company sit down, perfectly at ease in point of dress and address, to a good dinner, each attended by his own servant. And the moment the glasses are introduced, regardless of the company of ladies, the huccabadars enter, each with a houcca, and presents the tube to his master, watching behind and blowing the fire the whole time. As it is expected that they shall return to supper, at four o'clock they begin to withdraw without ceremony, and step into their palanquins, so that in a few minutes, the master is left to go into his bed room, when he is instantly undressed to his shirt, and his long drawers put on; and he lies down in his bed, where he sleeps till about seven or eight o'clock: then the former ceremony is repeated, and clean linen of every kind, as in the morning, is administered; his huccabadar presents the tube to his hand, he is placed at the tea table, and his hair-dresser performs his duty as before. After tea, he puts on a handsome coat, and pays visits of ceremony to the ladies: returns a little before ten o'clock; supper being served at ten. The company keep together till about twelve and one in the morning, preserving great sobriety and decency; and when they depart, our hero is conducted to his bed-room, where he finds a female companion, to amuse him until the hour of seven or eight next morning.—with no greater exertions than these, do the Company's servants amass the most splendid fortunes.

I am, &c,

LETTER

LETTER LVI.

To J—— M——, Efq; London.

Calcutta, Dec. 25, 1779.

THE prefent governor g——l of B——l is doubtlefs a perfon of uncommon abilities. He is a fine writer, and though his perfonal addrefs is fo far from being elegant and infinuating, that it is inelegant and forbidding in the higheft degree; yet, by a natural vigour of mind, and an haughty boldnefs, he is fitted to acquire an afcendant over minds more virtuous and delicate, but alfo more timid and irrefolute. His fuccefs in life has confpired with the natural haughtinefs of his temper to render him ambitious, imperious, refentful, and implacable.—You will be able to form fome idea of his great opponent, Mr. Fr——s, when I tell you, that this gentleman has uniformly oppofed the meafures of the overbearing g———r g————l, with the greateft firmnefs and fpirit, though, unfortunately for his country, not with fuccefs.

One of the great caufes of the erroneous conduct of Mr. H————s, and of thofe who fupport his meafures, is, as I conceive, an opinion that "fear and hatred are the univerfal fprings of action in the peninfula of Hindoftan." I fhall not controvert this opinion. The very fpirit and principle of defpotic governments is fear, which in its nature implies an hatred of its object: befides, the diffolution of the Mogul empire into an infinite number of petty ftates, has contributed, in an eminent degree, to eftablifh the truth of that odious doctrine. But if the

Hindoo

Hindoo princes, as well as their subjects, are chiefly governed by hatred and fear, it by no means follows that they may not also be won by gentle and mild treatment. If they are impelled in fact in their general conduct by the scourge of fear, does it follow that they may not, by the exercise of generosity and justice, be drawn by the cords of love? Let these opposite principles, of love and hatred, be united in a wise system of policy, the one to encourage and invite the good, and the other to check and controul the bad. The security of property will prevent prejudice and hatred from occupying good minds; and the fear of justice will deter the vicious. To govern kingdoms by a system founded in hatred and fear, can never be the project of a politician who looks beyond the present time, and studies the permanency of the state, as well as the happiness of the subject: for, while property, liberty, and justice, the plentiful sources of industry, contentment, and felicity, endear the governors to those that are governed, and secure the state at once from internal broils and foreign conquests; slavery, oppression, and injustice, the direful springs of human misery, in their very nature point to change and revolution.

I admit, and there is no doubt, that the British power in India is to be preserved only by a respect and dread of the British name: nevertheless, it should be an invariable maxim, to make a distinction between what degree of fear the exigency of affairs may require, and what may be thought necessary by an ambition of conquest.

It is much to be regretted, that the just and mild views which direct the conduct of Messieurs Fr———s and W———z, do not predominate also in in the mind of Sir E—e C———e, a name which fame had placed in an honourable and conspicuous light. This gentleman accepted a feat at the supreme board of India, and the chief command of all the Company's troops; diffusing hopes, as well to the nation as to the proprietary, that the successor to Sir J—n C———g would follow the footsteps of a man, whose unshaken integrity was stimulated by a native pride, and whose death will ever be lamented by the friends of Britain, of justice, and of humanity.

But to be grateful, by yielding returns in kind, would seem to have been the new-adopted creed of this general, and junior member of council; and to propagate so generous a principle, would seem to have been the chief end of his present visit to India. For, having an immense fortune in possession, formerly acquired there, and no actual posterity to inherit it; and having attained to the distinguished honour, title, and rank just mentioned, at a very advanced age, and in a very infirm state of health, he could have no other object in view, unless the usual companion of age and dotage, sordid avarice, urged him to a measure, which unhappily has tarnished the lustre of his former name; or that, perceiving by inspiration, or by private intelligence, the plain determined purposes of the principal leading servants in India, to subvert the constitution, and ruin the interests of the Company, he conceived the happy thought, that the sooner it was effected the better it would be for the Company's successors, of whatever nation, which his helping hand would hasten, while himself, as well as his friends, would partake of the spoils. Perhaps, as age and infirmity are known to reduce

men

men of first-rate abilities to a second state of infancy, it is more than possible, that baubles, composed of sparkling gems and precious metals, may have been deposited in his cabinet, as toys to amuse him; and being strongly tinctured with the enthusiasm of religion, he may naturally think it a religious duty, to do unto others as they have done unto him. This rare idea must have been deeply imprinted on his mind, when he expressed himself so elaborately in the conclusion of a minute, on the subject matter of the famous victualling contract, viz, " However, had I not these fundamental principles to induce me to support the governor general's motion, I should still most heartily join in it, from the long knowledge I have of the merits of the contractor, Mr. Belli." To comment on an argument and justification so consistent with the laws of personal friendship, and the abuse of a sacred trust, would be to arraign the capacity and understanding of those who shall happen to see or hear it. The whole tenor of the conduct of this once gallant officer, creates pity and astonishment, when it is considered as an infirmity peculiar to age, and an impaired constitution. But considering it in its effects, our charitable feelings are compelled to yield to others, which draw a veil over the splendor of military atchievements, stain the lustre of former merit, and insensibly beget contempt.

The knight militant had solemnly engaged, before he left Britain, to make the interests of the Company, and the dignity of the nation, the primary objects of his study and care; and to execute to the extent of his abilities, and the authority vested in him, the orders and instructions of his employers. At the Cape of Good Hope, on his passage out, at Madras, and even after landing in Bengal, he in the ſtrongeſt terms openly and frequently reprobated the conduct of Mr. Haſtings, with declarations expreſſive of a decided oppoſition to his meaſures. But alas! his reſolution failed him to that extraordinary degree, that he condeſcended to correct minutes, already recorded, which had originally ſprung from the conviction of an honeſt veteran, and ſervilely ſubmitted to faſhion them to the ideas and views of a man who had formerly aſſiſted to drive him out of India†. The firſt action in India, which diſtinguiſhed his public conduct, has already been mentioned, as a meaſure contrary to the laws of nations, and a violation of a ſacred treaty: I mean his inliſting, and placing as his body-guard, the natural-born French capitulant ſoldiers, taken priſoners at Pondicherry. His unmilitary, unjuſt, and abſurd regulations of the army, conſiſting of about one thouſand articles, and occupying as many folios of paper, had nearly been productive of very ſerious effects, at a very critical juncture; but the palpable inconſiſtencies contained in them, converted the juſt diſcontents and reſentments which at firſt agitated the minds of ſpirited officers, into pity in ſome, contempt in others, and ridicule in all‡. One of the objects of his

† Minutes after his arrival, concerning the miſcarriage of the expedition from Bombay againſt Poonah.

‡ One inſtance in general orders, which is literally taken from the Calcutta Gazette, will prove this allegation to any military gentleman.

" General Orders by the Commander in Chief.

" Futtygur, January 22, 1780.

" The commander in chief, with the moſt unfeigned pleaſure, adopts this method of juſtifying the ſatisfaction he has received, during his reſidence in this truly military cantonment. The common-place language of the his Afiatic expedition, appears to have been the claim and poffeffion of the lands and houfe of Ghyrotty, under a vague, or rather imaginary title, unfubftantiated by deed, or even oral teftimony; efficient in law or equity; which, however, was deemed fufficiently legal by his accommodated and accommodating colleagues, who granted the poffeffion to his fimple ipfe dixit.

To gratify, however, in more effential inftances, the ruling paffion of a perfon, whofe vote at the fupreme board became highly confequential at the very important crifis then approaching, by the power he poffeffed, of cafting the ponderous fcale to either of the contending fides, and which would of courfe, deprive the governor general of the double vote which he exercifed when the board, confifting only of four members, were equally divided; the knight, paufing, felt his own importance weighed in the flattering fcale of ambition, and fet upon it an Afiatic value.—People fcruple not (in India) to rate this newly-imported influence, at a price of enormous magnitude, under an appellation

the mere approbation of a reviewing general, bears no part in this addrefs; the fentiments flow from a more expanded and liberal fource, the effufions of Sir Eyre Coote's feelings, at proving the troops at this ftation fo highly diftinguifhed and finifhed in their difcipline, and fo worthy of every encouragement within the power of their commander in chief to beftow on them. Matters of fact alone appear the ftrongeft elogium that approval could direct on the fubject; we need only advert to the reviews and exercifes of this week, to afcertain the juftnefs of this action. Lieutenant Colonel Wilding, and the corps of officers, deferve the general's thanks for their unwearied attentions, that have placed the detachment at Futtygur in the moft confpicuous point of view. The laurel feemed always to the right of the reviewing corps, till the fucceeding day erafed every idea of diftinction, and left the military judge undetermined where to give the preference. The general defires, that both Europeans and natives may have his fentiments of their appearance and deferts, made known to them in the fulleft manner; and that their readinefs and difcipline, convinces him, that whenever actual fervice gives them opportunity, they will amply repay their officers for their pains taken, and approve themfelves highly difciplined troops in the fulleft extent of the word."

better

better underſtood in the language of the eaſt, than thoſe of Europe or the weſt.—Public gratifications appeared, firſt, in the advance of above twenty thouſand pounds ſterling a year, in addition to ſixteen thouſand pounds, to which his annual ſalaries and emoluments, as commander in chief of the army, and a member of the ſupreme council, were reſtricted by act of parliament, and poſitive orders from the Company.—Indeed, he ſhewed more moderation in the demand made by himſelf, of ſucceeding only to the emoluments of commander in chief, as enjoyed by Brigadier General Stibbert (who had no ſeat in council, nor eſtabliſhed ſalary fixed to the chief command) whom he had ſuperſeded, than his devoting friends ſhewed in his behalf. Theſe having the true knowledge of good and evil, of his importance, and withal, a grateful ſenſe of the advantages and ſecurity which they had already derived, and were yet to derive from his apoſtacy, freſh in their remembrance, eaſily over-ruled the principles of moderation and juſtice, and reprobated the unmercenary ideas of the general, by conſtruing the pretended ambiguity in the inſtructions which had accompanied General Clavering in 1774, and Sir Eyre himſelf ſince (1778) into a liberality very inconſiſtent with the Company's wonted moderation, and very different from the literal interpretation of their expreſſions. And Sir Eyre was humbly prayed, by his faithful friends, to accept and receive, as a mark of their gratitude and affection, the paltry ſum of 22,800 pounds annually, out of the revenues belonging to their conſtituents, in addition to his eſtabliſhed appointments; and alſo, to conſent that the ſecond

in

in command, Brigadier General Stibbert, be gratified in the receipt of near 10,000 pounds a year, over and above his legal appointments, to which he had no other claim than the profuse liberality of the dispensers of favours.

I am, &c.

LETTER LVII.

To J—— M———, Esq; London.

Calcutta, Dec. 29, 1780.

IN my letter of the 20th September, I observed, that about a third part of the Company's territories under the presidency of Bengal, had grown up into woods, and become the residence of wild beasts; the human inhabitants having been forced to abandon their native country by the unrelenting hand of European rapacity and oppression. I am now to give you some account of the Rohilla war, which was the chief cause of this melancholy event.

The extensive, fertile, and beautiful provinces called Rohilcund, are situated, for the most part, between the two rivers, Ganges and Jumna, from the boundary of Corah to the confines of Agra and Delhi. They also occupy a large district of country on the north side of the Ganges, reaching eastward to the provinces of Oude, and northward to uninhabited mountains. The annual revenues of these provinces, without oppression, exceeded two crores of rupees (two millions English) and

their

their military eftablifhment of cavalry and infantry was about eighty thoufand: a brave and warlike race. The body of the people were compofed of Hindoos, of ftatures, complexions, conftitutions, and difpofitions, infinitely fuperior to thofe of the low countries. But the fate of war fubjected them to the abfolute dominion of a number of martial Pytan Mahomedans, under the denomination of Chiefs or Rajahs. As thefe were very numerous, fingle chieffhips were not powerful; but united, as branches fprouting from the fame ftock, and in a common caufe, they were always deemed formidable.

Thefe people lived on good terms with the Emperor of Hindoftan, to whom they bore a loyal attachment. But the proximity of their fouthern provinces to the territories of the Marrattas, frequently expofed them to the ravages of that warlike and predatory nation. To the depredations of the Marrattas, the misfortunes of the Rohillas are juftly to be afcribed: for thefe depredations furnifhed a pretext to the afpiring ambition and reftlefs impetuofity of Sujah-ul-Dowla, the vizier of the empire, and Nabob of Oude, to ufurp the dominion of a country, whofe wealth, power, and vicinity would ferve him as fteps by which to mount the imperial throne of Delhi. He artfully infinuated to the Rohilla chiefs, that he was defirous to enter into an alliance with them, and to affift againft the Marrattas, as a common enemy; but as they were to reap the chief benefit, it was proper that a fubfidy fhould be paid for the fervices which his troops were to perform on remote expeditions. Previous to this meafure, he had caufed Mahomed Kouli Khan,

Khan, the Nabob of Illiabad and Corah, to be bafely affaffinated when at his religious devotion; and then he ufurped the dominion of his country. Thus bringing his own clofe home to thofe Rohilla provinces, which were fields of plunder and rapine to flying partiesof Marrattas.

The Rohilla chiefs, although they knew and fufpected his general character, doubted not his fincerity in a meafure which evidently accommodated himfelf; wherefore they confented to pay Sujahul-Dowla forty lacks of rupees, if he would fend a powerful army immediately to join their forces, in repelling and driving the Marratta marauders out of their country. The Marrattas, availing themfelves of the Vizier's flow movements, and of that fecurity which the promifed fuccours from the Vizier had created in the Rohilla chiefs, renewed their incurfions and depredations with redoubled fury, and with too much fuccefs. The Company's troops under the command of Sir Robert Barker, on the part of the Vizier, only entered the Rohilla country for its defence, after all the mifchief that could be done had been irretrievably perpetrated. The Rohilla chiefs were, by this means, fo reduced in their finances, that befides mildly ftating the non-performance of contract by Sujah-ul-Dowla, they were obliged by neceffity to defire a refpite in the complete payment of the ftipulated fubfidy, which however they promifed to make good by periodical inftallments, and propofed to fubmit the whole matter to the arbitration of the prefidency of Fort William. As all overtures were refufed, they at length yielded to the meafure of paying the whole original fpecific fum, upon conditions fuited to the reduced ftate in which the late Marratta incurfions, curſions, and the Nabob's own dilatory conduct, had left their country.

This was the very object of the Vizier's policy; and his ambition, treachery, and brutality, give room to ſuſpect and believe, that he had his emiſſaries amongſt the Marrattas, to ſtimulate them to commit the late depredations, upon a promiſe from him, that his armies, notwithſtanding the treaty he had concluded with the Rohillla chiefs, ſhould not obſtruct their operations until the year following; imagining, as it happened, that the pleas of neceſſity and equity, on the part of the Rohillas, would furniſh him with pleas for inſtant hoſtility and extermination.

Matters were in this ſtate of ſuſpence, when Mr. Haſtings and his council reſolved on a Committee of circuit to ſettle the revenues, adjuſt the adminiſtration of the Dewannee, and liquidate other commercial and revenue concerns in the provinces of Bengal and Bahar, and with Sujah-ul-Dowla, about the middle of the year 1773. A rupture, artfully contrived, ſeparated the members of circuit on the day of their departure from Calcutta, and it fell to the preconcerted lot of Mr. Haſtings to tune the inſtrument, and harmonize the diſcordant faculties of the Vizier Sujah-ul-Dowla. The governor repaired to Benaras, the field of action, charged with diſcretionary powers in relation to matters of trade, and the adjuſtment of the ſubſidy. There were ſeveral members of council, Sir Robert Barker the commander in chief of the army, and ſeveral ſenior ſervants of the Company, either by appointment, or in ſuite, at that time in Benaras. But ſecret deeds diſlike the light;

light; and, upon the principles of the negociation between the governor and the Vizier, it would have been impolitic and dangerous in the extreme, to have had affistants or witneffes. Sir Robert Barker refented the indignity offered to his military and civil ftations in the Company's fervice, and, as a man of probity, who fet a proper value on the faith and honour of his nation, reprobated the treaty as unjuft and difhonourable. The prefence and names of thofe gentlemen were only made ufe of, to witnefs the execution and interchangeable delivery of the public articles of the treaty, upon the 18th September, 1773. There were others of a much more intricate nature, not proper to be promulgated, referved for the influence which the governor's return, and improved condition, to the prefidency, could only bring to bear by his prefence in council.

By this public treaty, the Vizier was to be invefted (and immediately to poffefs, as an eftate in perpetuity) with the Emperor's rights to the provinces of Illiabad and Corah, which had been folemnly fecured to him by feveral facred treaties in 1765, and ratified by the Company openly, and implicitly by the nation: for this bold conceffion he was to give the Company forty lacks of rupees, as a confideration for a perpetual revenue of forty five lacks; and the tribute of twenty fix lacks to the Emperor, from the Nabobfhip of Bengal, was, by thefe two contracting parties, declared to have been forfeited from the 28th February, 1772, except two fums which the Vizier and Nudjiff Cawn (a colleague on this occafion) pretended to claim as a private debt from the King to them, both amounting to 92,800l. fterling.

The

The firſt part of the ſecret treaty which tranſpired, confuſedly, cautiouſly, and by piece-meal, ſeveral months thereafter, contained the barbarous and ſhocking tragedy, which a Britiſh commander in chief, and an army officered by Britiſh ſubjects, and paid by the Britiſh Eaſt India Company, were made to act, in maſſacring and exterminating a whole nation, diſtinguiſhed in Hindoſtan for many ſuperior qualifications ; and putting Sujah-ul-Dowla in the full poſſeſſion of their country, he paying the Company for the inhuman uſe of theſe mercenaries, the paltry pittance (in proportion to the annual revenue, and of the plunder) of fifty lacks of rupees, as a balſam to their wounded conſciences, by four annual inſtallments.

It is impoſſible to conceive, that Mr. Haſtings could have formed ſo firm and inſuperable an attachment, or perſonal friendſhip for a prince whoſe character was univerſally obnoxious, a perfect ſtranger to him, and who had received into his boſom thoſe perſons who not long before had inhumanly and perfidiouſly butchered, in cold blood, his own colleagues, and moſt intimate friends and companions, the members of the council of Patna and others. His ſecret motives or gratifications are ſubjects of ſuſpicion, but they are beyond the reach of legal proof. Every virtue that can dignify humanity, was ſacrificed to the ambition and ſanguinary thirſt of the moſt ſavage of his ſpecies†.

The

---

† That Sujah-ul-Dowla ſhould have protected and befriended Coffim Alli Cawn and Sombro, the murderers of Meſſieurs Hay, Ellis, Chambers, &c. will not be a matter of ſurpriſe, after the ſimple relation of the two following anecdotes, out of an hundred more.—Captain H——r, who was in the Company's ſervice, and alſo in the Vizier's, had a boat with ſome merchandize ſtopped by the revenue officers, for want of the proper permit. Without expecting any tragical conſequence, he mentioned it to the Vizier. He was

awakened

The governor general engaged deliberately in an unnatural, unprovoked, cruel war, to deſtroy an unoffending, induſtrious people, to whom the ſame mercenary arms had yielded ſuccour and friendly relief the preceding war, that were turned now againſt them. He ſacrificed the inherent rights of the Emperor to raiſe the Emperor's own ſervant and ſubject, by an act of open rebellion. He violated the ſolemn treaties upon which all the claims to trade, and the territorial revenues accorded to the Company and Britiſh nation, are founded and eſtabliſhed. He withdrew the tribute, which conſtituted the ſole legal and political conſideration for the Company's pretenſions to the Dewannee, and the rights of the Britiſh nation, without conſulting with his conſtituents, or his council, and againſt a ratified treaty; and ceded the Emperor's own provinces of Illiabad and Corah to the Emperor's own miniſter, a mere temporary officer, removeable at his pleaſure. He even, with an aſſurance and indecency ſcarcely to be equalled, avows, that the unauthorized treaty of Benaras, and the ſecret conditions which were known only to the two negociators, and not even committed to paper, were, to all intents and purpoſes, binding and obligatory on the Company; and in particular, he aſſerted, that the general tenor of the treaty im-

---

awakened at midnight, and the head of the Phouzdar (chief magiſtrate) of the diſtrict, preſented to him in a baſket: a circumſtance which ſhocked Captain H———r to that degree, that he ſcarce recovered his ſpirits while in. India.

Colonel G———d, hunting one day in Rohilcund, ſome villagers, whoſe hogs were killed by the dogs, threw a ſtick at one of the dogs. The colonel came to Sir R. B———r's tent, where the Vizier was at breakfaſt, and accidentally mentioned this trifling circumſtance. The Vizier whiſpered to one of his attendants, and before the breakfaſt was over, the attendant returned, and informed the Vizier, that the village was deſtroyed, and man, woman, and child, put to the ſword.

plied

plied a positive obligation on the Company to secure the Musnud to Sujah-ul-Dowla and his posterity; and the undisturbed possession of the Nabobship of Oude, together with the countries usurped by the sacrilegious murder of Mahomed Kouli Khan, and the treaty of Benaras; although in the same breath he acknowledges, that at the time of making the concessions, he had declared to the Vizier, " That he was acting and consenting to measures against the peremptory orders of his superiors."—All these doings are of so preposterous a nature, so much beyond the utmost extension of the Company's power, and so shameful and inglorious to the British nation, that they ought to be considered as the effects of madness, and as wholly null and void in their very nature. Nothing less than the vilest prostitution of trust, and the most consummate impudence, could have produced such a treaty, or dared to avow such a construction of it.

Mr. Hastings contrived to bring the majority of his council to approve the public treaty; and his subsequent equivocations and sophistry in council, concerning the secret conditions stipulated between the Vizier and himself, in relation to the conquest of the Rohilla provinces, demonstrated beyond a doubt, that he thought them of a complexion not proper for public disquisition.—This is pretty evident from his appointment of a resident at the Vizier's court, where none had before been deemed necessary, upon his own special motion, claiming, authoritatively, an independent right to appoint and call the proposed resident, of his own free will and mere motion; and that such resident shall

be

be confidered as his (the governor's) private agent, and correfpond only with him.— Mr. Haftings's minutes and reports upon this occafion, are to the following purpofe : " That it was my intention to convince the Vizier, that in his concerns with the Company, the immediate dependence was upon the governor alone, and to eftablifh a direct correfpondence between him and myfelf, without any intervention."—Could Mr. Haftings have adopted a furer maxim or language, or afferted a ftronger line of influence, to obtain an Afiatic recompence?—He then propofed, " To appoint a perfon for tranfacting fuch matters of correfpondence and communication with the Vizier, as he (the governor) fhall think proper to entruft to his management; and he offers it frankly, as his opinion, that if the board fhall entruft him with the fole nomination of fuch a refident, and the power of recalling him whenever he pleafes, it may be attended with good effects, but not otherwife."—What conftruction can be put on fuch declarations, recorded on the Company's own proceedings, but that the refult of the vifit to Sujah-ul-Dowla, had placed the author beyond the reach and power of his employers?—The confidential inftructions to the refident, and the correfpondence with him and Colonel Champion, corroborate thefe furmifes in pretty direct terms. By the inftructions to Mr. Middleton, the refident, he exprefsly " forbids any European, whether Englifh or not, civil or military, in or out of the Company's fervice, on any pretext, to vifit the Vizier, or the Rajah Cheytfing, but particularly the Vizier; not even the European officers in the Vizier's own fervice, except the commander in chief."—As Mr. Haftings obtained for

the

the Rajah Cheytſing, the zemindary of the provinces of Benaras, Ghazipore, &c. and to his poſterity, for twenty two and an half lacks of rupees yearly rent, it may be ſuppoſed, that the ſon and heir of the rich Rajah Bulwantſing, was alſo very liberal to his friend and benefactor; and therefore the prohibition to European viſitors was a neceſſary meaſure of prudent policy.—Mr. Haſtings, having written a private letter to Sujah-ul-Dowla, without any communication, as uſual, through the reſident, the jealouſy or fears of Mr. Middleton were rouſed, and he collected reſolution enough to complain with ſome bitterneſs, of the ſlight and diffidence which it implied, in a letter to Mr. Haſtings, dated the 4th June, 1774; wherein he ſays, "That having expreſſed his uneaſineſs to the Vizier, he was told by him, that it was only a private complimentary letter."—And Colonel Champion, in a private letter to the governor, before their quarrel, dated 30th May, 1774, uſes theſe very ſuſpicious and deep-meaning expreſſions.

" Dear Sir,

" In conſequence of what happened between us at parting, I have mentioned Colonel Upton's claim to the Nabob, and requeſted he would be kind enough to diſcharge it. His Excellency was very conciſe in his reply, that he had ſettled all money matters with Mr. Haſtings."

What can be inferred from this, but that Mr. Haſtings had undertaken to ſhut up all private claims and applications? And the reiterated ſtrenuous endeavours of Mr. Haſtings, by uncommon application, and indirect inſinuations, to prevail

on

on Colonel Champion to difmifs from his fervice as banyan, the very faithful and intelligent Collychurn, while upon the expedition in queftion, betrays a dread of his difcovering, in the courfe of bufinefs, and negociations with the army, and at Lucknow, the fecret fprings which led to the treaty at Benaras.

A Mr. Hall, whofe addrefs and management procured him a general intercourfe with the natives of condition in and about the Vizier's court and metropolis, having come down to Calcutta, fomewhat involved in difficulties, and finding no method of being extricated, bethought him of communicating the outlines of certain pieces of private knowledge to a confidential friend of Mr. H——s; declaring, that in his prefent diftrefs, if he was not relieved, he muft be under the neceffity of laying his mind open to General Clavering. It had the intended effect; his debts were forthwith paid. But Mr. Hall wifely faid, that he muft have future fubfiftence, and more money for immediate ufe;—he received an order on Coffimbazar for prefent fupply, and an appointment at Futtygur, upon exprefs condition of going inftantly, and remaining there to execute it in perfon.

Colonel Champion was appointed to the command of the Company's troops, on an expedition, near fifteen hundred miles by water conveyance up the country, againft the Rohillas, with peremptory orders to be directed in all his motions and actions by the Vizier Sujah-ul-Dowla, whofe commands he was implicitly to obey on all occafions. The Colonel put himfelf accordingly at the head of the army, and took the field, under the abfolute command of a prince, whofe object was favage bar-
barifm

barism and inhumanity, and who wanted manly courage to hazard, either his own person, his army, or even his artillery, in an action, to secure the success of what he was so solicitously ambitious to obtain.—The fatal battle was fought upon the 23d day of April, 1774, which iniquitously decided the melancholy fate of the brave, industrious, populous, and inoffensive Rohilla nation. In the mean time, Sujah-ul-Dowla withdrew with his army, artillery, and baggage, to a distance of several miles from the field of action: Nay, he positively refused to the application of Colonel Champion, a part of his cavalry in order to attack the enemy at a certain quarter, to which the numbers of the Company's troops could not extend without imminent danger to the whole; and he also pointedly refused to spare a few pieces of his artillery, to serve in another very necessary quarter. These refusals created uneasy suspicions in Colonel Champpion's mind, of foul treachery on the part of the Vizier, in case the success of the day should favour the Rohillas, which might place the vanquished army between a victorious enemy and a treacherous friend. Such an idea might not be wanted to animate the British General, but it might have pushed him to a determined resolution to conquer or fall.—The Company's brave general and their troops, unassisted, gained a decisive, but in truth, a disgraceful victory. Their artillery was so judiciously stationed and pointed, that, to the immortal honour of the brave Rohillas, it was asserted, they left four thousand men lying dead upon the field, before they retreated.

The surviving chiefs surrendered at discretion to the victorious army, and were delivered into the hands

hands of Sujah-ul-Dowla; except Fyzulla Cawn, who, yielding up his camp and towns as plunder to the Vizier, fled to the mountainous part of his country, by which means he was able to ftipulate certain conditions, though thefe were hard and inhuman.—The other chiefs were forced, together with their families, to fubmit to the moft difgraceful imprifonment, and the moft mortifying and humiliating treatment; their zenanas, which are facred fanctuaries in India, even againft the violences and outrages of favages, were plundered, and the wives, daughters, and fifters of princes, were violated and abufed. Children under puberty were facrificed to the luft of an old diftempered debauchee. Some fhocking circumftances have been alledged.—The plunder received into the poffeffion of the Vizier, has been eftimated at a crore and an half of rupees, or one million five hundred thoufand pounds fterling; and yet to this hour, twenty lacks fixty thoufand fix hundred and eight rupees, part of the fubfidy due for this conqueft, are yet owing to the Company, befides ten lacks promifed as a donation to the army, in lieu of the plunder, which he had treafured to his own ufe.

It is computed, that about five hundred thoufand induftrious hufbandmen and artifts, who were alfo, for the moft part, able warriors, together with their families, were deliberately driven over the Jumna, to receive an afylum from their late enemies and plunderers, the Marrattas.—Fyzulla Cawn was obliged to condition, that he fhould not entertain more than five thoufand perfons in his dominion.—The latter end of 1777, under the vague pretence that Fyzulla's country was flourifh-

ing,

ing, and becoming more populous than was stipulated by treaty, Mr. Middleton, as the Company's resident at Lucknow, in concert with his friends and protectors at the presidency, without any notification to the supreme board, or asking their consent, undertook to delegate Mr. Daniel Barwell, as an ambassador to the quiet, timid, Fyzulla Cawn; who, wrapt up in a garment of innocence, suspected nothing less than a charge of violating the compact, or the presence of an European ambassador to adjust the imaginary violation. It is said, that although the allegation appeared to have been without foundation, the minister found the means of procuring, by way of escort back to Lucknow, several elephants and camels, loaded with eight to ten lacks of rupees in specie. The minute of Mr. Francis, upon the occasion of the governor general's motion to approve the proceedings, as expedient, on the 9th March, 1778, is worthy of the space it occupies upon record.

He (Mr. Francis) calls it, " One of the gross-
" est pieces of management he met with in India.
" Mr. Daniel Barwell quits his station at Benaras
" without leave, and goes to Lucknow without
" leave; Mr. Middleton instantly discovers, that
" Fyzulla Cawn is carrying on some design preju-
" dicial to the interest of the Nabob, and that
" the Nabob gives cause for such designs, by his
" treatment of his subjects; at the same time,
" that nothing is more notorious, than that the
" Nabob has no more power in his own country,
" than he (Mr. Francis) has. To put a stop to
" these effects, which mutual jealousies must pro-
" duce, a treaty must be made; the guarantee of
" the

"the Company must be given; and Mr. Daniel Barwell finds himself very opportunely, at Lucknow, ready to execute the commission."

The Rohilla provinces are now a barren waste, and almost totally deserted by the inhabitants. The chiefs and their children are continued in the most miserable state of confinement, deprived of the common necessaries of life.

LETTER LVIII.

To J— M——, Esq; London.

Calcutta, Jan. 2, 1780.

ON how precarious a foundation does the British empire in India stand, when one daring individual can, at his pleasure, subvert every principle of the Company's government, violate their most positive orders and solemn instructions, contemn their authority, and set their power at defiance! The principles on which the Rohilla war originated, the Court of Directors unanimously condemned; yet, regardless of their most peremptory commands, Mr. H——s plunged them into another, the consequences of which threaten the subversion of the whole British power, together with the property and possessions of the English East India Company in Hindostan. Perhaps it is too late for that Company to weigh the disgraceful and dangerous consequences of uniting constant condemnation with constant impunity; and of continuing men in stations of the highest trust and dignity, whom, if we may rely on the opinion they have repeatedly

expressed

expressed of their conduct and character, they ought to think unworthy of the lowest.

The territories of the Marrattas, if we except that which was lately usurped by Hyder Ally Cawn, extend towards the sea from Travancore, near Cape Comorin, at the southern extremity of the peninsula of Hindostan, to the river Paddar, which discharges itself in the gulph of Scindy, and which divides Guzzarat from the dominions of Persia. On the east, they are bounded by the Carnatic, the Company's northern Circars, and the dominions of the Nizam-ul-Muluck, the Soubah of the Deccan-Bazalet-Jung: but the province of Catac stretches in a winding course to the bay of Bengal.

The Marratta states in the Deccan are the only people of Hindostan who were never effectually subdued, and who never unanimously acknowledged themselves fiefs to the throne of Delhi. The great Aurengzebe himself, unable to conquer the brave Marrattas, found it prudent, for the sake of peace, to yield to them the sovereignty of the Deccan. They even carried the terror of their arms into the heart of Delhi, whence they carried off vast treasures; and they continued their depredations, first in the country around that seat of empire, and then in the kingdoms of Bengal, Bahar, and Orixa; until, in consideration of the cession of Catac, and an annual tribute of twelve lacks of rupees, they concluded a peace with Alverdi Cawn, who had usurped the soubahship of Bengal, in 1750.

Their natural fastnesses and inaccessible mountains, which conspired with their native bravery to preserve

preserve the Marrattas from the Mogul yoke, account for their predatory habits, their neglect of agriculture, and invincible love of arms. Among this race of warriors, and among them only, that generous hospitality both towards strangers and each other, which in former times so eminently characterized the manners of the East, is still observed with sacred and even superstitious exactness.

The Marrattas, like the other nations of Hindostan, were originally governed by princes, distinguished by the title of Sou, or Ram-rajah†, whose throne was established at Setterrah. United under this head they were always powerful and invincible; but in process of time, each subordinate chief assuming the prerogatives of an independent prince, and one link of that chain which united them, being broken, they were separated into a number of petty states; yet they still continued to yield a kind of tacit allegiance to the Ram-rajah, who had a power of assembling the chiefs, and ordering out their troops as often as any public cause required their service.

The Marratta revenues were originally very great. Before the usurpations of Hyder Ally Cawn, in the kingdom of Mysore and around it, they amounted to about seventeen millions of British pounds. It is computed, that their annual revenue is equal still to twelve millions.

Their military establishment, which is composed of cavalry, is yet about three hundred thousand: but these are not to be considered as regulars, or permanent troops, but as an established militia. In

---

† There were among the Hindoos other titles of sovereignty; as, Ranah, Rajah, &c. Subordinate characters were known by the names of Paishwa, Surdar, Zemindar, Polygar, &c.—The titles of Vizier, Soubah, Nizam, Nabob, Omrah, &c. were introduced by Mahomedans.

judging

judging of the Marratta force, we are alſo to obſerve, that it is an invariable cuſtom among the troops, when an expedition is concluded, to retire with what plunder they have ſeized to their reſpective abodes, leaving with the chiefs only what may be called their body-guards.

The Sou, or Ram-rajah, exiſts now but in name. Nana-row, brother of the preſent Roganaut-row, commonly called Ragoba, ſeized at the ſame inſtant the reins of government and the perſon of the Ram-rajah : a revolution which was favoured by the Bramin caſt of the uſurper. The government he adminiſtered, under the title of Paiſhwa, or prime miniſter, and the prince he confined in a fortreſs near the metropolis Setterah. In this poſition the preſent young Ram-rajah and the government of the Marratta ſtate continue to this day.

Nana-row dying, left behind him two ſons, Mada-row and Narain-row ; the firſt of whom, being the eldeſt, ſucceeded him in the uſurped office of Paiſhwa. Ionogee-Booſla, or Bouncello, the father or immediate predeceſſor of Moodage-Booſla, Rajah of Berar, was one of the pretenders to the throne of Setterah, as neareſt of kin to the confined Ram-rajah ;. at the ſame time Roganaut-row was a pretender to the office of prime miniſter, even during the life-time of his nephew, for which Mada-row kept him under confinement.

But the Paiſhwa feeling in himſelf the ſymptoms of decay, and foreſeeing his approaching diſſolution, was moved with fraternal tenderneſs towards Narain-row, his young brother and lineal ſucceſſor ; whoſe youth and inexperience expoſed him to the machinations of his crafty and intriguing uncle, though in priſon.

Vol. II. L Had

Had Mada-row, on this occasion, observed the cruel policy of the cast, he might by a hint or a nod have removed the cause of all his fears concerning his brother; but he was a man of a humane disposition, and his mind was purged from all dark ideas of poison or assassination by the near approach of death. Divided between humanity towards his uncle, and affection for his brother, he embraced the generous resolution of effecting a reconciliation between the objects of his tenderness and his compassion. He caused Roganaut-row to be released: and, having made such arrangements as he thought the most likely to remove all uneasiness or dissatisfaction from the minds of both parties, he placed the hands of the youth into those of his uncle, and, shedding tears of joy, tenderly embraced them: "I intrust," said he, "the young man to your care: I recommend him to your protection. Give him your advice in the administration of government; guard him from the snares and plots of his enemies. He never advised your confinement: he was always an advocate for your enlargement: let all remembrance of former grievances on either side, die with me." The young man, it is said, and even Roganaut-row, on this occasion, dissolved in tears. But how fallacious are all momentary impressions on the heart, when the mind is not fortified by any principle of virtue! Ragoba promised to consider Narain-row as his own child; but this promise he kept no longer than he could procure assassins to cut him in pieces.

Mada-row died in November, 1772; and Narain row was allowed to live until the September following, when he was in the twenty-third year of his

his age. But concerning the cause and circumstances of this young man's death, you will not be displeased if I am somewhat more particular.

Gopincabow, the mother of Madah and Narain-row, had disgusted her eldest son by a dissolute and vicious life; in consequence of which, she withdrew to Benaras, in the dominion of Oude, then hostile to the Marratta government, and at a vast distance from Poonah. Just before his death, Madah-row expressed a desire to see her, which she refused with contempt, therefore, dreading her influence over the uninformed mind of his brother Narain-row, he earnestly cautioned him to beware of her artful councils. Some circumstances having appeared in the conduct of Roganaut-row, creating suspicions of a foul design upon his nephew, the rumour thereof reached Benaras, whence Gopincabow wrote to her son, cautioning him against the arts of his uncle, and even recommending to confine him again, as his brother Madah-row had found necessary to do for his own security. This letter in its way fell into the hands of Roganaut-row's adopted son, then under the care of Mudageepofla, in Berar, which he conveyed to his father at Poonah. Roganaut-row instantly determined to secure his own freedom, and the Paishwaship without a competitor, by one blow; as neither of the brothers had children, nor was it then known that the wife of Narain-row was pregnant. Two Subadars of the Durbar guard he made choice of for the accomplishment of his purpose. Simmering and Mahomet Issouff were consulted; who, after some consideration, engaged, for two lacks of rupees, and two strong forts for their future protection, to perform the horrid deed. An occasion

offered

offered to add a third to their plot. Tulajee, a fa
vourite servant, had been raised by Narain-row t
the command of a troop of horse near his ow
person. That young man having committed an a
of violence on a Soubadar of rank and conditio
upon complaint thereof, Narain found it necessar
to degrade and confine the favourite: howeve
upon application, he was not only released, but r
stored to rank and favour; but the disgrace sur
into his spirits, and he secretly menaced reveng
The conspirators associated him in their desig
and fixed the day, place, and manner of carryi
it into execution. On the 18th of August, 177
after the Paishwa had withdrawn to his retireme
as usual in the evening, he was alarmed by an u
roar and information that a body of armed m
were forcing into the apartments. He instant
suspected that his uncle meditated his death; a
he instantly flew into the apartment and arms
Roganaut-row, imploring him to take the gover
ment and spare his life. Ragoba was melted fo
moment, and he spoke to the Soubadars: but t
matter had gone too far to be receded from wi
security. Tulajee seized Narain-row's legs, and
sepoy disengaged his arms which embraced l
uncle. Tulajee struck the first blow, which w
followed by Simmer-sing and Mahomet Issouff.

LETTER LIX.

To J—— M——, Esq. London.

Calcutta, Jan. 5, 1779.

THE death of Narain-row was generally
mented, and the unnatural manner in whi
it was brought about, universally execrated by

he people. A powerful oppofition was formed, to he fucceffion of Ragoba to the office after which e afpired. The parricide was forced to fly from is country, indignant at his crimes: but he found rotection in the ifland of Bombay, in confideraion of a promife of the moft flattering conceffions, ;hich however he had as little the power as the ight to perform. The afylum thus granted to loganaut-row, incenfed the Marrattas on the one .and; while, on the other, it amufed the Englifh ith a profpect, not only of valuable territorial onceffions, but of the ufual fpoils which Indian evolutions prefent to the views of fuccefsful Euro- ean allies.

Hoftilities having quickly commenced, the maine of Bombay fuftained, with the bravery of Briifh feamen, the troops, in the reduction of the ifand Salfette, which was effected not without coniderable lofs to the affailants; while that of Baoach coft the life of General Wedderburn, one of he beft and braveft officers that belonged either to he Company or the Britifh army. The Company elt his lofs foon thereafter, in the defeat of the 3ombay army under Colonel Keating. Happily, 1owèver, by means of the eftablifhed enmity beween the Marrattas and Hyder Ally Cawn; of ealoufies and fecret enmities between the principal ind leffer ftates; and of divifions in the council of ?oonah, the Marratta government was inclined to)referve the friendfhip of the Company in preferance to all other connections: a difpofition in which hey would have continued, if the Englifh had not fforded fupport to the unjuft pretenfions of a paricide.

Such

Such was the situation of the Company with regard to the Marratta state, when the new government, composed of Mr. Hastings, General Clavering, Colonel Monson, Mr. Barwell, and Mr. Francis, commenced in October, 1774. The newly-arrived members, General Clavering, Colonel Monson, and Mr. Francis, entered on the duty assigned to them by the Company, and by their country, with alacrity: the sole object of their views being, to recover the affairs of their employers from confusion, debt, and discredit. These gentlemen, forming a majority in the supreme council, availed themselves of that superiority which the act of parliament gave them, in certain cases, over the other presidencies, and sent Colonel Upton to negociate with the Marratta court an honourable peace: which was at length concluded and ratified, on the first of March, 1776. This peace is known by the title of the Poorunder Treaty, and sometimes by that of the treaty of Poonah.

By this treaty, Salsette, Baroach, and other districts in the Guzzerat provinces, were ceded to the Company: they were to be paid three lacks of rupees at three fixed terms, to defray the charges of the war; as a security for which they got possession of several pergunnahs in mortgage; and an extent of territory of the annual value of three lacks, adjoining or near to Baroach.

On the other hand, it was stipulated, that Roganaut-row should be provided for according to his rank, in a private line, and withdraw immediately from Bombay; and that no protection or assistance should be given to him, or any other subject or
servant

servant of the Marratta state who might excite any disturbance or rebellion in that country.

This treaty was confirmed by the Court of Directors; who ordered a strict adherence to it in the strongest terms. They recommended special vigilance over the conduct of Ragoba, during the time he should remain at Bombay, that he might form no plans against what is called the ministerial party at Poonah: and positively commanded, that no intervention or scheme in his favour should be entered into, without the previous consent of the supreme council or Court of Directors. At the same time they admitted, that common humanity warranted the protection of Ragoba's person from violence.

In the mean time Roganaut-row, under the protection of the government of Bombay, entered into new intrigues, and fomented dissentions in the administration of Poonah†.

Unfortunately for the happiness of mankind, the will almost perpetually influences the judgment, and we too easily believe what we wish to be true. The history of all nations proves, that exiled pretenders to sovereignty are convinced, on the slightest grounds, that the body of the people is devoted to their interest, and ready in their cause to take-up arms. In the year 1715, the Pretender, with his adherents who attended him in France, were persuaded, that nineteen persons in Britain out of twenty, were what they called loyal subjects. The same language was held in the years preceding the famous 1745: and it is impossible to convince the British government, that the loyalists are not by far

† The seat of the Marratta government.

the

the greatest party in North America. A similar deception was the immediate cause of the Marratta war. Ragoba, deceived in all probability himself, by means of his partizans among the Marratta chiefs, beguiled the easy credulity of Mr. Mostyn resident from Bombay at the court of Poonah, into a belief, that a most powerful party was formed in favour of Roganaut-row, who were ready to advance him by force of arms to the supreme administration of government. This piece of intelligence was received with avidity, and credited without any hesitation by majorities in the presidencies both of Bombay and Calcutta. Having determined to reinstate Ragoba on the Poonah throne, they fortify their resolution with new arguments. The Marrattas, they asserted, had given countenance to agents from Austria and France. If report could be believed, formal engagements had passed between them and Monsieur St. Lubin, as agent to the crown of France, the object of which, whatever it was, must, if attained, prove destructive to the trade of the English Company, and to the British influence in India. Accordingly it was necessary, by a sudden and decisive blow, and particularly by seizing the island of Basseen, to curb and reduce the Marratta power, before it should be encreased by the accession of that of France. They flattered themselves with the greatest assurance of success in favour of Ragoba, as they expected assistance from Hyder Ally Cawn, who professed a friendship for his party. Thus the object of this projected war, was, to place at the head of the Marratta government, a man whose hands were dyed with the blood of his own

own kindred; whofe treachery had rendered him an object of execration over all Afia; and who was withal the avowed friend and partizan of Hyder Ally Cawn, an afpiring ufurper, whofe enmity to the Englifh and their allies, was as firmly rooted as his hatred of the Marrattas.

The circumftances then that excited or encouraged the governor general of Bengal to commence a war with the Marrattas, were chiefly three. There was, as he conceived, a powerful party at the court of Poonah, determined to hazard their lives in fupport of Ragoba; a majority of the Marratta chiefs had entered, or were on the point of entering, into a treaty of alliance with France; and Hyder Ally Cawn would not fail to join the Englifh in fupport of his friend Ragoba, againft his inveterate enemies.—How unfortunate was the governor, both in his fecret intelligence and his conjectures. In all thefe points he was deceived. While Mr. Haftings was haranguing at Calcutta, on the power and zeal of the partizans of Ragoba, the few adherents he had were pining in confinement at Poonah. There was not a man in the civil or military adminiftration of the Marratta government, either in thought or in action, ready to efpoufe the caufe of Roganaut-row. On the contrary, the whole body of the people in every ftation, feemed unanimous in their refolution to oppofe him, and the plan he had adopted. The Marratta government fhewed at firft every poffible difpofition to preferve the friendfhip, and to maintain an alliance with the Englifh: and if they entered into any negociations with the French at laft, we may eafily trace them to their proper fource

in

in the protection that was afforded to Roganautrow, in violation of a solemn treaty, and his intrigues at Bombay. The Marrattas, unwilling to irritate the English, entered into no treaty whatever with the French; but on the contrary, dismissed Monsieur St. Lubin from Poonah, where he had had partizans. This agent of France went therefore to Hyder Ally, who had, before this repulse of St. Lubin at Poonah, resented the offers he had made to the Marrattas. The rejection of these offers by the Marratta government, facilitated a treaty between St. Lubin and Hyder, and procured for the French the cession of Mangalore.

The pacific disposition of the Marratta court, and their refusal to treat effectually with St. Lubin, will appear from the following passage, in a letter from the governor general's friend, the Rajah of Berar: " I formerly intimated in my letters to Calcutta, the purport of what the Poonah ministers wrote to me; that they neither had nor would have, any friendship or connection with the French nation; and that the French agent came to Poonah, solely for the purposes of trade; and that out of friendship to the English, they had sent him away; that I should therefore write to the Nabob Amand-ul-Dowla (meaning the governor general) to be perfectly satisfied with respect to them, they being steady to their engagements."

Such being the state of affairs at Poonah and Mangalore, the simple exercise of justice and fidelity to engagements, would have detached the Marratta chiefs more and more from France and from Hyder Ally, and united them in a close connection and friendship with the English. But a breach of
public

public faith, and an infatiable thirst for power and unbounded dominion, so apparent in every measure of the Company's servants, united the discordant Marratta states, and jarring members in the administration of Poonah, Hyder Ally Cawn, the Soubah of the Deccan, the Rajah of Berar, Nudjiff Cawn, and all the lesser powers of India into a close association for the purpose of resisting the extravagant pretensions and views of the Company's administration in Asia, and even reducing their power. Impelled by the same motives, they discovered inclinations to hearken to the overtures of France, looking with wishful impatience for the day of deliverance from the iron hand of oppression.

LETTER LX.

To J——M——, Esq; London.

Calcutta, Jan. 10, 1780.

ON the 22d November, 1778, an army, amounting to 3910 men, officers included, moved from Bombay, with an immoderate quantity of baggage, and a train of nineteen thousand cattle, to place Roganaut-row at the head of the administration of Poonah. The conduct of this expedition was entrusted to a committee, consisting of Colonel Egerton, Mr. Carnac, and Mr. Mostyn. Thus the commander in chief was circumscribed in his designs and operations by the appointment of field deputies: a measure, the bad effects of which have been constantly shewn by experience. Debate and

execution

execution are in their nature incompatible. The succefs of military operations depends very much upon unity of command, without which there can neither be decifion nor timely execution. This maxim of war was not contradicted by any fuccefs attending the prefent expedition. The army had not got within two days march of Poonah, after having been about fifty days in their progrefs without any hoftile obftruction, before they were totally defeated, and reduced, by the neceffity of offering a carte blanche to the enemy, to the moft difgraceful humiliation. After a few days fkirmifhing, they capitulated at Wargaum, on the 16th of January, 1779. This mortifying intelligence was received at Calcutta in the month of February, in a literal tranflation of a letter to the Nabob of Arcot, from his Vakeel at the court of Poonah. Of this letter I fend you a copy. It will exhibit a new inftance of the perfidy of Roganaut-row; the folly of placing confidence in a treacherous character, and of allowing Ragoba to move with a feparate camp; and the generofity, moderation, and good fenfe of the Marrattas.

Intelligence from Poonah, contained in a Letter from Row Gee, dated 18th of January, 1779, to the Nabob of Arcot.

1. I have addreffed to your highnefs feveral letters of late, fome of which I hope are arrived; I have accounts of others having been intercepted on the road, and fhall therefore recapitulate fome of the moft important tranfactions here.

2. The Englifh Surdars†, as I have already wrote to your Highnefs, marched from Bombay to

† Or Chiefs.

the

the paſſes, and fortified that of Kodtichully. Roganaut-row took poſſeſſion of two forts which were in the road, and joined the Engliſh army, which I hear conſiſted of ſeven hundred Europeans, eight battalions of ſepoys, forty pieces of cannon, mortars, and a quantity of powder and military ſtores; they had beſides four lacks of rupees in money.

3. Siccaram Pundit, and Nana Furneſe, two Marratta Surdars, joined their forces, and ſatisfied the diſcontented chiefs Schindiah and Holkar, by giving them money, jaghires, and other preſents.

4. All the chiefs having met to conſult what was to be done in the preſent ſtate of affairs, they all with one voice agreed, that if Roganaut-row came with his own forces alone, they ſhould receive him, and give him a ſhare of the power as formerly; but ſince he came with an army of Engliſh, who were of a different nation from them, and whoſe conduct in Sujah Dowla's country, the Rohilla country, Bengal, and the Carnatic, they were well acquainted with, they unanimouſly determined not to receive Roganaut-row; as otherwiſe, in the end, they would be obliged to forſake their religion, and become the ſlaves of Europeans. Upon this they exchanged oaths; and Nehum Row, Apagee Pundit, and Scindiah, were ſent with an army of fifteen thouſand horſe, beſides foot, to the Gaut of Tulicanoon, and were followed immediately after by Siccaram Pundit and Nana Furneze, with 40,000 horſe.

5. It has been for ſome time the fixed determination of the Engliſh Surdars to give their aſſiſtance to Roganaut-row, in replacing him at the head of the government; an army was ſent from Calcutta, who made an alliance with Boofla, (Rajah

jah of Berar) and they were greatly encouraged by the news of the furrender of Pondicherry.

6. Mr. Moftyn, who went from Poonah, made them believe, that many of the Marratta Surdars were in their intereft, and that as foon as their army fhould arrive at the Gaut, Holkar would join them with all his forces.

7. The Englifh, trufting to this, marched their army to the Gaut, and waited impatiently for a whole month, but no one appeared to join their ftandard. The Englifh army marched forward from the Gaut, and were fo much harraffed by the Marrattas, as not to be able to proceed more than two cofs† a day, during which time they loft a great many of their men by the fire kept up on them by the Marrattas. When they came to Chockly, which is about fourteen cofs from the pafs, they were obliged to halt; Captain Stewart, one of their Surdars, was killed at this place.

On the twenty firft of January, the European army arrived at Tulicanoon, (feventeen cofs from the pafs) Mr. Carnac, fecond of Bombay, was with them. Siccaram fent a body of horfe to Tulicanoon, to harrafs them; twenty five Europeans, amongft whom was an officer, and one hundred fepoys, were killed on the firft day; The Marrattas had two hundred men killed.

9. On the fecond day, the Englifh were furrounded on all fides by the Marrattas, and all fupplies of provifion cut off from them. Seeing themfelves in this fituation, they determined, if poffible, to return back to the Gaut, and confulted upon the means to effect it. Roganaut-row hearing this, fent privately to the Marratta chief, Schin-

† A cofs is five Englifh miles.

diah,

diah, telling him, that if he would attack the English, he would join him with his two battalions of Sepoys, and six hundred horse. The English, it would appear, had intelligence of this; for, on the thirteenth of January, they suddenly marched secretly from Tulicanoon, taking Roganaut-row with them, and leaving their baggage and tents standing, under the protection of two hundred Europeans, and one battalion of sepoys, with eight pieces of cannon, to make the Marrattas believe their whole force was at Tulicanoon.—Siccaram, however, got private intelligence of their retreat; and, with Nana Furneze, Schindiah, and Holkar, went to cut off their march. At the same time he sent a body of horse to Tulicanoon, where the rest of the English were encamped. The Marrattas, as usual, fell upon the plunder, and a smart engagement ensued between them and the English. The detachment, who had marched with Roganaut-row, but had not proceeded far, returned to the assistance of those in their camp. A heavy cannonade was kept up by the Marrattas from midnight till four o'clock the next day; the English were not able to march one foot of way, and all their firing took no effect; one hundred and fifty Europeans, with many of their officers, and eight hundred sepoys, were killed. The Marrattas surrounded them, and kept patroles going all night, to prevent any from escaping. On the fourteenth, the Marrattas commenced their cannonading again, fifty Europeans and four hundred Sepoys were killed. The English ceased firing, seeing that it had no effect. In the evening of that day, the servant of Roganaut-row, and that of of Mr. Carnac, brought a letter to Madah Row, acquainting him, that they would fend a trufty perfon to confer with him upon fome matters, if leave was given. The Surdars read the letter, and fent an anfwer by the fame perfon, that they were willing to ceafe hoftilities, until a perfon was fent. They, however, took care to keep a ftrict patrole round the Englifh camp all night. On the fifteenth, the Marratta furdars went to the trenches, and began firing again; but it was not anfwered from the Englifh camp. Soon after, Mr. Farmer (a gentleman who was fome time ago at your Highnefs's court) came from the Englifh camp, and the fire of the Marrattas immediately ceafed. The Marrattas fent for him into the prefence, and Mr. Farmer faid to them, " We are only merchants.—When difputes prevailed with you, Roganaut-row came to us, and demanded our protection. We thought he had a right to the government, and gave him our affiftance. Nothing but ill fortune attends him, and we have been brought to this miferable ftate, by keeping him with us. You are mafters to keep him from us. We fhall henceforth adhere to the treaties that have formerly taken place between us. Be pleafed to forgive what has happened."

The minifter anfwered, " Roganaut-row is one of us. What right could you have to interfere in our concerns with him? We now defire you to give up Salfette and Baffin, and what other countries you have poffeffed yourfelf of; as alfo the Circars, thofe of the Purgunnahs of Baroch, &c. which you have taken in Guzzarat. Adhere to the treaty made in the time of Bajalee Row, and afk nothing elfe."—Mr. Farmer heard this anfwer, and returned to his camp. While this negociation was

carrying

carrying on, fifteen thousand Marratta horse were sent against some out-posts where the English had entrenched themselves, and set fire to them, putting every one they met with to death. They did the same at the fort of Choul, where the English had fortified. I heard all this from Nana Furneze; whether it be true or false, I am not certain.

On the 6th at noon, Mr. Farmer returned, and told Schindiah that he had brought a blank paper, signed and sealed, which the Marratta chiefs might fill up as they pleased. Schindiah told the ministers, that although they had it in their power to make any demands they pleased, it would not be adviseable to do it at this time. "For our making large demands, would only sow resentment in their hearts, and we had better demand only what is necessary. Let Roganaut-row be with us, and the treaty between us and the English will be adhered to. Let Salsette and the Purgunnah in Guzzarats, &c. be given back to us. Let the Bengal army return back. For the rest, let us act with them, as it is stipulated in the treaty with Bajalee Row; let the jewels mortgaged by Roganaut-row be restored, and nothing demanded for them. Let all these articles be wrote out on the paper which they have sent." Which was accordingly done. " It is likewise conditioned, that till this treaty is returned, signed and sealed by the governor of the Council and Select Committee, under the Company's Seal, and till Salsette and the other countries be given up, the nephew of Captain Stewart and Mr. Farmer shall remain in the Marratta camp as hostages for the due performance of the articles of this treaty."

Vol. II. M The

The English soldiers who have escaped with their lives, fasted for three days, and are now in a miserable condition. The Europeans and Sepoys have all grounded their arms.—On the 17th the treaty was sent to the Marratta camp. The articles were written in Persian, Marratta, and English, sealed with the Company's seal, and signed by Mr. Carnac and seven officers. After this the Marratta Surdars sent them victuals, which they needed much. The English marched out, escorted by two thousand Marratta horse; but Roganaut-row not finding a lucky hour, did not go to the Marratta camp, but will go after twelve o'clock tomorrow."

LETTER LXI.

To J—— M——, Esq; London.

Calcutta, Jan. 14, 1780.

IN my last I laid before you striking proofs of the moderation and good sense of the Marratta regency, on an occasion the most tempting that could be imagined to revenge and ambition. I wish now to impress the ideas that those proofs have made on your mind, by two letters from Siccaram Pundit, minister of the Marratta sovereignty, to Mr. Hastings, in his capacity of governor general.—There are many who write letters to extenuate the crimes and display the virtues of the Company's leading servants: let me do justice to those whom they have chosen to make their enemies.

Copy

Copy of a letter from Siccaram Pundit, prime minifter of the Poonah government, to governor general Haftings —Received in Bengal the 7th of December, 1778.

" At the time when fome of the Company's chiefs were engaged in difputes and hoftilities with the chiefs of this government, actuated by a wifh to promote the good and happinefs of mankind in general, which fuffered by thofe troubles, you interpofed your friendly mediation to remove the caufes of complaint, and to put a ftop to them ; and deputed Colonel Upton for this purpofe, to the prefence of my mafter Scriminift Row, Row Pundit Pinkham, Pifhaw Saib.

" At the time of the ratification of peace, I objected to there being no perfon of rank and credit prefent on the part of the governor general of Bombay ; to which the Colonel made anfwer, " That the governor and fupreme council of Calcutta were invefted with authority over all fettlements of the Englifh Company, and that their acts were binding on the chiefs of all the Englifh fettlements." On the faith of this declaration, I made peace between this government and the Company's chiefs, and concluded a treaty ; but the governor of Bombay has, in every inftance of his conduct fince, excited troubles and commotions, in violation of the ties of friendfhip ; and notwithftanding your exprefs orders to expel Roganautrow from the Company's dominions, and to fettle all points between the two ftates, in conformity to the treaty, he has performed nothing thereof. And an envoy from the king of France arriving here

here with a letter, interested persons, and inventors of falsehoods, conceiving this a lucky opportunity to obtain credit to their lying reports, without examination or reflection, represented it in the best manner calculated to answer their malicious purposes.

"I call God to witness, that out of regard to the friendship and alliance of the Company and the English chiefs, I dismissed the said envoy, without negociating, or even conversing with him.—I have lately heard, that some of our people have hostilely possessed themselves of the fort of Calpee, which belongs to this government. This measure is widely removed from the faith of the solemn treaty executed by the English.

"When the governor of Bombay, in former times, put on the mask of friendship for the purpose of deceit, and aided the enemies of this government; regarding you, Sir, as superior to all other chiefs, I made peace and friendship with you; and these are the fruits produced by this friendship.

"You write, that the maintaining of friendship and strict union between our states, is your resolve. Is it in effect for the preservation of friendship that you trouble the dominions of this government? Such a mode of conduct is inconsistent with the maxims and measures of high and illustrious chiefs. —It is mutually incumbent on us to preserve inviolate the terms of the treaty. Should any deviation arise therein, they are effects of the will and dispensation of God."

From

From the same.—Received in Calcutta the 12th December, 1778.

"I have been favoured with your letter under date the 22d Tremadee Affamee (17th July) on the subject of the preservation and increase of the friendship between the two states; and intimating that it is your resolve to maintain every article of the treaty, so long as it is adhered to by the Paishwa; that the troops have been sent solely for the reinforcement of the settlement of Bombay; and that the commanding officer had strict injunctions to observe such a conduct in every respect, as is consistent with the friendship subsisting; that the several letters you have lately received from this quarter, meaning from me, contain a declaration to maintain the treaty of friendship between us; yet that my having hitherto evaded to grant passes for the march of the troops through the government dominions, causes you great astonishment. That if I still refuse to comply therewith, you are remediless, and the blame will fall on me. This letter, containing the above, and other particulars, which I shall notice before I conclude, reached me on the 4th of Shabann (28th August) and afforded me great pleasure.

"It is universally allowed, that there is nothing in the world more excellent than friendship and harmony, which are blessings to mankind in general. The maintenance of every article of the treaty, is equally incumbent on both parties.— It is not stipulated in any article of the treaty, that either party may send forces through dominions of the other, without consulting him beforehand,

and

and cause trouble and distress to the people.—To what rule of friendship can be attributed the stationing of garrisons in the forts, and making collections in the country of the other party.—What has happened, is then agreeable to English faith. In proof of this assertion, be it observed, that Colonel Leslie, the commanding officer of the detachment, has kept with him Roganaut-row's Vakeel, and, in conjunction with him, collects money from the dominions of the government, by intimidating its subjects.—This being the case, what become of your assurances before recited, that the treaty should be scrupulously adhered to on your parts, so long as was maintained by my master? or what degree of credit can be given thereto?

" From time immemorial, no forces of the maritime European nations have marched by land through the dominions of the government; but the route of all the trading and European nations has been by the ocean. Nor is it stipulated in the treaty, that the English detachments shall have a passage through the government territories. Reflect maturely on this, and then determine, on whose side the blame rests.—That such unlooked-for acts should proceed from you, is a matter of the highest astonishment; to think that mighty and powerful chiefs should act in direct opposition to the faith of their engagements.—You are pleased to write, that if the presidency of Bombay shall still continue to require the troops, you can in no case agree to recall them.— The matter is briefly thus:—The king of England, and the English Company, have placed confidence in the supreme

council

council of Calcutta, and invefted it with authority over all the other fettlements. The acts of the council of Calcutta are binding on the government of all the Company's fettlements. Having given this affurance, he propofed the form of a treaty, fuch as the critical fituation of the times rendered neceffary.—You tranfmitted a treaty conformably thereto, under the feal of the Englifh Company:— It was from the beginning, the earneft wifh of the government of Bombay, that no friendly connection fhould be eftablifhed between the two ftates, and they have been, ever fince, ftriving to overfet it. And notwithftanding the conclufion of the treaty, they kept Ragoba with them. How then was it to be expected, that they fhould recall their troops, which were difturbing the peace of the government's dominions? It even appears, to a conviction, that they perfuaded Ragoba to the meafures he has purfued. How then does the fupreme authority of the council of Calcutta from the king of England, appear, fince the chiefs of the different fettlements do not regard engagements made by you as binding on them, but make no fcruple to break them: and you, Sir, paying no regard to your own acts, take your meafures on the reprefentations of the government of Bombay. This is indeed aftonifhing to the higheft degree!

" It is the dictate of found policy, that you withdraw your troops to your own territory. This will be a convincing proof of the fincerity of your friendfhip, and will fpread the fame of your good faith throughout the univerfe.

" From the commencement of the government of the family of the Paifhwa, they have entered into treaties with many of the chiefs of the eaft

and

and weft, and have never before experienced such a want of faith from any one; nor ever, to the present time, deviated from their engagements, or been wanting to the duties of friendship and alliance: the blame rests with you."

LETTER LXII.

To J—— M——, Esq. London.

Calcutta, Jan. 18, 1780.

WHILE one army was marching from Bombay, to place Ragoba at the head of the administration of Poonah, another was moving from Bengal, to raise to the same distinguished station Moodajee Boosla, Rajah of Berar. You start at this, as being incredible; nevertheless, it is a fact, as you will be convinced by the following narrative:

On the 23d of February, Mr. Hastings presented a letter from Bombay, representing the favourable circumstances at the court of Poonah, and other particulars, tending to induce the English to support the pretensions of Roganaut-row to the office of Paishwa. On this letter, he founded a motion to march a detachment over land to support the army of Bombay. The governor's double vote, together with that of Mr. Barwell, having over-ruled the single votes of their opponents, it was resolved, that for this purpose a detachment should be sent under the command of Colonel Matthew Leslie, consisting of one hundred and three

three officers, fix thoufand fix hundred and twenty four troops, nineteen thoufand feven hundred and twenty nine fervants, and twelve thoufand buzars or market-people. An army only of fix thoufand feven hundred and twenty feven troops, and a fuite of thirty one thoufand feven hundred and twenty nine fervants and futlers, was ordered to traverfe an unexplored country of immenfe extent†, abounding in faftneffes, interfected by defiles and navigable rivers, and inhabited by a warlike and hoftile people. This detachment began their march in the month of May.

It was now the wet feafon, and torrents of rain overflowed the country, deftroying the roads, and making even fmall rivers and brooks impaffable. The effect of the heat was fatally experienced by the troops and their numerous attendants, on the firft day's march from Calpee : for either through the ignorance of their conductors, or the obftinacy of the commander, they moved out of the right courfe ; and through fatigue and want of water, between three and four hundred perfons died raving mad. Captain Crawfurd, one of the beft men and braveft officers in India, died in that ftate, of two hours illnefs. Colonel Parker, Major Fullarton, Captain Afh, Captain Showers, and about ten fubalterns, happily recovered from dangerous illneffes.

The army having croffed the Jumna, notwithftanding the fierce oppofition of the Marratta ftates adjoining that river, and proceeded into the very heart of an hoftile country, its recall from which would be conftrued into a difgraceful re-

† Fifteen hundred miles.

treat,

treat, the governor general did not think it necessary any longer to disguise his real object in this expedition. The same army, which originally was destined to support the pretensions of Ragoba, is now to be made the instrument of placing Moodajee-Boosla at the head of the Marratta empire, as well in opposition to Roganaut-row, as his adversaries; and the Company is to join with that prince in invading the dominions of their own ally, the Nizam of the Deccan. And yet Mr. Hastings, in the month of December last, declared, that this Moodajee-Boosla, who was then dangerously ill, and expected to die, was not the real Rajah of Berar, nor the pretender to the Marratta imperial throne; but the Naib, or deputy Rajah of Berar, during the minority of the real prince.

In consequence of this change in the destination of the expedition, Colonel Leslie was ordered to take his route through Berar, instead of pursuing his journey directly through Malva.—At the beginning of a French war, and at a time when all India beheld the Company's growing power with jealousy and with dread, instead of providing for the security of Bengal, or any other of our possessions in the east, the governor general dispatches Mr. Elliot with powers and instructions to enter into a treaty of alliance, offensive and defensive, with the Rajah of Berar. By this treaty, Roganaut-row was to be set aside, and Moodajee-Boosla to be placed at the head of the Marratta empire, and to be supported in his pretensions against the Company's ally, the Souba of the Deccan, the richest prince in Hindostan. Mr. Elliot set out on this embassy; but dying on his journey, all the negociations

negociations intrusted to him were of course suspended.—And here let me digress from my narrative, in order to lament the too early fate of one of the most amiable characters, and elevated geniuses that ever distinguished humanity. All who knew him were his friends; even strangers, to whom report alone afforded an opportunity of admiring his talents and virtues, mourned for the death of Mr. Elliot. He fell a martyr to patriotism and fidelity to the East India Company. Afflicted with a disorder peculiar to the east, which originates in bilious obstructions, and the cure of which requires a copious application of mercury, his duty prevailing over every other consideration; he undertook a long and fatiguing journey, in the rainy season, without a possibility of enjoying such accommodations as might be suitable to his state of health. After leaving the Company's territories, he discovered, that governor Chevalier, who had secretly escaped from Chandernagore, was pursuing the same route before him. Knowing the ambitious designs of that man, and the accurate knowledge he had acquired of the politics of India, he strained every nerve to seize his person, dreading that his liberty and arrival in France might be attended with the worst consequences to the Company's affairs, and the views of Great Britain. He pushed onward by forced journies, still tracing and approaching Monsieur Chevalier. Unfortunately, just when he had the chase in view, his progress was obstructed by a sudden overflow of the waters of one of the large rivers of Catac. Regardless of the state of his health, and the medicines he had taken, by an extraordinary exertion of activity and strength, he encountered the rapid stream, and
swam

swam across the river with a few of his attendants and sepoys. He found Monsieur Chevalier at the metropolis of Catac: and, although escorted only by a few sepoys, he claimed the person of Governor Chevalier with such sensible arguments and manly eloquence, that the Rajah surrendered him.

As Mr. Elliot had but a small escort, and the longest and most dangerous part of his journey was yet to be performed, he could not, without sacrificing the object of his commission, return a guard to conduct Monsieur Chevalier and his companion Monsieur Moneron, to Calcutta; wherefore he engaged their paroles in writing, to surrender themselves prisoners of war, within a limited time, to the governor general.—Monsieur Chevalier and Monsieur Moneron performed their engagements. Mr. Elliot pursued his route to Berar; but died a few days afterwards.—

Chatterpore, the capital of Bundlecund, the country of diamonds, is situated near the western confines of that province. Its distance from Calcutta may be computed at twenty days journey for a native courier. Here Colonel Leslie had lain near three months, committing in the country around many hostilities and depredations. A letter from this officer was laid before the supreme council upon the 19th of October, wherein he stated the cause which retarded his march; and accounts for his not having been hitherto more explicit in his communications to the board, by saying, that he had furnished Mr. Hastings, at his own special desire, with a particular journal of occurrences, and therefore had trusted to him for such explanations as the board might require. The Colonel, notwithstanding his delays and depredations, expressed

pressed not the least apprehension of Mr. Hastings's resentment, or of any effects it could produce; but, on the contrary, he set him at open defiance in plain terms, and refused to hold private correspondence with him any longer.

LETTER LXIII.

To J——M——, Esq; London.

Calcutta, Jan. 21, 1780.

COLONEL LESLIE died at Chatterpore on the 3d of October, 1778. He was succeeded in the chief command of the detachment by Colonel Goddard; who received a charge to renew the negociation with Moodajee-Boosla, on the principles of Mr. Elliot's instructions, with full power to conclude a treaty.

The power that had been delegated on the 15th of October, to the presidency of Bombay, of commanding the march of the detachment, was revoked, and Goddard was to be directed only by orders from the supreme council. The governor general, on the 12th of October, had violently censured the presidency of Bombay, for not pushing matters to extremity against the Marratta regency, in order to reinstate Rogunaut-row in the office of Paishwa; he now takes a measure inconsistent with the ostensible object of the expedition, which was to cooperate with the Bombay army in favour of Ragoba. For, without a preconcerted coincidence of movements, how can two armies act for one end?

end? and, how can there be a coincidence of movements, where armies are under feparate commands? But, notwithftanding Mr. Haftings's warm approbation of the plan for raifing Ragoba to the Marratta throne, he confidered his caufe as defperate; and even while he approved the refolutions of the Bombay prefidency, to accompany him with an army to Poonah, he declared, that he confidered them as refolutions to do nothing: an opinion for which an extreme fluctuation in the councils of Bombay, had indeed given good ground. But though he entertained no hopes in the meafures of that prefidency in favour of Ragoba, he probably trufted that they might fave at leaft his detachment; a conjecture which the event fully juftified. It is certain, however, from the uniform tenor of Mr. Haftings's minutes, as well as the letters to and from the Rajah of Berar, that the real object of that expedition was an alliance with the Rajah, and an embaffy to folicit him to become a candidate for the fovereignty of the Marratta empire. Yet the expedition over land was planned and refolved on the 23d of February, 1778; and by the fixth article of the inftructions to the prefidency of Bombay, to treat conclufively and effectually with Roganaut-row, bearing date the 18th of the enfuing month of March, the fupreme council were folemnly bound to perform every condition which any fuch treaty might contain. And if violation of faith was not intended from the beginning, why was not the government of Bombay commanded to forbear entering into any treaty with Roganaut-row, the moment that it was refolved to enter into a negociation with Moodajee-Boofla; and to avoid all overt hoftilities againft the

Marrattas,

Marrattas, unlefs in felf-defence, until they fhould be exprefsly authorifed by the fupreme council, or court of Directors ? Or, why was it not confidentially intrufted with the defign in favour of the Rajah, and directed to contribute to its fuccefs when it was ripe for execution ?

In profecution of his views of exalting Moodajee-Boofla to the Marratta imperial throne, Mr. Haftings wrote the following letter to his prime minifter, Dewagur Pundit, dated in Calcutta, 23d November, 1778: " In the whole of my conduct I have departed from the common line of policy, and have made advances when others in my fituation would have waited for folicitations: as the greateft advantages to which I can look, cannot in their nature equal thofe to which the profperous iffue of our meafures may conduct the ftate of the Maha-rajah's government. But I know the characters to which I addrefs myfelf. I truft to the approved bravery and fpirit of our chief, that he will ardently catch at the objects prefented to his ambition; and to your wifdom, of which, if fame reports truly, no minifter ever poffeffed a larger portion, that you will view their importance in too clear a light to hazard the lofs of them, by attempting to take an advantage of the defire which I have expreffed for their accomplifhment. This intimation is not fo much intended for a caution to you, as for an explanation of my conduct to thofe who may be lefs able to penetrate the grounds of it."

But Moodajee-Boofla did not catch at the objects prefented to his ambition, with that ardour which the governor looked for; nor does it appear that he ever had an idea of the nature and extent of

Mr.

Mr. Hastings's views; much less that he entertained any design of waging war against the Marratta regency and the Soubah of the Deccan, or of entering into any engagements, with the Company, that would lead him into a rupture with either of those states, his neighbours. The Rajah, tottering on the brink of the grave, wisely preferred peace in mediocrity to the flattering, but uncertain alurement offered to his ambition. He undertook to vindicate the Paishwa from the charge brought against him by the Company's servants, of maintaining a secret connection with the French; and offered, with great earnestness, his own mediation to effect, between his countrymen and the English, a perfect reconciliation.

LETTER LXIV.

To J—— M———, Esq; London.

Calcutta, Jan. 25, 1780.

IN the beginning of January, 1779, Colonel Goddard, with the detachment, crossed the Narbudda, and encamped on the southern banks of that river, within the territory of Berar; where he waited to be informed of the final resolution of Moodajee-Boosla. He deputed Lieutenant Weatherstone to Naig-pore, in order to press the Rajah to conclude the proposed treaty, and immediately to enter on the execution of it; but without the smallest success. That prince declined entering into any treaty, or taking any active part whatever,

ever, till further accounts fhould arrive from Calcutta. As a pretext for this refufal, he pleaded the part taken by the council of Bombay, in favour of Roganaut-row, and not only recommended, but earneftly entreated the Englifh to abandon that chief, and accept of terms from the minifterial party in Poonah.

The government of Berar had a thoufand arguments to oppofe to thofe urged in favour of the plan for their affuming the dignity of Ram-rajah of Setterah; particularly, " their pledged faith, and the friendfhip they had fworn to the prefent Paifhwa. Their afferting their pretenfions to the fovereignty, they affirmed, would be encountered by numberlefs obftacles. A victory could not be obtained without fhedding much blood, and violating the moft facred engagements." The fupport afforded by the Englifh to Roganaut-row, they confidered " as highly impolitical, and predicted, that in the end it would be found to be fo. Roganaut-row, they faid, was held in univerfal abhorrence; and the prejudices in the Deccan againft that chief would not eafily, if ever, be removed."

The fentiments of the Maha-rajah and his minifters, being communicated to governor Haftings, very much difconcerted and diftreffed him. He fent a letter to Moodajee-Boofla, in which he laments rather than complains, of the diftruft entertained by the Rajah; and declares, that had he accepted of the terms offered to him by Colonel Goddard, and concluded a treaty with the government of Bengal, he (Mr. Haftings) fhould have held the obligation of it fuperior to that of any engagement formed by the government of Bombay; " and fhould have thought it his duty to have maintained

maintained it againſt every conſideration, even of the moſt valuable intereſts and ſafety of the Engliſh poſſeſſions intruſted to his charge†. To you," continued the governor general, "I had unreſervedly committed all my views, partly and indiſtinctly by letters, but very fully in repeated converſations with your Vakeel Beneram Pundit, as it would have been very improper to have the affairs of ſuch delicacy and importance committed to letters, and to the hazards to which theſe would have been expoſed in a long and doubtful journey. Your caution was ſtill greater, and perhaps more commendable, although I may regret the neceſſity which preſcribed it; for neither your letters, nor the letters of Beneram Pundit, afforded me the leaſt clue to judge of your ſentiments or inclination reſpecting the particular points of action which were to form the ſubſtance of our projected engagements. And although from your general profeſſions, and the warmth and ſincerity with which theſe were manifeſtly dictated, I had every reaſon to conclude that you approved of them; yet, without ſome aſſurances, common prudence required, that I ſhould not precipitately abandon every other reſource, and irrevocably commit the honour and intereſts of this government in a doubtful meaſure. Precautions were taken, that nothing ſhould be undertaken by any of the governments dependent on this, which might eventually interfere with thoſe actually concluded with you."

The governor's letter had no effect on Moodajee-Booſla; and Colonel Goddard, having received

† This declaration of Mr. Haſtings ſurpaſſes the bittereſt accuſations of his adverſaries, and expoſes views and purpoſes totally inconſiſtent with duty and fidelity.

a letter

a letter from General Carnac and Colonel Egerton, bearing date the 11th of January, advising him not to continue his march towards Poonah, but to proceed either to Baroach or Surat, or to remain on the borders of Berar, wifely followed their advice. He moved with his detachment from Brahmpore, on the 6th of February, and arrived at Surat about the 26th of that month, without having met with any oppofition, or fo much as even feeing an enemy; and, had the army been commanded by a man of lefs bravery and activity, this expedition might not have been fo fuccefsful. The Marrattas called in all their troops to oppofe the Bombay army; and the treaty made with Mr. Carnac, lulled them into a fecurity, until it was difavowed in Bombay; and in the mean time, Colonel Goddard preffed his march, and efcaped.

LETTER LXV.

To J——— M———, Efq; London.

Calcutta, Jan. 26, 1780.

EUROPEAN nations falfely imagine, that all the delicacy of tafte and refinement of fentiment that are to be found in the world, are poffeffed by themfelves; other nations, they confider as rude and barbarous. It is true, that a few men of enlightened underftandings are ready to allow a degree of cultivation to certain Afiatic nations: but I am apt to think, that even thefe men underrate the talents as well as the virtues of the sons of the east; at least, I have scarcely met with any author who speaks on this subject with any degree of enthusiasm. Every body seems willing to give a tacit consent to that vast superiority, in all respects, which European vanity and arrogance have assumed over all the rest of the world.

The following letter from the Maha-rajah Moodajee-Boosla, to Mr. Hastings, for good sense, a spirit of justice, humanity, and delicacy of sentiment and taste, may justly be compared with any of Pliny or Cicero.

Copy of a letter from Moodajee-Boosla to Governor Hastings, dated the 5th December, 1778, and received the 2d January, 1779.

" Your friendly letter of the 19th Ramzam, (11th October) informing me of your having received advice of the death of Mr. Elliot, in his way to Naigpore†; your concern at that event, and at the unavoidable suspensions of the negociations which that gentleman was to have conducted with me on the part of your government; and the delay in the establishment of a strict and perpetual friendship between the Company's state and mine (concerning which you had exerted yourself so warmly) by reason that the present situation of affairs would not admit of the delay which must attend the deputation of another person from thence, without injuring the designs in hand; but that in your conviction of my favourable disposition, from the knowledge that my interests and the

---

† The capital of Berar.

Company's are inseparably connected; and in the zeal of Beneram Pundit, whom, during the long period he resided with you, you found so deserving of your confidence, &c. &c. That the plan proposed, and what you have written, is to promote our common advantage, not for the interest of one party only, being convinced, that no public alliance or private friendship, can be firmly established without reciprocal advantages: That it is on these principles you had long ago planned an alliance with me, the time for the accomplishment of which is now come; for you conceive it to be equally for my interest as for yours, our countries bordering on each other, and our natural enemies being the same: That, in a word, you required nothing but the junction of my forces with yours, by which, though each is singly very powerful, they will acquire a ten-fold proportion of strength: That the delay of the progress in the detachment intended for Bombay, had not arisen from the opposition of an enemy, but from other causes improper to mention; but that it will now shortly arrive in my territories, and its operation be determined by my advice: That you have given directions to Colonel Leslie, to co-operate with the forces which I shall unite with his: That as you offer me the forces of your Circar to promote my views, you in return require the assistance of mine to effect your purposes; with other particulars which I fully understand, reached me on the 26th Shawand (16th November) and afforded me great pleasure. I also received duplicate and triplicate of this letter.—In the latter part of it you express, that as you had made me acquainted with your views, it is necessary that I also communicate to you, without reserve,

serve, the ends which I look to for my advantage in this union: That the good faith of the English to every engagement they contract, so long as it is observed by others, is universally known; and that it has been the invariable rule of your conduct, to support this character in all acts depending on you, and never to relinquish any design of importance formed on good and judicious grounds, but to persevere steadily to its completion: That having thus explained to me your sentiments and views, you wait only to know mine; and on the knowledge of these, you shall form your ultimate resolution.—

" It is equally a maxim of sincere friendship and good government, steadiness, magnanimity, and foresight, that a plan, formed on good and judicious grounds, should be conducted in such a manner as to end happily. You desire to learn my sentiments and views; and deferring to form your ultimate resolutions until you heard further from me, is the same thing as if you had consulted me primarily on your first designs.

" Since, after the strictest scrutiny and researches into dispositions and vices of the multitude, it has been determined, on proofs of mutual sincerity and good faith, that a perpetual friendship and union be established, it will, like the wall of Alexander, for the happiness of mankind, continue unshaken until the end of time.

" The having caused a translation to be made into English of the Hindoo books, called the Shaster and Poran, and of the history of the former kings; the studying these books, and keeping the pictures of the former kings and present rulers of Hind, Deccan, &c. always before your eyes, and
from

from their lifeless similitude to discover which of them were or are worthy of rule, and possessed of good faith; from which to determine with whom to contract engagements, and what conduct to observe to them respectively;—also, the endeavour to preserve the blessing of peace, until forced to relinquish it;—the supporting every one in his hereditary right; and revenging the breach of faith and engagement; but on the submission of the offenders, the exercise of the virtues of clemency and generosity, by pardoning, and receiving him again into favour, and restoring him to his possessions;—the not suffering the intoxication of power to reduce you into a breach of faith—and the giving support to each illustrious house in proportion to its respective merits, and in matters which required a long course of years to bring to perfection;—the forming your conduct on mature deliberation, and the advice of the Company and Council,—are the sure means of exalting your greatness and prosperity to the highest pitch—The intention of all this is to recommend universal peace and friendship in the manner following: The Almighty disposes of kingdoms, and places whomsoever he chuses on the seats of power and rule; but makes their stability to depend on their peaceable, just, and friendly conduct to others.—It is not every one that is equal to the task of government, on the plan designed by the Almighty Ruler, and of ensuring his stability by a wise and just conduct.—Hind and Deccan possess, at present, very few enlightened, but a great multitude of weak and ignorant men: The English chiefs, and you in a superior degree, possess all the virtues above recited,

cited, who coming from distant islands by a six months voyage on the great ocean, by their magnanimity and fortitude, gained the admiration of many Soubahs on this continent. It is easy to acquire a kingdom; but to become a king over kings, and chief of chiefs, is a very difficult matter. The attainment of this is only to be effected by the means of friendship, by which the universe may be subjected. My conduct is framed on these principles.—The residence of Beneram Pundit at Calcutta, was solely to effect the establishment of the most intimate friendship; and by the blessing of God it has taken such deep root, that through your means it has reached the ear of the Company and King of England: And our connection and correspondence, carried on under the veil of the vicinity of our dominions, has been discovered by the Poonah ministers, and by the Nabob Nizum-ul-Dowla; yet, though they form various conjectures and doubts, and have sent a trusty Vakeel, and written repeated letters, to endeavour to find out the motives of our union, yet they remain a mystery, as I make the plea of our ancient ties, and the junction of our territories.

"I was impatiently expecting the arrival of Mr. Elliot, who being endowed with an enlightened understanding, and invested with full powers from you to conduct the negociations, and determine on the measures to be pursued, would have established the ties of a perpetual friendship, and have settled every matter on the firmest basis. It pleased God that he should die on the journey; and the grief I felt, at his unfortunate loss, who would have been the means of settling all points between us, to our mutual content, and by his negociation with me,

giving

giving satisfaction to the Paishwa and Nabob Nizam-ul Dowla; all which have been by his death thrown back many months; my grief is not to be described, and only serves to add to your afflictions. I have not yet recovered the shock which that event gave me, as you will learn more fully from Siccaram Pundit. There is no remedy for such misfortunes, and it is in vain to strive against the decrees of Providence. Had Mr. Elliot arrived, such strokes of policy would have been employed, that the Poonah ministers would have adhered more scrupulously than before to their engagements; and the French, who are the natural enemies of the English, would have been theirs likewise; and their suspicions from apprehensions of support being given to Roganaut-row, which never was, nor is designed by the English chiefs, as I learn from Beneram, who had it from your own mouth, and which has caused them great uneasiness, would have been entirely removed by Mr. Elliot and my joint security.

" The Nabob Nizam-ul-Dowla,—who wrote you repeatedly on this subject, and received for answer, that you had no idea of aiding or supporting Roganaut-row ; that your enmity was solely pointed against the French ; and that whoever assisted the French were your enemies, —would likewise by these means have been thoroughly satisfied, and your detachment would have reached Bombay, without meeting the smallest interruption; and had the Poonah ministers then acted a contrary part, I should have withdrawn myself from their friendship. But by the death of Mr. Elliot, all these designs have fallen to the ground, and must be suspended till another opportunity, and the

knowledge

knowledge of your sentiments. It is a proverb, "that whatever is deliberately done, is well done." In reply to what you write respecting your framing your ultimate resolutions, I have communicated to Beneram Pundit whatever I judge proper and eligible, and which may promote them in such a manner as may not be subject to any change from the vicissitudes of fortunes. For those points which I fixed on, after minute deliberation, as the most eligible that can be adopted, I refer you to the letters of Beneram Pundit. If, notwithstanding, you have any plan to propose for the reciprocal benefit of our states, be pleased to communicate to me.

POSTSCRIPT.

"To your letter respecting sending an army to overawe the French, and to reinforce the government of Bombay; and setting forth that the Poonah ministers having broken the treaty with the English, and in opposition to the rights of friendship received an envoy of the French king, and granted the port of Choul to that nation, thereby enabling them to form an arsenal, and collect military stores; and of their having written to their officers, to permit the French ships to enter their ports; and that it being therefore incumbent on you to take measures to counteract their designs, you had determined to send a strong detachment for the reinforcement of Bombay, by the route of Berar; and that in consideration of our antient friendship, and the vicinity of our dominions, you requested, that on its arrival in my neighbourhood, I would cause it to be instructed in the route, and, providing

providing it with provisions and neceffaries, have it conducted in fafety through my territories, and join a body of my forces with it, which would increafe and cement our friendfhip; and that you have, at the affurance of Beneram, fixed on this route for its march in preference to any other: In reply to this letter, actuated by its dictates of the fincereft friendfhip, I waited not to take the advice of any one, but without hefitation wrote you, That where a fincere friendfhip exifted, the paffage of troops through my country was a matter of no moment; that they fhould proceed immediately through my country. I likewife informed Colonel Leflie of the difficulties and dangers he would meet with in the way, from dangerous mountains, extenfive rivers, &c. And alfo difpatched Lalla Jadda Roy, with a chief of note, to the banks of the Narbudda, to fupply the detachment with provifions as long as they were in my territory, and to treat them with all the duties of hofpitality; where he waited in expectation of their arrival for fix months to no purpofe. They loitered away their time in the Bundle Cund countries, contrary to every rule of policy. At that time all the Poonah minifters were feparately employed in their own private affairs, or in the war with Hyder Naig, infomuch that they had no time to turn their attention to the concerns of other parts, and the march to Bombay might have been effected with the greateft eafe. The time is now paft. The arrow is fhot, and cannot be recalled. As I have repeatedly written to the Poonah minifters, with whom I keep up a correfpondence on the fubject of their encouraging a French envoy, and breaking their faith with the Englifh chiefs, acts highly inconfiftent

confiftent with honour and policy; the anfwer I received from them. I have communicated to you. The fubftance of what they fay in their own juftification is this : That the French Vakeel came for the purpofe of traffic, not to negociate ; yet, for the fatisfaction of the Englifh, they gave him his difmiffion : That the account of the grant of the port of Choul, and an arfenal, is entirely without foundation; and that they have not the leaft indifpofition towards the Englifh : That I will therefore write to Calcutta, that you may be perfectly fatisfied refpecting their difpofition.—My letters did not produce the effect of fatisfying you on the fubject of the Paifhwa, but your doubts ftill remained. And, actuated by wifdom and prudence, you determined to fend Mr. Elliot to me; and wrote to me, that on his arrival at Naigpore, after he had an interview with me, and learned my fentiments and views, he would, in conjunction with me, form a plan for our mutual honour and benefit, and give directions to Colonel Leflie in confequence, who would be guided thereby. — The event of this gentleman's deputation is too well known; and Colonel Leflie likewife, after engaging in hoftilities with the Paifhwa's officers and Zemindars of thefe parts, and collecting large fums of money, died. Colonel Goddard fucceeded to the command, and purfued the fame line of conduct, with refpect to the Talookdars, as his predeceffor ; and arriving at Garawale and Garafur in the territory of the Afghans, whither he was obliged to march with the utmoft caution, being furrounded with a Marratta army, who conftantly feized every opportunity to attack him, wrote me from thence, that he fhould fhortly reach the
Narbudda,

Narbudda, where I would be pleafed to caufe grain and other neceffaries to be prepared, and a party of my forces to be ready to join him.—I wrote him in anfwer, That Lalla Jada Roy, and Shao Baal Hazaile were waiting on that fide the Narbudda which is within my territories, and that the Gaut where the troops fhould crofs was two cofs from hence, under Haflingabad; that Janojee Boofla forded it with his army at that place, on his expedition to Malawa, and that I did not doubt it was now fordable; that he fhould therefore crofs his army there, and repair to Haflingabad: That Lalla Jada Roy fhould exert his utmoft affiduity in fupplying him with grain and other provifions, and treat them with every degree of hofpitality; but that, as the road forward was very difficult and dangerous, and thoufands of the Balha Caftes were concealed in the holes in the mountains; who, though not able to oppofe him openly, yet would do it by ambufcade and ftratagems, and cut off his fupplies of provifions; and that, beyond that he would enter the Soubahfhip of Barhampore, dependent on the Paifhwa: That near four thoufand of Scindia's cavalry were waiting at the fort of Affur, for the arrival of the Englifh on the banks of the Ganges; ten thoufand more were under the command of Bagarut Sundiab; Scindiah himfelf with the chiefs in readinefs at Poonah, waiting to hear of the approach of the Engiifh; and moreover in Berar, in which the Nabob Nizam-ul-Dowla poffeffes a fhare with me, all the Jaghirdars were in readinefs with powerful armies; and although the Englifh poffeffed the greateft magnanimity in battle, yet as every ftep they took would be juft into the mouth of danger, and all the above mentioned

chiefs

chiefs would set themselves to cut off and destroy his provisions, and take every opportunity of attacking him when they saw an advantage, and of harrassing him night and day, constantly surrounding his army with their numerous forces, the junction of a body of my forces with his, would avail nothing in the fate of such large armies, but would only involve me in the greatest losses: That it neither was adviseable for him to return, which would diminish the awe and respect in which he was held; that I would therefore write the particulars explicitly to Calcutta, and that whatever you should think proper to intimate to him and me in reply, it would be adviseable to abide by, and act accordingly. All which time I would recommend that he continued at Hossingur.—That I have received letters from Calcutta, filled with the warmest friendship and confidence to the following purport: "That the detachment should come into my neighbourhood, and be guided in its operation by my advice: That it is incumbent on every chief who enjoys the confidence of another, to give such advice as may be most advantageous to the party reposing trust, and most consistent with the faith of engagements; and that with such conduct the Almighty is well pleased." That I had also written to the Poonah ministers my advice on the situation of affairs, to this purport: "That Mr. Elliot was deputed hither to negociate with me, but dying in the journey, all the negociations intrusted to him were suspended; that had he arrived at Naigpore, I had determined from principles of attachment, to have removed from the minds of the English the doubts and apprehensions which had arisen by reason of the supposed encouragement of the French

French envoy at Poonah, and the agreement to support that nation, who were the inveterate enemies of the English, which had given rife to the quarrel between the two ftates, by proving to them under the fanction of folemn oaths, and becoming myfelf guarantee, that all thofe reports were groundlefs, and that the Poonah minifters were fteady and zealous in their engagements with the English, and on feveral accounts highly obliged to them. And I would have taken from Mr. Elliot, engagements, that the English had no idea of affording fupport to Roganaut-row, but were refolved to maintain their treaty inviolate; and that their apprehenfions related to the French; and that when I gave the English fatisfaction relating to the French, and became guarantee, all his doubts would be removed; and that if it was requifite, a frefh engagement fhould be executed, to which he would be a guarantee: That, in brief, each party entertained a reafonable doubt; the English, that the Poonah minifters would join with the French; and the Poonah minifters, that the English fupport Roganaut-row: That when thefe fufpicions no longer remained, all caufes of difpleafure would of courfe ceafe; and that they could have no objection to a detachment of English forces, fent for the reinforcement of Bombay, and to overawe the French, not for the fupport of Roganaut-row, repairing thither; and to oppofe them would in fuch cafe have been highly improper," &c. &c.

Second Postscript.

" Baboo-row, the Paifhwa's vakeel, has obferved to me in the courfe of converfation, that his
master

master has not the slightest idea of failing in his engagements with the English, or of contracting any friendship with the French; but that the treaty forbids the march of English forces through the Paishwa's dominions; that therefore the appearance of the detachment now on its march, is an infringement of the treaty.

Third Postscript.

"Although it may appear improper to repeat the same thing over again, yet the importance of the subject may plead in my excuse. On either part a doubt subsists. The Poonah ministers suspect that the English forces on their march to Bombay, though ostensibly for the purpose of opposing the French, are in reality intended for the support of Roganaut-row; and that the English at Bombay, who were not included in the treaty with the Paishwa, which was concluded through the governor of Bengal, with the advice of the chief at Calcutta, are desirous of breaking with the Paishwa, and supporting Roganaut-row; and that the detachment had been sent at their requisition. They alledge, that the chief of Calcutta writes to them, that he is firmly resolved to adhere to the treaty with the Paishwa; and that the detachment he has sent to Bombay, is solely to awe the French, without the least design to assist Roganaut-row; and that since it is forbidden in the treaty to dispatch troops over land, the march of the troops is a breach of it: That if it is necessary to send troops to Bombay to awe the French, they ought to be sent by sea.

"The

"The English on their part suspected the Poonah ministers of joining the French, in consequence of receiving a French vakeel. As the Paishwa formerly wrote me, that he had no idea of failing in his engagements with the English, and that he had given no encouragement to the French vakeel, who came for the purpose of traffic, and that he had dismissed him, therefore requested that I would satisfy you in that respect; I, in consequence, formerly wrote you all these particulars. As I have a voucher in my hand from the Paishwa, that he has no connection with the French, and is steady to his engagements with the English, I am able, by this voucher, to give you complete satisfaction on this head, but I have no voucher, or intimation from you, by which I may be able to give satisfaction to him.

"As he pleads a prohibition in the treaty, to the march of forces over land, and likewise complains respecting the money collected by Colonel Leslie in his territories, what answer can be made thereto?

"As the time requires that a reconciliation take place with the Poonah ministers, you will consider and determine what reply shall be given to these two points of which they complain; and by what means they will be satisfied; and communicate your resolution to me, that I may write conformably thereto, and remove all doubts."

LETTER LXVI.

To J—— M——, Esq. London.

Calcutta, Jan. 24, 1780.

THE Company's concerns in Europe and in India, are now reduced to a state, by much too critial not to alarm every person whose mind is not callous, and tainted with deliberate treachery†.

The nation, engaged in a general war in Europe and America, must, ere now, have contracted with the Company to continue their charter, and the possession of all territorial revenues in India, in consideration of a gift and loan of several millions.

The Company were fully justified, by the confident asseveration of their governor general and the second in supreme council, on the tenth of August, 1778, to conclude with certainty, that near three millions sterling are now unappropriated in their treasury in Bengal, without any reduction of the current investments; and therefore, to make these very important and seasonable concessions to the nation.

The nation, equally confident in the truth of what the Company's principal ministers abroad had asserted, and the Directors at home believed, must have implicitly trusted to that resource; and either advanced proportionably in the measure of expence, by prosecuting the war with vigour, or seasonably relaxed in taxing the people.

† The substance of this letter on the subject of an intended coalition, was also sent to a member of government in Bengal.

The measures, obstinately and perversely pursued in India, have consumed all the Company's treasures in Bengal; and in some establishments have increased their debts, without the probable means of removing the causes, or of retrieving their circumstances; insomuch, that it is to be apprehended, the very investments must be curtailed, if not wholly stopt, instead of making an extraordinary remittance of three millions to Britain, to answer the Company's engagements to the nation.

The weight of this disappointment will embarrass government, and operate as a double tax upon the nation, already depressed in means, and in credit: The minister will throw it upon the Company; the Company will justify themselves by the baseness and treachery of their principal servants abroad; the nation will accuse the Directors, as accessaries in the guilt of their servants, whom they might have removed, as their malversations had repeatedly been communicated to them; the Directors will retort upon administration, by recurring to the censures, which they had freely thrown from time to time upon the majority of their principal servants; and alledging that, under the secret influence and protection of ministerial power, the delinquents were not only kept in their stations, but encouraged in contemptuous disobedience, and a continuation of abuses.

The nation will view it in its true light; it will become a subject of impeachment; the perfidious authors will be abandoned to their fate. A bill of pains and penalties will pass unanimously, because no minister will dare to support so bad a cause; pri-

.vate property will be sequestered, and the offending person arrested.

The chief author of these great evils sees the approaching event with dreadful alarm; he dreads again the apostacy of Sir E⸺ C⸺e; again he beholds all the powers in India roused, and united to oppose the unabating ambition of a foreign people, under the guidance of men, who have proved themselves strangers equally to public and private faith, and to the purity and sacredness of solemn engagements. He fears the premature arrival of French auxiliaries, to incorporate with, and to direct the offended native states. He knows that all the powers in India have lost confidence in himself, and that pacific overtures are therefore needless. He desires, now, to lessen the odium against himself, and to elude a part of the public censure, by associating his opponents in all his pernicious measures, by a late coalition. He wishes also to associate them in support of his foul, destructive, and illegal contracts—in the misconduct and enormous depredations of the late resident at Oude. And he dreads that old practices, even antecedent to the present government, will burst out into judgment against him. Craft, subtilty, temporizing, and self-possession, are peculiar to a thirty years education under wily Rajahs, Banians, and Circars in Hindostan. He is not only insincere, but premeditately intent on deception, the instant that a breach of faith can gratify his resentment, because he is implacable; or his purposes, because he is political; or his power, because he is imperious; and would rather part with existence than with authority, or cease to be idolized or flattered.

He

He sees no alternative, but to pursue the war; he sees, that to pursue the war, besides the chances of being worsted at all quarters, he must stop all investments; and he sees, that to stop the investments will be followed with the immediate bankruptcy of the Company in Europe. Nay, he must see, that such is the miserable state to which his measures have reduced trade, that all the current years investment being already in store, it cannot be converted into money; and that money is now indispensably wanted to carry on the war. And his discernment points out clearly to his view, the intire destruction of the Company's power in Bengal, Bahar, and the Vizier's provinces, if the manufacturers are thrown idle, and consequently forced to emigrate for bread.

In this critical dilemma, he calls artfully for relief from those, whose arguments against his own perfidious measures he had hitherto treated so contemptuously, as not to deign answers to them.

He knows, that to secure success in any overtures to Indian princes, he himself cannot appear as ostensible minister, or as contracting party, because they will place no confidence in his promises, engagements, or faith. That therefore, a new administration, in which he bears no leading part, can alone gain access, even to treat.

After so long, so honourable, so faithful, and so steady a resistance, to save the Company, and to benefit the British nation, † however wearied with want of success and protection, to yield now, unless with a firm and unalterable purpose to support the same measures and principles, will be, to release

---

† Alluding to Mr. Francis's conduct.

the active aggressor from more than a third part of his guilt; and to become not an accessary, but a principal in all the mischiefs and crimes he has committed.

It may be possible to divert Hyder Ally and the Nizam from the union with the Marratta junction. A common cause, to oppose a common enemy, only could have connected men whose enmities are inherent, inveterate, and deep-rooted. A speedy and judicious embassy may effect an alliance with these two princes: and the Rajah of Berar is so contiguously situated, that the movement of a brigade over the Jumma, will withdraw him from the Poonah alliance, after the alliance is effected with Hyder Ally and the Nizam. In all, and every other respect, it will be prudent to act only on the defensive, until those connections are firmly established: and then the Marrattas will hearken to such just and reasonable terms, as will not dishonour the British name, tarnish its military fame, or weaken its influence in Asia.

Before matters are reduced to extremities, or, that the critical situation of the Company's affairs is published, it might be expedient to open the treasures of Bengal and Madras, to receive a loan of a crore of rupees. If it cannot be effected at five per cent. as it might have been last year, to give six, seven, or even eight per cent. per annum interest, on what shall be made payable in India; or four per cent. payable, periodically, in Europe.

I shall set out from this place within a day or two, to embark in the ship G—s, now lying at the Barabutta, near the entrance of the Houghly. My next

next shall be from Madras, whence we are to have convoy. I shall continue this correspondence during the passage home, from the several places of refreshment. Adieu.

LETTER LXVII.

To G—— L——, Esq; in Calcutta.

On board the ship G—s,
Madras Road, Feb. 23, 1780.

SINCERITY, my dear Sir, is too firmly implanted, both by nature and habit, in my constitution, not to command an implicit observance of such promises as are also the spontaneous offspring of esteem and friendship. I am willing to believe, that your motives in asking, were as candid as mine in promising to converse with you from the several places of refreshment.

I do not know what orders were given to the captains R——— and H———, about keeping company (although one was detained a whole fortnight, for the avowed purpose of security to both, by which the fair season for a safe and quick passage to Madras was lost) but they parted and lost sight of each other the second night, as if by mutual inclination, and by previous compact. Calms retarded our progress; so that our passage hither was tediously protracted from the 6th to this day. The want of accommodations to sit or lie, and far less to write (for I am now writing upon one knee over the other) added to the unceasing noise of eighteen children of all complexions, who are, for the most part, under no kind of government, are circumstances which have proved so exceedingly unpleasant, and opposite to my desire of retirement, that if I cannot be relieved from some of these local inconveniences, I must endeavour to procure an accommodation in some other ship at Madras, better fitted to all my views, and more consonant to the indulgences which I have ever been accustomed to enjoy at sea, even when a prisoner.—Nor can I, with an exertion of pains, persuade myself to admire the generality of our aged society. We have, however, some mild, agreeable, and sensible ladies, who, to the other pleasing advantages to be derived from their conversations and dispositions, add the particular tendency of checking a species of entertainment, which has ever proved peculiarly disgusting and nauseous to me, and to which, otherwise, I plainly perceive that the bulk of our company would be very prone; that is to say, obscene and profane language.—It has fallen to my lot to make many voyages and tours; but I never remember to have seen a company so completely resembling what hath been delineated in a stage coach in Britain, or a diligence on the continent of Europe, as that of which I now compose one. To the ladies, I have found a great acquisition in Captain C———e, who is a frank, honest, intelligent man, with a proper knowledge of men and manners, and a heart which does equal honour to his country and to humanity. If our friend should ever preside in India, I wish, for the sake of both, that he was his aid de camp, with rank and emolument suitable to his merit and capacity. Major W———r improves upon acquaintance by a superior propriety of demeanour, which a knowledge of of life gives him over others of our little community.—I need not tell you who I mean; but you will readily recollect a wish which I had entertained, to have a certain person, for his own sake, of the party. These ideas have vanished, and I can see nothing now in that visionary superficies, but self-conceit, self-love, drivelling repetitions of wit, insincerity, and a character approaching to misanthropy. Thus we find, my good friend, how difficult, and how improper it is to judge of men, from early, or even late appearances. Men hackneyed in deceit and dissimulation, who have power to possess themselves, can long conceal the cloven hoof, when they find it necessary to carry their ends by hypocrisy. I have often had occasion to make an observation, from experience, that men having sinister views, disguise themselves with too much art to be easily detected; and that a combination of ambitious criminals, are not only impenetrable, but irresistible, by means of mutual support and encouragement in the greatest enormities. Vices, which at first might have struck them with horror, become at length, by insensible degrees, not only familiar to themselves, but infuse their contagious influence to all their dependents, until every sense of honour and virtue is absorbed in avarice, and her concomitant passions.—This digression has insensibly led to a subject, which has incessantly occupied my thoughts. By fresh discoveries, in consequence of new researches, and by probing the cancerous ulcer which has contaminated the infectious air of Bengal, I have discovered additional causes of disgust, as well as of serious apprehensions of damnable, dark designs to circumvent their opponents to their iniquitous practices,

into

into a participation of the very measures which they had so honourably and faithfully pursued; and consequently, of their own guilt; as the most effectual means of escaping the punishment so justly due to the enormity of their own crimes. What greater curse can the justice of Providence denounce on criminals, than an ambition to acquire that kind of reputation in life, which the keen testimony of their own consciences continually belies?—This must be the tormented state of a set of men, who now practise deceit in Calcutta with envenomed art, to wound the spotless reputation of the only guiltless members of the supreme administration of India, in the hope of reducing them, in respect to guilt, to a level with themselves, because they now begin to believe, that the application of eastern riches will not be able to protect them from the justice of a much-injured nation, and deluded constituents. I wish I could, with equal ease as I write, convey some recent ideas of an incredible magnitude, which, under all local inconveniences, I have cursorily committed as memorandums to paper, since I left the Barrabutta. I only dread, that a coalition will tarnish the glory inseparable from honour, justice, and virtue.

I cannot avoid to express my hearty desire to know in what degree, upon what conditions, and to what purposes, the so much (by me) dreaded coalition has taken place. Indeed, it may be proper and useful to keep friends truly advised, as well to guard against misrepresentations of the general system, as to be able to refute allegations of particular or personal natures.

LETTER

To ——— ———, Efq; in Calcutta.

Madras, March 28, 1780.

THE day after my arrival here, I ufed the freedom of conveying, inaccurately, fome ideas which occurred on the paffage from Bengal hither. Having an invincible attachment to my country; conceiving the moft fanguine ideas of the unbounded advantages which the productions of Hindoftan are capable of yielding, in return for the production of Britain; and expecting to return with that kind of fupport which may enable me to accomplifh my views with honour to myfelf, and benefit to the Company, to the nation, and to the natives; I am moved by a natural impulfe to dwell upon a fubject, which may appear foreign to my ftation and character.

Much information and knowledge of India politics, acquired by inveftigations in Europe, and confirmed by local evidence in foreign eftablifhments, and in Calcutta, have directed my lateft thoughts to future events, which have prefented themfelves to my view, big with evils to the Britifh empire in Hindoftan. I had been but a few weeks in India, when the vapour with which the partiality of my moft familiar connections in Europe had obfcured my underftanding, was reluctantly difpelled. I foon beheld, not only the errors into which mifreprefentations, and confequent prejudices, inferfibly led ftatefmen to defeat the objects they wifhed to attain, and to ruin the faireft hopes of a nation, by that dreadful combination of

native

native princes, which the imperious law of nature dictated as the only refuge from slavery, and the only means of preserving their religious tenets and customs from the insatiable grasp of wild ambition and sordid avarice, and from the wanton scourge of relentless oppression and injustice. Driven to despair, which often inspires resolutions big with hope, the native powers of India resolved to oppose, resist, and by a united blow to annihilate the faithless authors of violated engagements, the unprovoked disturbers of the peace of Asia; and whose successes had raised in their brains, the frantic idea of omnipotence and universal monarchy. This is the substance of what those powers inculcate, to excite a general commotion against the English. They have succeeded but too well. Instead of venerating the English, they now execrate them: instead of being solicited as allies, the English now solicit in vain: instead of receiving bribes, bribes are now offered to petty rajahs to mediate for the English. And yet the authors of these calamities, most unaccountably and preposterously, continue perversely, to pursue the same hostile iniquitous measures, and by every possible means endeavour to incense the greater powers, and to cement the combinations already formed against the English Company and nation. These things frequently occupied my thoughts, and as often prompted me to communicate what I dreaded would be the consequence, in the hope, that through you, they might contribute to confirm the honourable stand made by your friends Messieurs F—— and W——, who, I believe, see matters through the same medium that I do.

The

The return of Mr. George Gray to Madras, from an embassy with which he was charged to Hyder Ally Cawn, with a variety of other circumstances, do sufficiently prove, that a native compact, of a very general extent, is concluded under the auspices of four powerful states, the Marrattas, Hyder Ally Cawn, the Nizam of the Deccan, and Nudjiff Cawn, representing the Emperor and himself; that it is no longer meant to be concealed; that persons of opposite and inveterate principles, have thus astonishingly drawn together, and linked the chain of union; that the destructive storm is gathering fast, and ready to burst on the heads of a deluded and devoted people, who are incapable of enjoying felicity with temper and moderation. However, the means perhaps might yet be found, in a speedy and judicious application from the supreme board to one or other of the chief conductors of public affairs in Poonah or Seringapatnam, to rescue the British reputation in Asia from perdition.

You have heard me often predict, that the game was lost irretrievably, unless the men and measures now in power in India were speedily and exemplarily changed; to shew to the natives, that neither the Court of Directors, nor the administrators of Britain, were the authors, or even abettors of the unwarranted proceedings of the Company's principal servants abroad. If that doth not happen quickly and effectually, Hyder will claim and obtain the observance of his late treaty with France; he will avail himself of the scattered state of the Company's troops, the reduction of the Nabob's army, and the impoverished state of his finances and country, to revenge the infraction of the treaty of 1769 in 1770, and the hoftility commenced by the Company in 1766: and he will wreak his vengeance with redoubled fury on the Nabob, to whom he very properly imputes the whole of this conduct, equally unjuft and unprovoked. This he never would have dared to attempt, if the Company's arms had not been engaged againft the Marrattas, and had not the Marratta overtures to all the native ftates fucceeded in forming the defired combination.

The chief of this prefidency has at length declared in council, his fixed purpofe of withdrawing, as the means to fave his life; the bilious attack being more frequent and more dangerous.—He has a competent portion of enemies here, many of whom are fo, not from principle, but difappointment, which they have not temper to conceal. If all that his foes impute to his ambition and avarice be true, he has judged wifely and politically in withdrawing; becaufe, in the prefent diftracted ftate of the Britifh nation, his prefence may be materially ufeful to fecure his acquifitions, fince it is more than probable, that a parliamentary difquifition may extend as well to the adminiftration of Madras as that of Bengal; although the confequences and effects of the former are but as a molehill, compared to a mountain of enormities of the latter. Contrarily to every opinion which I have ever heard, I cannot but think that nature has been extremely liberal in endowing this chief with very powerful faculties; and that, if the charge of abufe in refpect to the natives were not juft, he had capacity and firmnefs to do a great deal of good. I have fpoken with firmnefs and candour to his fucceffor, recommending a line of conduct the

moft

moſt likely to co-operate with the views of your friends, conſequently the true intereſts and ſecurity of the Company and the Britiſh nation; and as the means of removing any unjuſt ſuſpicions that may have been entertained of himſelf, in carrying on an illegal trade with the French. He has determined not to improve his fortune, during the period of his power, by any means but by the ſtrict legal emoluments of his ſtation. Sir Hector Munro preſerves his name and hands as immaculate and fair as you wiſh the perſon to do, for whom you entertain the moſt friendly ſentiments. I have ventured to inſinuate to him and Mr. Whitehill, that Hyder having confidence in Sir Hector's integrity, knowing that he does not pay court at the Chepauk Durbar, and knowing alſo, that Mr. W——— is not devoted to that palace, he will receive overtures for an accommodation and alliance through them, ſooner than through any other; but that the miniſterial Plenipotentiary muſt be a perſon not known to favour the Nabob; and that the aſſiſtant and interpreter ſhould be Mooda-Kiſtna: That all theſe meaſures ſhould be ſecretly recommended, as a neceſſary political manœuvre, to the old Nabob—Forgive this dry ſubject; it ſhews a deſire to converſe familiarly with you, even at a diſtance, and I cannot deviſe any other, though I know that it is one which you underſtand better than I do.

- Adieu.

P. S. Our day of departure is fixed for the 3d of April. I hope it will hold, for I am impatient to be gone.

LETTER

LETTER LXIX.

To J———— M————, Eſq; London.

Cape of Good Hope, Sept. 25, 1780.

I LEFT but two letters in Madras, to be forwarded over the iſthmus of Suez to Europe, and one of them was for you.

I embarked on the evening of the 6th of April at Madras; and next day the fleet, conſiſting of four Indiamen under the convoy of three line of battle ſhips, ſailed for Europe.—The ſenior captain acting as commodore, under a diſtinguiſhed pendant, ſeemed watchful of his charge; but whether he was guided by his inſtructions or by wrong information, after having croſſed the equator, he ſteered a courſe ſo far to the eaſtward of what experience and common reaſon had eſtabliſhed, that to this ſimple miſtake all the procraſtinations and loſs of ſeamen during the reſt of the paſſage is to be imputed†. The time waſted in regaining what we had thus loſt, would have carried us into the Cape of Good Hope, and we ſhould probably have avoided the ſtorm which diſabled the Rippon's main maſt. Inſtead of making, or at leaſt approaching within ten or twenty leagues of the ſouth ſide of Roderigue (by ſome called Diego Rays) or erroneous courſe led us about five degrees

---

† There ſhould be an underſtanding between the admiralty and the Company, concerning the routes of convoys, both out and home; to be founded on the experience which the Company's navigators have had in theſe eaſtern ſeas, and contained in their private inſtructions from the Admiralty to their ſea commanders going to preſide in India.

to the south east of it; so that before we made the
island of Madagascar, the crew of the Asia man
of war, who had been then six years in constant
service in America, Europe, and Asia, were laid
up, and dying fast, of the sea-scurvy, in spite of
the judicious and humane exertions of Captain
Vandeput to save them, by the use of his own fresh
provisions and liquors, keeping the ship aired,
freshening their water by air-pumps, and by every
other act which his feelings as a man, and a strict
observance of duty in his station, could dictate.
Sir Thomas Rumbold was not wanting on his part,
by sending bountiful supplies of wines, and fresh
provisions from his own table, to them, from the
ship in which he was passenger. When the fleet
came to anchor in St. Augustin's bay on the 15th
June, the Asia had not a sufficient number to ma-
nage her sails; and the Rippon and Bellisle had near
half their companies either dead or sick in their
hammocks.

The evening of the 13th, sailing along the south
end of Madagascar, we had a narrow escape from
losing the fleet upon the Star-bank; but Captain
Vandeput, by a fortunate signal from the Asia, discovered the position in which we were, which at
length, by good fortune, operated (though after
eight at night) upon the commodore, to tack and
stand upon the other course; the only ship that had
not observed the night signal, although the wind-
wardmost and the best sailing ship belonging to
the Company, with a fixed steady gale, and with
every possible exertion, was found to be in a critical situation the next morning, and required the
exercise of skill and firmness in the seamanship,
and trimming her sails. A few days thereafter, we

Vol. II. P were

were joined, in St. Auguftin's bay, by four of the Company's homeward-bound China fhips, and in a few days more by a fifth, which had fprung a leak. Thofe feamen belonging to his Majefty's fhips, whofe diforders had not already feized the vitals, foon recovered; the dry feafon, and refrefhments, together with the affiduous attention of the captains and furgeons, produced rapid effects. Several little difficulties occurred in the negociations with the king and the people, which might have been attended with manifeft inconveniences hereafter; but the good fenfe and addrefs of Captain Vandeput and Captain Blanket, eafily removed every obftruction. Thefe gentlemen, upon true political principles, did not limit their views to the prefent occafion; but always had in their eye the means of removing unfavourable impreffions from the minds of the natives, in order to fecure fuccours and good treatment to fuch Britifh fhips as fhould, fingly or in fleets, hereafter have occafion to call for them.

After much lingering, and wafting time, the fleet, now confifting of twelve large fhips, took leave of Madagafcar, to the inexpreffible joy of all the paffengers, on the 28th July, having been fix weeks at anchor in St. Auguftin's bay. We proceeded with a fair wind, but were a good deal delayed by the flow failing of the Morfe and Norfolk, whofe commanders endeavoured, by a preffed fail, to keep up, but they could not get to windward: Captain Elliot of the Morfe fhewed evident fuperiority in his profeffion, and confirmed his general reputation of an artift; but he was unfortunate in difplaying his fkill on a veffel which baffled his endeavours. Nor had he and the Norfolk fair play; for on the evening of the 4th Auguft, gust, they were a great distance to leeward, nor could they approach the fleet: the course and wind would have admitted of the fleet's bearing away one or two points towards them; but by some unaccountable conceit, at six o'clock in the dusk of the evening, without a signal being made, when those ships could not perceive the change, the commodore hauled his wind, and those who were near him did the same, thus enlarging the distance from the leeward ships, and destroying every probable hope of their joining the fleet again. Accordingly, they could not be seen from the topgallant mast-head the next morning. The Rippon was ordered to back her course, to look out for ships that must now have been many leagues to leeward of her, instead of steering to the southwest, the course in which they might have been intercepted, and reunited to the fleet. We made the land of Africa that evening, Cape Natal bearing north west of us, distanced by little more than the width of Natal bay. Here again we were thrown out of our right course by the false judgment, or fears, or perverseness of our conductor. It has of late years been well understood by experienced navigators, that there is less risk of encountering the storms peculiar to those seas, and that there is little danger of a lee-shore, by keeping the land of Africa close on board, from Cape Natal to the Cape of Good Hope; and that a strong current setting to the south west, generally favours navigation. But, unfortunately, without the preparative of a signal, on the evening of the 7th, the fleet stood out to sea, whereby the Asia, whose station it was to bring up the rear, did not perceive the motion, and by that means lost the fleet; but which

which the active prudence and vigilance of Captain Vandeput remedied, and happily joined the fleet next evening. Although the commodore had been cautioned on this head, by all the commanders of the Company's ships, who even communicated their journals to him, yet he persevered in standing out to sea, until we entered into the tempestuous latitude; and on the 11th we encountered a very smart storm. The storm continuing, on the morning of the 13th we found ourselves under the protection of the Asia only; the Bellisle and Rippon, together with the Company's ship Talbot, being quite out of sight. And as the sea was more dreadful than the tempest, we were not without apprehensions for the Bellisle, as by her form she laboured exceedingly in the water, and some of her seams had been filled up with small hawsers. The storm abated on the 15th: on the 21st we were joined by the Morse and Norfolk: on the 23d we were also rejoined by the Rippon, carrying all the sail she could on the mizen and fore-masts, having sprung her main-mast in the storm: and the next day made Cape la Guilla's, and coasted it, until we were joined, on the 25th, by the Bellisle and Talbot, under Penguin island, at the entrance of Table bay, where we anchored in the course of that night and next morning.

 The well-timed and judiciously applied address, and superior good sense of Captain Vandeput and Captain Blanket, extricated the King's ships and the Company's, from difficulties into which the conduct of the Commodore had precipitated them; having indispensably occasion for masts, spars, ironwork, cordage, and provisions, to qualify them for the remaining part of the voyage.

Contrarily

Contrarily to the uniform ufage of all admirals, commodores, and captains of the Britifh navy, touching for refrefhment at the Cape of Good Hope, fince the commencement of the Englifh trade to India, although their inftructions were filent upon the fubject, Captain Barber declined to falute the citadel, where the colours of the Seven United Provinces were flying; he declined to pay a complimentary vifit to the governor; demanding fupplies in a peremptory ftile, menacing to obtain them by force, if not freely granted; refufed obedience to the revenue laws of the country, in the examination of packages landed from his own fhip; made his demands by writing in the Englifh language, and refufed to receive the anfwer, becaufe the direction of a letter, bearing the Dutch Eaft India Company's armorial impreffion, was in the language of the people, the Dutch, and returned it unopened to the council-board whence it was fent, actually granting the fupplies he had defired; and he burned a proteft which was officially delivered to him, without reading it. Even the private mediation of Captain Vandeput and Captain Blanket, doth not take away from the merit which the governor and council have difplayed in the great portion of moderation and confideration fhewn, in accommodating both the King's fhips and the Company's with every neceffary which they had occafion for, notwithftanding the public and private infults which had been lavifhed upon them. Nor did their condefcenfion appear to have proceeded from motives of fear, as their conduct throughout was fpirited, fteady, and juft, and wifely and generoufly applying the meafure to the

man,

man, and not the country which he reprefented by mere chance, not choice.

The difcontents which prevailed at the Cape, between the people and the government, when I was here before, I found, on my return, had broke out into difaffection, and a refractorinefs bordering on hoftilities. The people, fuffering under the iniquitous and relentlefs oppreffion of the Company's government and tyranny, folicited redrefs by reprefentations, and by deputies, in vain; and at length openly deputed fome of the principal perfons to lay the enormities and exactions open to the States General, for redrefs; and to be enfranchifed from the fervitude extorted by the Company's government.

After unneceffary procraftinations, neglects, and delays, the fignal for weighing at laft was difplayed on board the Bellifle, on the 12th October; and the fleet having been joined at the Cape by the Company's fhip the Ceres, failed that day out of Table bay, with a fair fteady gale; and arrived at St. Helena on the twenty ninth October, where we found the Hannibal, Captain Caldwell, of fifty guns, and the Prothée, Captain Buckner, of fixty four guns, and the Company's fhip Hawke, from Bombay.—The accompanying letter will furnifh you with my obfervations on the ifland and natives of Madagafcar.

LETTER LXX.

To J—— M——, Efq; London.

Cap. of Good Hope, Oct. 1, 1780.

THE Ifland of Madagafcar needs no defcription, as it is well known to have been efteemed the fecond largeft ifland in the world, before the difcoveries

veries made by the late able and ingenious navigator Captain Cooke, that New Holland, &c. were iflands. It lies under the latitude of 12° to 26° South, and between the 43° and 51° longitude, Eaft from London.

The force of prejudice, even when founded upon the fabulous conceptions of illiterate and incurious feamen; and for the moft part upon the catch-penny voyages and fufferings, hatched in the brain of a garret compofer, of pirates and buckaneers, have overcome reafon and juftice, in imputing to the aborigine inhabitants of countries remote from Europe, ferocioufnefs, barbarity, ignorance, ftupidity, irreligion, and a complication of immoralities. Thefe ideas are in truth rank and unjuft prejudices. The oppofite qualities belong more naturally to moft of the remote nations, which are, by Europeans, denominated favage.— The natives of Madagafcar, and the Hottentots of the Cape of Good Hope, have been confidered as poffeffing no one quality to diftinguifh them, except in figure and articulation, from the brute creation; and thofe of Madagafcar as ferocious tygers.

The French are the only nation of Europe, who have attempted to make eftablifhments on the ifland of Madagafcar. They fet out on their Eaft India fyftem by attempting it; but after feveral years indefatigable perfeverance and expence, the climate aided the fteady refiftance of the natives to deftroy many French fubjects, and they gave up the conteft. About the year 1770, Count Benowfki, a Polifh nobleman, of a bold and enterprifing genius, having efcaped from the exile to which he was fent by the Emprefs of Ruffia to Siberia, travelled thence to Kamfcatcka, and there built a

kind

kind of vessel, in which he committed himself, and a few desperate companions, steering along the coast until they arrived at Canton river in China, whence he took a passage to the French islands; and informed himself of many particulars relative to the natives, &c. of Madagascar; and, following the natural bent of his own eccentric disposition for achievement and enterprize, when he came to France, he laid a plan before government, for reviving the idea of an establishment in Madagascar. He was attended to; and was impowered to raise a regiment to consist of three hundred men, composed of all European nations and religions, and to be uniformed and accoutred according to his own mind. He chose the Russian livery, green, and the same kind of arms. He completed his corps, was transported to Mauritius, and thence embarked to Fort Dauphin in Madagascar, to the command of the garrison and settlement; having prevailed on a considerable number of civil settlers to follow his fortunes. He treated with the natives, who consented to the forming of a settlement at a bay near the sea side, but proscribed his intrusions into the country. He had a stockaded fort and garrison built, and huts to lodge his people, stores, and provisions in. The inhabitants never molested him while he kept within the limits they had set to his dominion, and to the letter of their treaty. But the Count wanting to make roads into the country, they immediately opposed his progress, and hostilities commenced. This establishment having been injudiciously formed on a low marshy ground, or near it, his troops and settlers were dying fast; discontents and murmurs sprang up among themselves; complaints were sent to Mauritius,

ritius, the supreme government; bickerings arose between the supreme chiefs of the islands and him; an appeal was made to the court of Paris; and leave was given to the Count to come home. When he arrived in France, his conduct was disapproved; and although he was not professedly dismissed from the service and stations he held, his reception and treatment was tantamount thereto. It is said, he has had addrefs since to recommend himself into a respectable military station in the service of the Emperor of Germany. In October, 1778, there were but four officers remaining in the island, and three under confinement for military offences; and about fifty privates and non-commissioned officers. All the settlers were dead.—Thus ended the establishment, and the natives were inveterately hostile, even to private traders from the islands; a circumstance very injurious, as they were supplied with rice and horned cattle, on reasonable terms, and in abundance, from St. Mary's, Foul-point, and St. Antongil, large bays, which are opposite to the islands. The run down from Bourbon or Mauritius, to either of these places, is from two to five days; but the return is more tedious, by reason of the trade wind and currents, which oblige them to stretch far to the northward or southward, to be able to fetch the islands.

Our fleet anchored in Augustine Bay on the 14th and 15th of June. The natives soon came on board, and began a traffic by a judgment matured by experience. Their ingenuity is far below the medium in every mechanical art; but they are sufficiently knowing in bartering: fine bullocks as any in the world, sheep, goats, dunghill fowls, Guinea fowls, milk, and such vegetables as they raise in the

the proper seasons; for powder, balls, flints, muskets, and spirituous liquors, which are the staple of their commerce. On the N. N. E. and S. S. E. sides, they cultivate great quantities of an excellent rice, and have plantains, yams, limes, lemons, oranges, tamarinds, &c. in plenty. The largest and clearest crystals of rock-salt in the world, are in the bowels of the earth in this island. Their bays abound with fish, excellent in their kinds, together with most sorts of shell-fish upon and under the rocks, and on the rivers. There is a wide field in the woods of this country, for naturalists to display their faculties upon. The island is divided, it is said by the inhabitants, into seven distinct kingdoms, each governed by its own king, who enjoys his authority and title by inheritance. These princes commit hostilities in proper form; but it consists in plundering and carrying off the horned cattle, and the prisoners are sold to the French and Dutch traders as slaves. The men are of the middle size, clean made, agile, and active; they are bold and brave to a high degree, not able to brook an insult, even from the highest superior, which is instantly resented with the musket or the lance. They are dexterous at throwing the lance; it is with a dart of the lance, from a considerable distance, that they kill their bullocks, which produces the most instantaneous death I ever beheld; the dart enters near the shoulder, and the beast drops down in a moment. They are fond of spirituous liquors, and are apt to be riotous when drunk. They are a steady, judicious, penetrating people, and jealous of liberty; but in general they are not faithful to their engagements, so that it will be imprudent to advance before-hand, unless

al prefents to the king, and other
proftitute their women to ftrangers,
ofe inferior ones as princeffes, to en-
mium. But the French on the Eaft
/ith the chiefs and princes for their
a weekly or monthly contract, dur-
e, they are not only diligent and at-
paring food, and in the houfehold
iithful in preventing any harm to
ofitions in their dealings with other
y are much troubled with the vene-
, which doubtlefs was introduced by
ut they have found a perfect and
fimples. For the moft part they
efcendants of the Caffrès on the fouth
, by their woolly hair, features, and
There is a tract of country in the
iarter, the inhabitants of which are
n the Arabs; and although that na-
continually at war with fome of its
t is more than probable that their
; extended to render the features of
; but it is remarkable, that notwith-
quent intercourfe of their women with
iever faw a Mulatto or Meftiff upon,
gafcar. I fufpect that fuch progeny
d to exift, from a political jealoufy.
ld learn that there are any wild fero-
this ifland. There are alligators in
They have a great many dogs and
here are feveral fpecies of ducks and
the ifland, which are not to be met
:: they are large and beautiful.—I
that it is neceffary to wifh for an
ablifhment on this ifland, becaufe,
by

by establishing prudent regulations, to be obligatory on the captains of ships, every want may be supplied, at a price and in a manner infinitely more easy and desirable than if an European settlement was made upon it. Garden vegetables, such as cabbages, turnips, carrots, and the like, is all that they have not to supply; and a little pains would bring them into the practice of raising these also. Good treatment, and a strict observance of engagements on the part of Europeans, would soon inspire the natives with a similar disposition and conduct.

As I had been reduced to the lowest state, and confined to my cabin for six weeks, by a bilious complaint, and incapable of digesting any solid food, I had every reason to apprehend, that I should leave my bones at Madagascar.—I found, however, a speedy and effectual remedy on this island: A stream of mineral water issues, at low water, out of a solid rock in the bay of St. Augustine, about one hundred yards north of the Tent Rock: at first, it produces a kind of dizziness like Bath water; but in less than a week, it effectually removed all bilious obstructions. I used it all the way to the Cape of Good Hope, with continued effect: with a vigorous appetite, I could dine upon the steak of a bullock that had been killed that same morning, without feeling any inconveniences from indigestion. — Beeves are excellent, weighing from five to eight hundred weight each, and the meat delicate, tender, and well flavoured. Their sheep have broad tails, like those of Africa, and are as large —The hospitality of this people, is a mark of their humane disposition. A young gentleman went ashore with one of them, the day

after

after our arrival, in the canoe of the natives; but the evening breeze and the strong current of the tide, preventing their return, the man conducted him to his house. One of the princes of the country, and a guardian to the minor king of Baba, visited the stranger, and supped with them, inviting him to his own house: a Guinea fowl was killed, and dressed after their manner, for his supper: the host and his wife lay upon the ground, and the stranger was made to sleep upon their own bed. We met with various other instances of a natural hospitality. And it was easily perceived, that they could distinguish between persons who deserved respect, from those who did not, in their conduct, and selection of the captains of the men of war from each other.

LETTER LXXI.

To J—— M——, Esq; London.

St. Helena, Nov. 5, 1780·

YOU will be so unreasonable, I suppose, as to require a description of a place, which the unjust partiality of persons in the East India Company's service, have represented as a perfect paradise. — On general topics, I would be ready to yield to the opinions of the multitude; but upon this occasion, satisfied and confirmed in the propriety of my own sentiments, I cannot subscribe to representations which are contradicted by all human faculties, and by common sense.

The

The island of St. Helena, which appears to hav[e] arisen above the surface of the great Atlantic ocea[n] by an eruption, or convulsion of nature, in th[e] latitude of sixteen degrees south, and six of we[st] longitude from London, is composed of one entir[e] rock of a circular figure, and measures abou[t] twenty four miles in circumference. That th[e] whole island has undergone a conflagration, is b[e] yond a doubt; the interior mass of solid rock shew[s] that it has yielded to the force of fire, and h[as] been dissolved; in which waving figure, after t[he] fire was extinguished, the horizontal veins or str[a] ta remained hardened, as glass, when on the ver[ge] of becoming liquid, bends by heat to its o[wn] weight, and retains that form if the fire is wit[h] drawn, and even loses its lucid quality. The par[t] nearest the surface resemble the ordinary la[va] emitted from volcanos; the strata of mould [or] loam, which were burnt to ashes, in many plac[es] retain the original appearance and colour of ashe[s] and those of clay retain their stations with t[he] firiness of burnt bricks in the first or second stra[ta] The eminences, if placed upon a continent or lar[ge] island, would bear the name of hills; but up[on] so circumscribed a base as St. Helena, they cla[im] that of mountains. There is scarce a flat of [a] dozen acres in the island; and for the most part, [it] has been difficult to find a plain extensive enou[gh] to build a house and offices upon. The thin s[ur] face or soil upon the rocks, is loose and ligh[t] but of a kind and vegetative quality, if blest w[ith] seasonable showers, and aided with a little manu[re] of which they have plenty upon the island in a v[ery] rich marle, both white and blue: I do not find t[hat] the inhabitants have discovered the use of it [as I] perceiv[e] perceived it on the high road, and put two pieces in my pocket, to examine the quality on my return to town; and when I mentioned its excellence, it seemed as if they understood me not. There is now but one spring remaining, from which ships can be supplied with water; and even that is so insignificant, that they are obliged to collect a body of the water in a large reservoir, to await the arrival of the Company's ships. There are but two places where it is possible to land; they are at opposite sides of the island, and both are most powerfully fortified; that to windward is too dangerous a navigation to be hazarded by any ships; and the other to leeward, which is at the metropolis, would prove a dangerous undertaking, not only from a number of batteries most judiciously and skilfully arranged, but from the difficulty of securing anchorage upon the bank, which is narrow, and near to the shore; because the current being strong, if the anchor is dropt upon or near the edge of it, the ship will drive, and fall to leeward in an instant, so as to render it a laborious and tedious business to regain the island.—Exclusive of the inhabitants, which, comprehending all sexes, ages, and complexions, may be two thousand four hundred (chiefly slaves) there are from five to six hundred regular troops, maintained by the Company; and as they even send, in the annual store-ships, most of the necessaries of life from Europe, if they are not brought at the Company's expence from India, China, and the Cape, its annual charges, for several years last past, may be computed, on an average, at thirty thousand pounds; while at the same time it yields no benefit to the Company, or to their navigation, except as a place of rendezvous.

vous. Of late years, the island has been so subject to continual droughts, that it has not been able to yield any refreshing succours to the shipping; even the water is become scanty. The cattle have perished of famine, and the gardens scarcely produce vegetable food for the inhabitants. In short, it cannot ever be an object of conquest for the enemies of Britain, unless in a war with Holland. The temporary conquest of it by the Dutch would distress the British commerce. And if the troops and people of St. Helena were situated upon any fertile spot upon the continent, the Company's ships would benefit by the change, and the settlers would enjoy the sweets of their industry. I cannot but imagine, that by explosions with powder, undermining the rocks where the main spring rises, the concussion would probably divert the current of the water, and in that case, the island would not be habitable. At present, it appears to be a useless incumbrance to the Company, and a perpetual prison, threatening lingering death by famine to the inhabitants.

I embarked last evening, and the signal for weighing is now hoisted.

LETTER LXXII.

To J―― M――, Esq; London.

Dublin, Jan. 29, 1781.

I TOOK leave of you on the fifth November, in the road of St. Helena, with the signal for sailing displayed on board his Majesty's ship Bellisle, with eleven of the Company's ships, escorted by five capital ships of war.

To give you a comprehensive idea of the whole passage, without descending to particulars, as a passenger, it may be deemed sufficient for me to say, that chance, not conduct, hath brought this valuable fleet in safety to a British port. It is the duty of the Company's immediate servants to lay their journals, together with their opinions, before their employers, not with a view of remedying the past, but to guard against future error and misconduct.

On the 12th day of November, we sailed close to the island, or rather the cinder mountain, of Ascension, so famous for the salutary refreshment it affords in the proper season, to voyagers, by an abundance of turtle, which are esteemed superior in flavour and size to any others, and for the quantities of fish and birds which it furnishes in profusion. It yields no other supply; for want of soil, it is incapable of throwing up grass; nor is there any stream of water upon it that I know of, although I have been informed by a French gentleman, that at a considerable distance inland from the common landing-bay, he saw a very pretty spring, whence a stream of pure water flowed.

We were fortunate in carrying a fair wind along with us into soundings, near the entrance of the English channel, on the sixth day of the present year. But alas! a succeeding calm terminated in a contrary wind on the same evening, which induced us to direct our course for Ireland, without any effort to stretch into the channel. By mistaking even this plain course, although the wind was favourable for any port in Ireland, we steered so wide of the right mark, that the next morning we could not stand up for the Shannon, nor for Corke; but pushed in for the little harbour of Crookhaven, near Cape Clear, on the 7th instant.—Thus I arrived in the British dominions, after suffering the severities of three winters in one year; one in January, in Bengal; another after crossing the line, in August, at the Cape of Good Hope; and a third in December last, after recrossing the line, at the entrance of the channel.

The hospitality of the gentlemen of this nation having long been proverbial, I anticipated the pleasures which, in my hurried excursion, I was to enjoy; but description hath fallen short of the hospitality, liberality, and humanity, to which I can now bear testimony. I enjoyed a happy introduction to that uncommon civility, characteristic of the people of condition in Ireland, by means of the favourable opinion, and virtuous confidence, of two amiable fellow-passengers, who had entrusted to my endeavours on this journey, a charge, in the care of themselves and their children. The genteel appearance and deportment of both, and the superior sense, address, and conversation of one, would have proved irresistible inducements, in a country less distinguished for polite assiduity to oblige the fair sex than this, to bestow on these ladies every mark of respect and attention; but it would be unjust to insinuate even this consideration, as a motive for actions which, I am sure, originated in nature.

Having less influence to procure a boat to Crookhaven, than the smallness of the village and the number to be accommodated in it, rendered necessary; it was late before a country conveyance did

me

me that favour at the price of a dollar. After diving into several mean houses, chance directed my steps to the second house in the place. Sir T. R. having been the first to land, secured the best quarters for himself and family, with the surveyor of the customs. I made my wishes known to the wife of the deputy surveyor, whose husband was absent on custom-house service in Corke. She consented to accommodate myself and an old gentleman, but declared against ladies, who (she said) were not to be pleased: I assured her, that the ladies which I would have the honour to introduce into her house, were so amiable and affable, that they would compel her to change her opinion of her own sex. She, however, persisted in her negative. The clergyman of the village, who boarded and lodged in the house, a truly good man, being present, with his landlady's daughter, I made my addresses alternately to the daughter and mother, and attacked the reverend old clergyman, in a stile adapted to his holy function, and interested both his feelings and the self-importance of the daughter in my suit; until, after long pleadings and rejoinders, the good lady agreed to receive my fair fellow-passengers :—and in a few days, she did them the justice to tell me repeatedly, that she never again would judge so injuriously of strangers, because her present lodgers were too good, even better than I had represented them. The honest clergyman, who was as full of goodness as he was of learning, was also full of expressions of esteem and satisfaction; and took leave with the tenderest respect, when a chaise arrived from Corke, on the 14th, at the opposite side of the

the bay, to receive the two ladies and their four children.

My miftaken liberality to the poftillion, was productive of ferious alarms, and might have terminated in a melancholy cataftrophe.—He had neglected his horfes, but not himfelf; for, being overcome with liquor, he was incapable of conducting them. There were many fteep pafies in the firft ftage, and the firft one led by a precipice which hung fufpended, many paces perpendicularly, over the fea. When he came to this fpot, the famifhed, fatigued horfes, were unable to draw the carriage, and the poftillion, under the influence of liquor, inftead of coaxing them up, beat and pufhed them, until, in the very middle of the bank, they gave way. Apprehenfive of danger, I rode clofe behind the carriage, when happily, on the turn of the off-wheel, it was ftopt by the hind-quarter of my horfe; I feized the other wheel with my hand, and by chance dexterity, not ftrength, gave it a turn which gave a footing to the carriage, and eafe to the yielding horfes; and by that means, the whole were faved from precipitating into the fea. I held my horfe to fuftain the wheel, and the weight of the carriage, until I could alight, and was able to lodge a pretty large ftone under each wheel, and then, letting go my horfe, I ran to the upper fide of the chaife, and, without much ceremony, pulled out the affrighted ladies and the four children. Thus fecure and happy, I took out the reftiff horfe, and without the ufe of a whip, coaxed one horfe only to pull up the empty chaife.—After a fhort refpite, the ladies and children refumed their ftations in the carriage; but had not gone far, when the drunken poftillion again ran the chaife into a

deep

deep gutter on the fide of an eminence, and nearly overfet it.—After difengaging my companions a fecond time, and calling the aid of about a fcore of country peafants, we again got to a level road.— The ladies entreated me to return, and I urged to pafs on, becaufe we were near to the houfe of the reverend Doctor Townfend, where I would venture to introduce them, though I had only had the pleafure of being once in his company. After walking until they were out of breath, I prevailed on them to go into the chaife; but upon condition that I fhould not feparate myfelf from its fide; the drunken poftillion having pofitively refufed to let me drive the chaife, and to ride my horfe. In this pofition, we encountered a private chaife and four horfes.—I was determined to accoft thofe who were in it, for relief to my fellow-travellers, when happily I beheld the worthy old gentleman, Doctor Townfend. I went up to him, and without ceremony, after felicitating my company, I told him my fituation. He threatened our poftillion in his magifterial capacity; and upon exprefs conditions that we fhould go to his houfe and pafs the night, he detached his principal fervant and beft pair of horfes from his own chaife, harneffed them to ours, requefted a gentleman (Mr. Jermyn of Millbourn) to conduct us to his houfe, and introduce us to his lady, promifing to follow us in an hour; thus conferring a twofold obligation on us, fo as we fhould not feel the weight of either. My amiable fellow-travellers, with uplifted eyes and hands, enjoyed the fweet relief, and bleft the liberal and hofpitable mind of the Doctor, and his brother, a commiffioner of the cuftoms, who accompanied him in the chaife, and who fhewed an equal defire to accommodate

modate us. We arrived at the Doctor's house, and were first received by a most agreeable young gentleman, Mr. Robertson, the Doctor's nephew, who was also in orders. An excellent cold dinner, and choice liquors, were set before us, together with a chearful fire, and a bountiful welcome.—Mrs. Townsend soon appeared; and although infirm, discovered a genteel mien and conversation, and was a just representation of an hospitable and social husband. The Doctor and his niece returned within the promised time, and three hearty neighbours soon joined us. After an elegant supper, a chearful glass, and the essence of jollity, at two o'clock in the morning we separated into our respective apartments; and after breakfast next morning, we parted from a family whose goodness will ever remain imprinted on our minds.—I enjoyed the praises that had been liberally bestowed on my fair fellow travellers, by every person.

We enjoyed the most polite hospitality at Skibberton, from Mr. Jermyn, where Mrs. Wright (the collector's lady, and the sister of Doctor Townsend) came in person to Mr. Jermyn's, to invite us to her house. We proceeded, without further interruption, except from the officers of excise, to Corke.—There the mayor, Mr. Carleton, and his lady and nephew, shewed us every mark of attention. The second day we proceeded on our journey for Dublin, young Mr. Carleton having previously written to his house, to have lodgings ready for our reception.

It was a pleasing surprise to me, to find throughout the road, accommodations and entertainment which would be thought respectable on the principal roads of England. The country appeared destitute

titute of that cultivation which diftinguifhes th
regions of freedom. Although it is, for the moft
part, of a turfy or peat quality, yet it is capable
of high improvement, particularly by draining;
and I doubt not, but a few years, under the happy
ftate of freedom which they now enjoy, and which
they fhould have had long before, will exhibit the
happy effects of this bleffing, by adding largely to
the wealth, commerce, power, and population of
the Britifh nation. Then we fhall fee difplayed the
tranfcendent virtues which are infeparable from political liberty: the civilization, induftry, and ingenuity of the common people, who are as yet more
rude and impofing, than any Indian, American,
or African nation I ever had occafion to fee; and a
flourifhing change on the face of a country, capable
of receiving every improvement which hufbandry,
arts, and canals can produce. A very diftinguifh-
ing proof of this opinion occurred upon the road.
The evening of the fecond day after our departure
from Corke, I was all at once fo fenfibly ftruck
with the inclofures by walls, fences, and ditches,
the fubftantial neat farm houfe and offices, and the
lefs indigent garbs, and diffufive contentment
which appeared in the people, that I obferved to
Mrs. M———t, the lady in whofe company I had
then the honour to fit, that the proprietor of the
lands over which we were travelling, was a munificent and good landlord; and that, if I could fuppofe that Lord Cahir poffeffed any part of that country or province, I fhould, from the high commen-
dations which I had heard of that great and generous nobleman's conduct, as a fubject, as a mafter,
and as a man, conclude that we were at that inftant
travelling through his eftate. We entered a town

very

very soon after, where plenty and tranquillity were signalized in every object which prefented itfelf to our view. We ftopt to breathe the horfes at a handfome inn; I called for fome cakes for the children, which were brought by a handfome, genteel, well-drefied landlady: I afked the name of the place? She faid, " Cahir." I afked to whom the furrounding eftate belonged? " To Lord Cahir."—My fair, fenfible companion, after expreffing a furprife, repeated what I had faid about an hour before. The landlady poured forth his Lordfhip's praife in the grofs. As I had had the honour of being a little known to his Lordfhip, and his brother, Mr. T. Butler, I begged the landlady to deliver a meffage to his Lordfhip, concerning a relation in the Eaft: fhe faid fhe would; but that my Lord would be very glad to fee me, or any lady or gentleman who was travelling. I had always admired the exalted character which my Lord Cahir was eminent for in England, and in France; but I was at this time impreffed with fentiments of veneration for him, and only lamented that he was not fo young, as to give hopes of his living as an example to others, for the benefit and happinefs of all, for fifty years to come.

The partiality of a worthy friend having introduced me handfomely to Mr. Longfield, the member for the city of Corke, whofe mind is as independent and unincumbered as his fortune, as well as to the Mayor of that city; and having had the honour of being formerly known to Lord Carhampton, Sir John Blaquiere, and Sir Richard Heron; the only caufe of regret I could poffibly have in Dublin, was, that I could not pafs fix or eight weeks in it. The juft and independent principles

ciples of Mr. Longfield, and the liberal ufe to which he applied a clear annual revenue, exceeding tenthoufand pounds, procured him a choice of conftituents and of friends.

It was pleafing to hear the great orators and geniufes of this nation, fpeak the true language of pure patriotifm, with arguments and energy which are irrefiftible, and which carry conviction to every heart. It was not the inflammatory language of men foured by difappointment. It was not an effort to remove thofe who were in, in order to fucceed to their places; they were the glowing expreffions which iffued from the unaffected feelings of patriotic virtue. It is a pleafure to look forward to the field that is opening to receive the improvement and ingenuity of the moft learned men, and the greateft geniufes in Europe. It is not to benefit Ireland only that thefe fenators ftand forth : in every word which they utter, in their martial garbs, and in their voluntary affociations, they breathe true loyalty to the extended Britifh empire.—They are jealous of honour, and out of the way of corruption. To render them as ufeful as they are difpofed to be, they fhould receive impartial and unbounded confidence ; and they never will betray it. The public buildings, the private houfes, the new ftreets, the fquares, the finifhings, the furniture, and the entertainments in Dublin, are elegantly modern. Our obligations to the family of Mr. Carleton of Corke, cannot be defcribed ; civilities were heaped upon us by his nephews, niece, and fifter-in-law, in Dublin ; and they afforded me an opportunity of being acquainted with his fon, Mr. Carleton, the folicitor-general of Ireland. But to particularize

rize the proofs of kindness we received among a people justly celebrated for their hospitality, though not an unpleasing, were an endless task. As I am to embark in the packet at one o'clock in the morning, I shall bid you adieu, until we meet in London about a week hence.

APPEN-

APPENDIX [A.]

THE original stock of the Dutch East-India Company consisted of 2100 shares, at 3000 florins * each: they afterwards encreased the number of shares to 2130, without advancing the stock proportionably; so that the original stock of 6,300,000, florins divided into 2130 shares, valuing each share at 3000 florins, increases the estimation of the capital to 6,390,000 florins. Their singular good fortune in stepping, without loss or expence, into all the Portuguese settlements and fortifications in Asia, except Goa and Damain; the rich prizes made of Portugueze ships; the justice rendered by their agents abroad to their constituents at home; and the enormous advantages arising from their unconscionable oppressive treaties with the princes of Java and Ceylon, together with the superior influence which the intire property of cinnamon, cloves, mace, nutmegs, and two-third parts of the pepper trade in India, have indispensably yielded to them in Asia, at one time raised the value of their stock to 650 per cent. thus encreasing their capital of 6,300,000 to 40,950,000 florins. From this magnitude, avarice, and an ill-judged severity exercised over their allies or dependants, and a false parade of dignity in Batavia, &c. exceeding that of any crowned head in Europe, have reduced their stock from 340 to 355 per cent. A still delusive and pernicious estimation, which, by dividing the principal instead of the profits, together with various other concurring circumstances, must, at length, lay them prostrate, as bankrupts and delinquents, at the feet of the States General; who will then be as little capable of sustaining them, as of upholding their own credit.

* Each florin of Holland, according to the par of silver, is worth 22d. sterling nearly—but the course of exchange varies according to the fluctuations of trade, &c.

The

APPENDIX [A.]

The benefit arising from the sale of cloves, cinnamon, mace, nutmeg, and pepper, will appear from the following distinct calculation, viz.

	lb. wt.	Florins.	Sale in India.	lb. wt.	Florins.	S. in Europe.	Gen. Sale.
They fell							
Cloves in India	150,030	at 5 : 0	750,000	350,000	at 5 : 0	1,750,000	2,500,000
Nutmegs in do.	100,000	at 2 : 16	280,000	250,000	at 3 : 15	937,500	12,175,000
Mace do.	10,000	at 6 : 8	64,000	100,000	at 6 : 8	640,000	704,000
Cinnamon do.	200,000	at 5 : 5	1,050,000	400,000	at 5 : 6	2,100,000	3,150,000
Pepper do.	13,500,000	at 30 per ct.	1,050,000	5,000,000	at 50 per ct.	2,500,000	3,550,000
		in Europe.					
Current Guilders in Holland			f. 3,194,000			f. 7,927,500	f. 11,121,500

Equal in British money to 299,437 l. 10 s. in India; and in Europe to 743,223 l. 19 s. 2 d.; making the general sale to amount to 1,042,661 l. 9 s. 2 d.

From bad cinnamon they extract a rich oil, which they either fell to great account, or by presents, answer all the purposes of money in their political engagements with native princes *.

It is computed, that as the following are the average costs of these spiceries, the profits annexed to each species, arise to the Company from the sale, viz.

APPENDIX [A.]

	Quantity	Cost and Charges		Gr. Cost.	Profit.	
	lb. wt.	Florins.		Florins.	Florins.	
Cloves	500,000	at 2 3 per lb.		1,075,000	1,425,000	Amboyna.
Nutmegs	350,000	at 1 5 do.		437,500	780,000	} Banda Isles.
Mace	110,000	at 2 14 do.		297,000	407,000	
Cinnamon	600,000	at 0 6 do.		180,000	2,970,000	Ceylon.
Pepper	8,500,000	at 0 18 per cent.		1,530,000	2,020,000	Java chiefly.
				f. 4,219,500	f. 5,502,000	

	£.	s.	d.
f. 11,121,500 or sterl.	1,042,661	9	2
f. 3,194,000 - - - -	299,437	10	—
f. 7,927,500 - - - -	743,223	19	2
f. 4,219,500 - - - -	395,578	2	6
f. 5,502,000 - - - -	515,812	10	—

By this calculation it appears, that the grofs sale of spiceries doth amount annually to

That those they sell or barter in India, by reason of which they have the exclusive power of influencing markets

That the rest is sold in Europe, and becomes almost a clear remittance, and nearly a balance against the other European nations who consume it

That the first cost and charges paid generally in merchandize, are

That consequently there is a gain, exclusive of the gain on the merchandize bartered for them, of

---

* It is supposed that Ceylon yields a million pounds of cinnamon annually; and as the half only is sold, the rest is destroyed, in order to keep up the price.

APPENDIX [A.]

Let any minister of a commercial nation, revolve this recapitulated view of the Dutch East India Company's trade in his mind, and draw all the conclusions which such a manufacturing nation as Britain, would derive from it, and it will furnish an extensive field for political speculation.

It is not only presumable, but certain, that the merchandize given in barter for many, or all of these goods, has borne a considerable profit; and that the other commodities extorted under value from the people of Ceylon and Java, and resold to very great advantage in India, will render the remittance in spiceries to Europe the only gain and clear remittance belonging to the Company; or that the establishments necessary (according to the Dutch system) to command the monopoly of these commodities in Amboyna, Banda, Java, and Ceylon, being deducted out of this remittance of 7,927,500 florins, the surplus will be equal to all the other exorbitant charges appertaining to their settlements, leaving a balance of 3,500,000 florins, which is a high estimation of the annual profits of the Company.

The Company's capital in India, &c. comprehending their shipping, goods, good and bad debts, provisions, ordnance, all kinds of warlike stores and ammunition, plate, and cattle, exclusive of territorial properties, are computed not to exceed   f. 47,000,000

They owe in Europe 11,250,000, which doubtless bears an interest of 3½ per cent. per ann. or f. 393,750
They owe in Asia 7,000,000, where the interest is seldom under 10 per cent. per annum; or, these two principal debts added make — f. 700,000   18,250,000

                             28,750,000

The surplus 28,750,000, being a real advance out of the original gains of the Company, will bear 8l. 13s. 5d. per cent. f. 2,406,250l.

The annual gross profit, by estimation   f. 3,500,000

Of this surplus (28,750,000) it is presumable, and indeed confidently believed, that bad and doubtful debts and dead effects will consume   —   —   f. 15,250,000

The real commercial or moveable effects of the Company will therefore be — —   f. 13,500,000

APPENDIX. [A.]

The eſtabliſhed prime value of 2130 ſhares of the Company's ſtock, at 3000 florins each, being 6,390,000, bearing a proportion of f. 211. 5s. 4d. per cent. to their real commercial or moveable capital of 13,500,000 florins, which is f. 138. 14s. 8d. ſhort of its current value, at f. 350 per cent. according to which they divide; it is therefore evident, that even without reſerving prudential allowances for caſual loſſes and charges, wars, &c. they are injudiciouſly dividing a fixed proportion of their capital annually, as a real, although in faƈt an imaginary and deluſive profit. As the ſtocks of public companies riſe in their prices, in exaƈt proportion to the intereſt that is divided, or in proportion to the equal increaſe of capital and intereſt; and as in every country, the uſe of money bears a certain fixed value, in proportion to the reputation of the ſecurity; if therefore the Dutch Eaſt India ſtock be eſtimated at f. 138. 14s. 8d. per cent. more than the intrinſic value of their capital, it muſt follow, that exceſſive dividends alone originated, and have ſupported that falſe, or nominal value; and conſequently, that they have been in the baſe practice of dividing as a profit, from $4\frac{1}{2}$ to 5 per cent. annually, out of the real capital. A conduƈt, which, by a progreſſive calculation, will conſume the entire capital in about fourteen or fifteen years, without the aid of a variety of other evils and enormities, which haſten that event, as well as the annihilation of the Company.

The 23,000,000 florins, ſaid by themſelves to have been expended in the eſtabliſhment of the Cape of Good Hope, of which f. 10,000,000 may moderately be ſtated as an irretrievable loſs; the f. 15,250,000 (making together f. 27,725,000) added to the real commercial and moveable capital, f. 13,500,000, fully accounts for the former riſe of their original capital to 650 per cent. and at the ſame inſtant avows, that in proportions conſiderably leſs offenſive, than thoſe which have either enhanced their expences, or reduced their profits, their deſtruƈtion is inevitable, if they do not wiſely and ſpeedily adopt the only rational means of evading it.

APPENDIX

APPENDIX [B.]

OBSERVATIONS on Mr SMITH's "Nature and Caufes " of the Wealth of Nations ;" on a curfory reading thereof, at the Cape of Good Hope, in Africa, April, 1779.

Vol. I. p. 39. Lond. Edit.

MR. SMITH fays, "That labour alone, never varying in its own value, is alone the ultimate ftandard by which the value of all commodities can at all times and places be eftimated and compared. It is their real price; money is their nominal price only."

OBSERVATIONS.

Since all nations have at length concurred in reducing the labour and ingenuity of men to a value, and fixed gold and filver, when ftamped by authority, as the intermediate vehicle or mark of univerfal exchange, and thence a ftandard to regulate the value of labour, may not this be confidered as a mere commercial commodity, equally liable to fluctuations as many others, according to local circumftances, the prices of the neceffaries of life, and the commercial demand?

P. 40. He obferves, "That college-leafes, by ftatute, are payable one-third in corn, at the current market price, or in kind. And that this third is now become near double the value of what arifes from the remaining two-thirds referved in money. This (Mr. Smith calls) finking the old money-rents to a quarter-part of their ancient value."

Although ancient money-rents are not more than a quarter-part of what the fame lands now rent for, yet, may it not be more properly faid to arife, not from finking the old money-rents, but, from evident caufes, increafing the value of corn, and the neceffaries of life, the confequence of arts and improvements, and particularly of luxury?—The increafe of luxury having increafed the wants of land-holders, they have proportionably exacted greater rents; and thefe exactions have obliged tenants and fub-tenants to advance, in an equal degree,

gree, the prices of their commodities; which, falling heavy on the common neceffaries of labourers, have advanced, in the fame proportion, the price of labour. Thus money might have retained its original weight, quality, intrinfic value, and currency; but the fluctuation of the neceffaries of life hath claimed a larger quantity thereof, to keep pace with the labours of the hufbandman, and artift. But, may there not have been a coincidence, the one decreafing in its value, as the other increafed in demand, and both from natural and unconnected caufes?

P. 85. He fays, "That the money price of labour is higher in America than in Britain, and provifions cheaper; yet, that the real price of labour is alfo higher in America; its real price, the real command of the neceffaries and conveniences of life, which it conveys, muft be ftill higher in a greater proportion."

This I conceive, with fubmiffion, to be a kind of contradiction of his former principles, as well as of the immediate affertion.—If provifions are cheaper, cloathing only can be underftood to be dearer; yet linen and woollen drapery, imported from Britain, have been retailed in America for lefs than in Britain. The low value of land, the encouragement prefented fettlers, and a natural love of freedom and independence, are the probable caufes of the high price of labour in America.

P. 86. He fays, "That population in Britain and Europe, doubles only in 500 years."

One would wifh to believe, that this is an erroneous computation. Britain, freed from war, emigration, the pernicious extenfion of the city of London, and monopolies of farms, its population would increafe in near the fame proportion as in America. Throughout thofe ftates in Europe where the Romifh faith prevails, population decreafes by the evident confequences of impolitic conftitutions, and the want of manufactures, by the rigour of religious tenets, and by wars. In the northern kingdoms, Sweden, Denmark, and Norway, where induftry, peace, navigation, and commerce are encouraged, without the advantages of colonization, population increafes rapidly, notwithftanding the intemperature of climate and fterility of foil.

P. 99. Mr. Smith, with great penetration, defines the several conditions of the great body of the people thus, " The condition of the labouring poor is moſt happy in the progreſſive ſtate of the ſociety, hard in the ſtationary ſtate, and miſerable in the declining ſtate. In all the different orders of the ſociety, the progreſſive ſtate is hearty and chearful, the ſtationary is dull, and the declining melancholy."

P. 201. He attributes " the want of ſtrength and form in the labouring people in Scotland, compared with the ſame claſs in England, to the difference of bread food, or, between oaten-bread and wheaten-bread."

Should it not rather be imputed to the quantity of animal or fleſh-food, and ſtrong beer, which Engliſh labourers eat and drink plentifully, and the Scots but ſparingly, or very ſeldom?

P. 202. He ſays, " That as it is difficult to preſerve potatoes, the fear of not being able to ſell them before they rot, is the chief obſtacle to their ever becoming the principal vegetable food of all the different ranks of people."

Query.—Whether by kiln-drying, potatoes would not keep long, without either rotting or loſing their nutritive quality? Or, might they not be ground to meal or flour, and preſerved by hard packing?

P. 244. He ſays, " That the nominal ſum which conſtitutes the market-price of every commodity, is neceſſarily regulated, not ſo much by the quantity of ſilver, which, according to the ſtandard, ought to be contained in it, as by that which, it is found by experience, actually is contained in it."

This is an aſſertion againſt practice and experience. It is the value which the government of every country ſets upon its current coin, and the proportion thereof to the exchange with other countries, operating in the way of commerce, that conſtitutes its price: for example, in Holland, the ſilver and copper coins current by tale and authority, are not intrinſically worth three fourth parts of their current value; yet with that baſe inferior compoſition, a bill of exchange upon London is

bought,

APPENDIX [B.]

bought, with which guineas are commanded, worth twenty one shillings on any exchange or in any mint in Europe.

Mr. Smith would seem, in my humble opinion, to treat the real and nominal prices of labour, and of current coins, throughout, too philosophically; which, in reality, the subjects will not admit of.—Philosophy had very little share in their establishment. Commerce was a more active agent.— The value of coins is upheld by authority; and the prices of labour and ingenuity are estimated by the prices of the common necessaries of life in the first instance; by the consumption in luxuries and parade at home, in the second; and, principally, by the balance of trade, which guides the rate of exchange with other nations, in the third instance. In Britain, the value of a pound sterling, or of a penny, by either of which the exchanges with Europe are ascertained, fluctuating according to the immediate demand for remittances, are founded upon the sale of its manufactures, and the commodities of its colonies and settlements in America and Asia, or by the excesses of its supplies from other states, or sums foolishly wasted in foreign dominions.—When the standards of its gold and silver coins are higher than the standards of other neighbouring states with which it communicates by commerce, to a greater extent than the risque, insurance, commission, and charges of exportation, the price of exchange is then affected, because it becomes an article of commerce, hurtful to the nation.

P. 248. Mr. Smith says, " That it would be more proper to consider the variation in the average money price of corn as the effect rather of some gradual rise in the real value of silver in the European market, than of any fall in the real average price of corn."—He alledges throughout, " That the rise of the price of corn at the several periods, has been owing to the increase of silver by the discovery of the South America mines, which diminished the value of coins."

The last idea appears natural; although in other places Mr. Smith observes, that the coinage of silver has at different periods diminished in weight, without altering the name, or in fact the nominal value of that species. It may be thought, and it is acknowledged to be presumptuous, to oppose an opinion to that of so eminent an author; but these, surely,

appear

appear as contradictions, and the entire system seems adverse to daily experience. The nominal value of coins in all nations, which is derived from the supreme authority, has undergone very little alteration (except in the gold coin of France) since mankind attained a distinct idea and knowledge of universal commerce, and the force of luxury invented new wants; which is of a modern date. Until then, the uses of coins were imperfectly understood; and it is only since they were accurately understood, that their nominal and intrinsic values have become the objects of political and commercial disquisition. The advance prices of corn may rather, therefore, be imputed to an increase of luxury in the middle and inferior classes of the people; to an increase in the number of manufacturers, navigators, and citizens, who become necessarily consumers, not in barter, as before the invention of coins, but in exchange for money; and to the monopoly of farms, which are converted into meadows for pasturage. In other countries of Europe, where manufactures are less known, the prices of corn have advanced only by the demand for exportation, operating as a manufacture, and creating an essential commodity in the scale of trade.

P. 250. He says, "That from 1740 to 1751, Britain exported 8,029,156 quarters and one bushel of all sorts of grain, for which a bounty was paid of 1,514,962l. 17s. 4d. h.

This is an important subject to the state. A nice calculation, founded upon true principles, is requisite, to determine the propriety or impropriety of a measure which hath consumed so much of the public wealth, and might prove dangerous, in certain events, to the existence of the nation. The conversion of corn land into meadows, may have been attended with two national evils, by creating a losing balance against it in trade†, and consuming the public revenues; and particularly, by raising the prices of the essential necessaries of life upon labourers, manufacturers, and the poor, and by that means enabling foreign states to supply themselves and their neighbours, by underselling Britain in those commodities which formerly produced the chief articles in the balance of trade.

† A balance against the trade of a nation may, in some local circumstances, be considered as a gaining balance, when it is necessary, without indulging luxury, and procured for less than it can be manufactured at home.

Doubtless,

APPENDIX [B.] 253

Doubtless, the enormous export and bounty mentioned by Mr. Smith, must naturally have advanced the prices of grain at home, to the detriment of useful commerce, and the increase of the national debt; because it is a fact, that, notwithstanding these occasional exports, the imports have, of late years, been considerably greater than the exports, without bringing back a penny in duties, in lieu of the bounty paid on exportation†. The wisdom of parliament should devise expedients to encourage husbandry, without granting a bounty on the exportation of corn, and without the monopoly of farms; then the manufactures of Britain would resume their stations in the markets of Europe, as their qualities have ever been, and continue acknowledged to be superior to those of all other countries.

P. 269. Mr. Smith alledges, "That silver has increased in its value, since the present century."

Whether it has or has not, or shall hereafter, either increase or decrease in its quantity or value, as a commercial commodity, essential also to the gratification of luxury and pomp, will make no alteration necessary in the nominal values of silver coins current by authority in the several kingdoms and states of Europe, while it is considered and used merely as the vehicle of exchange in commerce, without any direct or critical retrospection to is quality or intrinsic value. If silver or gold in bullion, either rises or falls in its commercial price, a greater or lesser quantity of alloy will be compounded in the current coins, without varying in any instance the currency thereof, in the country where it is stamped by legislative authority.—Doubtless, a nation labouring under discredit by a heavy load of public debt, may justify the calling in the current coins, and recoining with a greater proportion of alloy, by way of seignorage, to reduce it to an equality with coins of the neighbouring states; and by that means, reduce the public debt; while it will secure the national coin

---

† It has been computed with certainty, that the balances paid by Britain, for corn imported, after deducting the value of exportation, stood thus:

	£
In 1771,	105,200
1772,	84,400
1773,	569,820
1774,	1,922,230

and considerably more in 1775.

within

within itself, without affecting either its political or commercial credit. In France, the seignorage is eight per cent. on gold coins, besides that the standard, which is twenty one carats, three quarters, is a quarter of a carat worse than English sterling. By reducing the gold now in circulation in the British dominions, to the circulating standard of French gold coins, it will yield about one million and a half sterling to the treasury.

P. 272. Mr. Smith says, " That it is scarce in the power of human industry to multiply game and fish."

If Mr. Smith had visited the royal dominions of France, and those of the princes of the blood royal, he would have perceived, that human power, by the simple exercise of political despotism only, can increase and multiply game; and that wild birds will resort to, and admirably increase, in a greater proportion than dunghill fowls, and become equally tame, where shelter and security is yielded to them from human violence and invasion.

P. 300. He alledges, " That the increase of the quantity of gold and silver in Europe, and the increase of its manufactures and agriculture, are two events, which, though they have happened nearly about the same time, yet, have arisen from very different causes, and have scarce any natural connection with one another."

Though the abolition of the feudal system originated in Europe at the same period of time that chance effected the discovery of the American mines, it is, nevertheless, equally true, that the increase of the quantity of gold and silver, which were, long before that period, the intermediate mark of exchange whereby to ascertain the prices and values of all commodities, was partly the cause of the improving progress in manufactures and agriculture; without which no adequate compensation could be made by other nations, either to increase miners, or to obtain the valuable metals from those nations who had the sole possession and monopoly of them, as the means of giving value to any larger quantity than was before necessary in the then imperfect state of commerce. I conceive it to be a fixed principle, in judging of the laws of commerce, that the improvement of manufactures and agriculture are

are not only inseparable in their own natures, but actually dependent on each other; and that their united influence is the true source of wealth and population, and the springs of commercial action.—Another principle, in affixing an affinity between the increase of precious metals, and of manufactures and agriculture, is, that the quantity of species in circulation, must bear a certain proportion to the manufactured commodities, and these commodities to the success or improvements in agriculture; and that the superfluous metals, by means of these improvements, have become also articles of manufacture, whereby their values are enhanced.

In support of this allegation, Mr. Smith instances Poland, "where the feudal system still continues, which, notwithstanding the increase of precious metals, continues as beggarly as before."—Doubtless, the unhappy system of its aristocratical government, operates as a mill-stone, perpetually weighing down and oppressing the great body of the people, or all below the rank of nobility, and discouraging industry and the arts. Yet it should also be considered, that Poland is so situated, as to be unfortunately removed out of the line of commerce. It wants freedom, without which neither commerce or agriculture can flourish: and its having been so often the wretched seat of ambitious wars, has interrupted agriculture, and occasioned depopulation.

Mr. Smith says, "That the value of the metals is lower in Spain and Portugal, than in any other part of Europe, because they come into all other parts loaded with a freight, insurance, and the expence of smuggling." I think this is an erroneous mode of judging and calculating, proceeding from Mr. Smith's not having accurately considered the nature of the commerce of Spain; which makes the precious metals scarcer, and in reality dearer, in those countries, than in other parts of Europe; since the same quantity of metals is capable of procuring less of the necessaries and conveniencies of life in their dominions, than any where else; as those countries receive all their supplies, even to the necessaries of life, from other states, and the very mines are carried on by means of the manufactures of other nations. Do not these goods, therefore, come loaded with heavier charges of freight, insurance, duty, commissions, and other charges, than bullion; which, by taking up less space, pays less freight; by being less liable to receive damage, is insured cheaper; and freed from a list of other charges, to which every other merchandize is incident?—and, as almost all the merchandize, and even.

the

the shipping which produce and transport the metals, are the production of other nations, to whom the metals are re-exported in the quality of manufactured merchandize, leaving little more than the duties and commission in the nations to which the mines belong?—Their poverty originated in the decay of industry, with the discovery of the mines†; which, by creating a nominal influence and false idea of wealth to the people, rendered them, at first by successes, and since by habit, proud, indolent, and totally negligent of agriculture and manufactures, whereby the population of Spain has, in that space of time, sunk from fourteen millions to seven and an half; and Portugal has dwindled from above three millions to one and three quarters.

P. 308 and 309. In support of his opinions concerning the difference in the values of labour and money, he quotes the high prices of superfine broad cloths formerly, compared with the present.— ☞ See the passages.

Arts have arrived to a greater degree of perfection since, and luxury have proportionably increased. The same cloths, made of the same materials, are now manufactured, by means of new inventions in every part of the progress, at a much cheaper rate; the very materials are now bought for a less nominal price, by means of foreign commerce and domestic improvements; but, as a hundred persons now use cloths of that quality, for one that used them in former times, the increase of the demand increases the profit, although the price be considerably less.

P. 330, &c. Mr. Smith's definition of 'the division of stock, is ingenious and judicious. The idea is new, and exceedingly proper for the study of persons in private life, and should be well understood by persons in the administration of public affairs, and by legislators.

P. 396. He says, " That the paper-currency of North America was made payable only after several years, without

† Query.—Whether Britain is not likely to fall by the luxury which originated in the wealth and power acquired by her great successes?—and Holland also?

interest

APPENDIX [B.] 257

interest: That therefore it was a violent injustice, and a tyrannical regulation, to force it in payment when the interest of the colony was six per cent. per annum, and only due in fifteen years, creating a loss to the holder of sixty per cent:—That one hundred pounds sterling was occasionally considered as equivalent, in some of the colonies, to one hundred and thirty pounds, in others, to eleven thousand pounds currency:—That this difference in the value arises from the difference in the quantity emitted in the different colonies, and in the distance and probability of its final discharge and redemption."

I have already observed, that the nominal value of coins in any country, or of that public emission which supplies the place of gold and silver, will not bear to be treated philosophically; because even the gold and silver coins are, in every country, founded upon a discretionary estimation, guided sometimes by the force of laws, and at other times by the voluntary agreement and pleasure of merchants.—Notes circulating under the sanction and security of government, and to continue in circulation for a limited term, in which it is computed that the public will be able to extinguish its debt by the redemption of paper with actual money; and that the sum in circulation is limited to the amount of the debt;—if the credit of government be good for that amount, there can be no inconvenience to the individuals, and it should pass as current as metal coins. By custom, and by tale, a half Johannes of Portugal, worth in England but thirty six shillings, when of full weight, is current in some of the American colonies, after repeated clippings, at sixty six shillings currency, when one hundred pounds sterling is rated at one hundred and sixty pounds currency; which is rating the gold at twenty three one-third more than the current exchange for bills upon England.—And yet, as it passes current, without the compulsion of any law, and only by the voluntary agreement and pleasure of merchants, who are willing to receive it at that rate, in paying for British and other goods, it is not deemed an injustice or tyranny, although the security is not so good as that of government, and although it produces no interest, but on the contrary loses daily in its real value by wear.—Spanish dollars are likewise rated in the same exact proportion above the current course of exchange. Mr. Smith has not (I apprehend) truly investigated the nature and causes of colony-exchange, and their fluctuations.—In the West India islands, where no paper has ever been emitted, and for the

most

most part, gold and silver coins of Portugal and Spain circulate in payment, the exchange varies from one hundred and twenty five to one hundred and seventy five per cent. in favour of British sterling, and the par of silver and gold is proportionably the same throughout, bearing above twenty per cent. more than bills. In the French islands, the exchange upon France is one hundred and fifty currency per one hundred pounds Tournois; yet the value of gold and silver is constant at one hundred and eighty three one-third per one hundred Tournois.—These instances may suffice to shew, that the emission of paper-money on government security, is neither unjust nor tyrannical, provided that there is not more thrown into the circulation than is requisite to maintain its commerce, and to supply the necessary intercourse of the colony within itself.

P. 431. He says, " That interest has sunk in Europe, since and by reason of the discovery of the silver and gold mines in America."

This assertion has a direct retrospection to what has been investigated (page 251) " concerning the increase of gold and silver in Europe, and the increase of manufactures and agriculture, though happening at the same time, having had, nevertheless, no natural connection, and arising from very different causes." In like manner, the same mode of reasoning may justify the reduction of interest for the use of money, as the principal, if not the sole cause, since the progressive improvements in useful arts and sciences have, by equal progressions, expanded the intellectual faculties of men.—As the arts of improvement and of commerce, have approached to perfection, so the prices of goods, and the labour bestowed on them, became less; and as the arts became general, the profits became so also, and in consequence less; therefore the use of money sunk in the same proportion.—Thus it will be found; and Mr. Smith acknowledges, that in new colonies, or upon any new undertaking, the value of money is higher, as well as the rate of interest, and diminishes in proportion to the improvement; and that in commercial states, and states far advanced in improvements, the interest is always lower than in those where there is less commerce and fewer manufactures, or which are, in general, very far back in the knowledge and property of the useful arts. Thus the rates of interest have been governed more by the improvements made in manufactures, trade, and navigation, than by the discovery of mines; because the active invention of mankind would have substituted some other metals, as the universal mark of exchange, to which time, use, and authority, would have given the same importance and stability, that are now given to silver and gold.

Mr. Smith explains himself afterwards, in opposition to the opinions of Locke, Law, and Montesquieu, who asserted, " that interest sunk by reason of the increase of gold and silver only;" and he says, " that the profits of stock are in proportion as the actual species in a country is to the capital employed; and that the common proportion between capital and profit would therefore be the same; and consequently the common interest of money."—This is declaring an effect without a cause: but surely, if the borrower did not obtain a greater profit than what he was obliged to give for the use of money, together with the bare value of his labour, the estimation of use is over-rated, because the borrower gets only a bare subsistence, without any reasonable consideration for risques, casualties, and genius; therefore the rate of interest should, and must, always be lower than the exact proportion between the capital and the profit.

☞ Whether it be that the subjects are less intricate, and better adapted therefore to my conception, or that they are more familiar to my knowledge and ideas, in the subsequent reading of this laborious performance; or that Mr. Smith draws the latter conclusions from facts and experience, and therefore ceases to treat them philosophically, I know not: but henceforward, his observations appear more clear and distinct to my comprehension, tending to elucidate the minds of administration, and instructing them to view the real state of the nation through a true perspective, and to disclose the means of restoring the whole to its original vigour and texture.

Vol. I. p. 479. Mr. Smith says, " That yeomanry is regarded as an inferior rank of people throughout Europe; and that they are most respected in Britain. That in the republican governments of Holland, and Berne in Switzerland, the farmers are said to be not inferior to those in England."

Upon a general principle, Mr. Smith's observations are just. Constitutional liberty ever encourages agriculture, as well as manufactures and trade. In England, farming is not only encouraged mechanically in those who profess it, but it

has

has of late years become a branch of liberal science, and the practice thereof fashionable among the first rank of commoners. It is very much respected and caressed in its general and mechanical capacity.—Mr. Smith might have ascribed self-importance, ease, and skill, with greater propriety to the farmers of the Austrian Netherlands, and to some districts of French Flanders, than to those of Holland and Switzerland; though probably the distances at which those provinces are happily placed from the over-bearing vices, tyranny, and ambitious emulation of their respective courts†, together with the remnant seeds of their own original constitutions‡, may have as yet preserved them from the wretchedness of their fellow-subjects.

Vol. I. p. 495. Mr. Smith has asserted with equal confidence and judgment, and it is an incontrovertible truth, "That commerce and manufactures gradually introduced order and good government, and with them the liberty and security of individuals, among the inhabitants of the country who had before lived in a continual state of war with their neighbours, and of servile dependency upon their superiors. This, though it has been the least observed, is by far the most important of all their effects."

P. 509. He says, "That a merchant is not necessarily the citizen of any particular country."—This remark is as pithy and just as it is liberal, under the idea of a general merchant, and the sacred reputation, honour, and commercial credit, which formerly belonged to a profession, which contributed more than any other to civilize remote nations, and establish a sociability. But the term merchant hath submitted to abuses since.

Vol. II. p. 2. He says, "That it is a popular notion, which supposes wealth to consist in gold and silver species, arising from the double function of money as the instrument of commerce and the measure of value." This is a very sensible observation, and a true one: and on the same principle, in the 20th page, he says, "That bullion is the money of the great mercantile republic."

Vol. II. p. 43. He says, "That to prohibit, by a perpetual law, the importation of foreign corn and cattle, is, in

† Vienna and Paris.   ‡ The Flemish.

reality to enact, that the population and industry of the country shall at no time exceed what the rude produce of its own soil can maintain."

If Holland, Venice, Genoa, the Hans-towns, and other free governments, were to adopt such a maxim, their declension would be rapid indeed. Mr. Smith's remark is so just, that it were happy for the British empire if every minister and legislator would submit to make it an unalterable part of his political creed, and remember it before he assents to the passing of any perpetual law whatever, as the effects of all general laws are deducible from the principles of industry and population.

Vol. II. p. 48 and 49. He says, with great justice, " That taxes upon the necessaries of life, have nearly the same effect upon the circumstances of the people, as a poor soil and a bad climate; provisions being thereby rendered dearer, in the same manner as if it required extraordinary labour and expence to raise them. When taxes are grown to a certain height, they are a curse equal to the barrenness of the earth, and the inclemency of the heavens."

P. 51. He says, " That to judge whether retaliations by one nation, for restraining the importation of its goods or manufactures in another, are likely to produce a repeal of the restraints, does not, perhaps, belong so much to the science of a legislator, whose deliberations ought to be governed by general principles, which are always the same, as to the skill of that insidious and crafty animal, vulgarly called a statesman or politician, whose counsels are directed by the momentary fluctuations of affairs."

However just Mr. Smith's distinction may be, in ascertaining the separate duties of a minister and legislator, in matters of trade, it nevertheless belongs to the legislator to be informed, as well of the particular principles which actuate the minister on any particular subject, as to understand the general principles of commerce, and the distributive relation of the manufactures of one nation to another. A particular knowledge of manufactures, and a general knowledge of trade, together with the universal and relative principles of navigation, are the equal, and should be the indispensable provinces of both statesman and legislator. This subject is more immediately applicable to the rivality between Britain and France, than any other countries in Europe.—The ba-

lance

lance of trade is the pivot upon which the rivalship turns.— A question will naturally arise upon this subject, whether a treaty of commerce with France, upon limited, but liberal grounds, would not prove more effectual in removing those retaliating restraints, reciprocally, than any other mode whatever, with peculiar advantages in favour of Britain.—Britain chiefly imports wines from France; its other imports consist of luxuries. These are commodities which corrupted gouts and minds have, by habit, rendered indispensable in the first and second classes of the nation, and will continue, therefore, to be obtained by licit or illicit means. France, more despotic and effectual over the minds and actions of all her subjects, can restrain the importation of contraband goods; and by that means necessity, the parent of invention, will devise means to force the manufacture of goods at home, which, in time, are brought to such perfection as to render the restraining laws unnecessary. Thus Britain loses in a two-fold sense, viz. by not vending her own manufactures, and by being obliged to take French wines avowedly paying duty, and three times as much clandestinely, without any duty, and by yielding encouragement for smuggling other luxuries. The balance of trade, for the same reason, will continually be against Britain. It is an unerring maxim, which experience should have demonstrated long ago to financiers, that when any commodity is taxed immoderately, the certain consequence will be, the diminution of that branch of the revenue; which arises from two self-evident causes, viz. the diminution of the legal imports, and the temptation to run contraband goods, the high duties operating as a seducing premium for the risque.

Without bringing the enormous sums expended by British subjects residing and travelling in France, into the computation, it must be acknowledged, that the general balance has of late years turned considerably to the side of France, notwithstanding the tobacco contracts, and the large exportation of the gold coin of Britain since the recoinage in 1773, which appeared conspicuously in the rate of exchange, having augmented the number of pence for a French crown above the par, which formerly had been generally under it.—The exportation of the British gold coin into France, arose from the very great superiority in the standard, and some also in the weight, of guineas over Louis d'ors; though in general they are reputed, in tale, of equal value. The Caisse d'Escompte in Paris had agents in Dunkirk, Calais, and Boulogne,

logne, who gave twelve fols and a Louis d'or for each new guinea, and fent feveral thoufands every month to Paris, where they were immediately diffolved into Louis d'ors. Would it not, as well in revenue, as in a commercial point of view, be political to reduce the Britifh coin-ftandard to an equality with the French gold ftandard? And, like them, and all the other commercial ftates in Europe, to increafe the quantity of filver coin in circulation, reducing the latter coin to the ftandard of Holland? Such a meafure, keeping to the exact ftandard of France and Holland, would raife a confiderable revenue; would retain the current fpecie in the nation, to the great encouragement and benefit of commerce, manufactures, and agriculture; and would do away many of the temptations to counterfeit and clip the coins. If, by thus reducing the real quality of coins to the ftandard of other commercial nations, the price of labour, or the productions of labour, fhould advance in a retrofpective progreffion, (which, however, is not very probable) the evil would in that cafe fall, as it ought in juftice and good policy to do, upon the intemperate or avaricious rack-renting landlords; provided a legal mean is devifed to reftrain them from a continuation of unreafonable exactions, or otherwife diftreffing their tenants; the confequences of which would be, that the future prices of the neceffaries of life would be fixed, unlefs remarkably good or bad feafons fhould occafion a temporary fluctuation.

The mode of computing the balance of trade in Britain, by the Cuftom-houfe entries, is erroneous and deceitful. The rate of exchange between one country and another, is the true criterion; becaufe the prices of bills are always governed by the furplus demand, which elevates or depreffes, like mercury, by the warmth of the creditor, or the frigidity of the debtor.—Thus, for example, if a greater quantity of any foreign coin is allowed for a pound fterling, than the par of exchange (according to their refpective filver ftandards) it denotes a greater demand to remit to England, and confequently that the balance of trade is in favour of England†.

The

† This fubject leads me to th obfervations that Mr. Smith, in treating of the commercial fyftem of Britain, and the connection thereof with the American colonies, although juft in almoft all his remarks, feems not to have fixed his attention with fufficient energy to the chief rational bulwark, "the acts of trade and navigation," particularly the 12th Car. II. Thefe two fubjects, to wit, the general commercial fyftem, and its immediate connection with the American colonies, confidered generally, will furnifh a political queftion—Whether, upon a ftrict enquiry into the flow, and often-times uncertain

APPENDIX [B.]

The subject of coinage is capable of useful discussion. A guinea, of full weight, passes in common currency but for twenty four livres, in France; although, by a comparative estimation, a Louis d'or of full weight is worth no more in England than about 18s. 4d.$\frac{12}{89}$, estimating the par of exchange at twenty two livres and ten sols per pound sterling.—I have made the computation thus:

	£	s.	d.
In France a mark of fine gold is worth	740	9	$1\frac{1}{11}$
The standard of $21\frac{3}{4}$ carats is worth	671	0	10
Less than pure gold, per mark	69	8	$3\frac{1}{11}$
The standard mark is coined into 30 Louis d'ors, equal to 720 livres, which is worse than standard	48	19	2
	£.118	7	$5\frac{1}{11}$

Thus coined gold is worse than fine, per mark 118 7 $5\frac{1}{11}$
Which will be found to be about 32l. sterling per mark, or   per ounce; of inferior standard by $\frac{1}{4}$ carat; and the English standard is valued at   -   -   -   3 17 $10\frac{1}{2}$
per ounce ; making a difference of
per ounce   -   -   -   -   -   -   0   2 $1\frac{1}{4}$
Eight per cent. signorage in France on 8ol. is   0   6 $6\frac{8}{10}$
$\frac{1}{4}$ carat in the standard is,   -   -   -   0   0 $11\frac{1}{2}$

The whole difference per ounce   -   -   £. 0   9 $7\frac{1}{4}$
nearly: which, proportioned to the guineas and Louis d'ors contained respectively in an ounce, constitutes a difference in the value of a guinea above a Louis d'or of 2s. 7d.$\frac{12}{89}$

Vol. II. p. 206. He says, " That Virginia and Maryland sent to the British market above 96,000 hogsheads of tobacco; whereof about 14,000 was said to be consumed in Britain."

It is a pity that Mr. Smith did not shew the public advantages reaped from this single branch of the American trade:

certain returns for British manufactures from the colonies in America, and the quick and frequent returns from the European foreign markets, the latter may not enable the manufacturers to undersell the manufacturers of other countries, with surer and greater advantages to themselves and the nation?

Each

Each hogſhead may be rated at 7l. 10s. neat, or the whole at 720,000l. ſterling; whereof the Britiſh conſumption was but 105,000l. the remaining 615,000l. created a balance of trade in favour of Britain; beſides that, by employing at leaſt 330 capital ſhips, it gave bread and encouragement to upwards of five thouſand ſeamen. The duties on the 14,000 hogſheads conſumed in Britain, produced a revenue, at 26l. 1s. per hogſhead, of 364,700l. beſides ſome fractional parts of the ſubſidies, which were retained at exportation, of the duties paid on importation.——The whole of theſe ſums, as alſo an increaſe of debts by way of loans, were returned to America in Britiſh manufactures and India goods from Britain. The debts owing by the coloniſts, in Britain, and the quantities of bullion annually remitted from the colonies to Britain, conſtitute the ſmalleſt part of the balance in favour of the trade of Britain with her colonies; the moſt important object hath been, the happy advantage of not being ſubjugated to other nations, for the rich and indiſpenſable commodities with which the colonies ſupply the Britiſh market.

P. 226. Mr. Smith ſays, " That the aſſemblies can never be managed, ſo as to levy upon their conſtituents a revenue ſufficient, not only to maintain, at all times, their own civil and military eſtabliſhment, but to pay their proper proportion of the expence of the general government of the Britiſh empire, ſeems not at all probable."

It ſhould be firſt determined by Mr. Smith, whether the Americans ſhould pay all their own civil and military eſtabliſhment, together alſo with a proportion of the whole expences of the general empire; or, under what quantum he means to define the proper proportion of the general expence. But in the form in which the meaning at preſent appears, it ſeems to be an idea founded only on conjecture. The people of America having paſſions like other men, after long and fruitleſs humble ſupplications, have become, in their turn, callous, as well as turbulent, refractory, and vindictive; infinitely more ſo than was natural to their conſtitutions, and their diſtinguiſhed loyalty and attachment to the mother ſtate; which proves, that no people are more dangerous than thoſe who preſerve a phlegmatic character, when driven to deſperation, and their reſentments are raiſed; nor a more dreadful and implacable enemy than an enraged friend; and it equally proves, that numberleſs political errors, when once adopted, become,

become, unhappily, fixed principles. But the people of America, being fensible, reasonable, and open to conviction, may easily be made to behold the happy state in which they once were, as subjects to the crown of Britain, and the miseries which independence will intail, inevitably, on themselves and their posterity; and they will, consequently, adopt the happy medium of contributing, in a reasonable proportion, to the exigencies of the general empire, for general security, as general subjects of the same great state.

P. 237. He says, "That it is alledged the Spanish and Portuguese colonies consume three millions sterling a year, in the article of linen alone, from Germany, Holland, Flanders, and France."

This allegation corroborates what I have already remarked, concerning the value of precious metals in the mine-possessing countries, (p. 255) but it also seems incredible; it being more than a probable proportion of the rich commodities, of every kind, imported into Europe from the Spanish and Portuguese colonies. It should likewise be computed in this estimate, that the galleons from South America to the Philippine islands bring back rich cargoes of fine cottons; that the Portuguese ships from India fell cottons on the coast of Brazil; that the Dutch, French, and English traders in the West Indies, supply the Spanish main with linen and cotton cloths; that vast quantities of superfine woollen cloths and silks are annually imported from Europe and Asia for the consumption of these American colonies; and that, after all, the whole export of bullion seldom exceeds the value of six millions sterling in any one year.

P. 248 and 249. Mr. Smith says, "That the Cape of Good Hope, and Batavia, are at present the most considerable European colonies in Africa or the East Indies, being peculiarly fortunate in their situation; that their situations have enabled them to surmount all the obstacles which the oppressive genius of an exclusive Company may have occasionally opposed to their growth, and, in Batavia, the additional disadvantage of perhaps the most unwholesome climate in the world."

Mr. Smith has trusted to a false information, in the idea of superiority which he has ascribed to these two Dutch settlements. The oppressive genius of an exclusive Company, hath wholly obstructed the growth of public and private opulence, and

and of induftry, at the Cape of Good Hope, where nature hath bountifully furnifhed the means of making it a moft delightful and flourifhing colony. Batavia is alfo cramped by the fame evil genius; and the natives, the Chinefe emigrants, and Malays, are rendered difaffected by the fcourges of wanton and impolitic tyranny and oppreffion. Even the unhealthfulnefs of Batavia, is an evil of Dutch invention, becaufe they cannot exift out of water; and they have introduced unneceffary canals into the town, the ftagnation of which is the chief caufe of the mortality that hath depopulated the place, and contributed greatly to the bankruptcy of the Dutch Eaft India Company.

Mr. Smith's obfervations in pages 236, and in 252, 253, &c. vol. ii. on the mercantile government and orders of the Englifh Company to their fervants in India, claim attention; and on the future government and influence in the Eaft and Weft Indies, are juft and prophetic.

Chap. II. Book V. upon the duties and excife, is, probably, the moft ingenious and perfect difquifition and conclufion on that fubject, that has yet appeared in print.—Great and many advantages may be derived from a juft and fteady application of the principles which are deducible from the objects laid down by Mr. Smith, as political improvements on the national finances and trade. In page 518, his obfervations on the falaries and perquifites of officers employed in collecting taxes, duties, and excife, call for the fpeedy attention of parliament.—The perquifites of office are more grievous than the tax levied, in as much as they are arbitrary and oppreffive: but, in many inftances, greater than the impoft collected; and are, moreover, the means of frequently defrauding the revenue by connivances.

In the 419th page, he ftates, "the ordinary revenues of Britain, for the current expence, intereft of public debts, and for finking a part of the debt, above ten millions; whereof the land-tax quota is near two millions, or one-fifth part."—By this mode of eftimating the land-tax, the grofs landed revenue of Great Britain does not exceed ten millions a year.—The rent referved is always fuppofed to be no more than one-third part of the grofs production of the land; and it is alfo conjectured, that when the land-tax is at four fhillings, the proprietors, on an average throughout the kingdom, pay no more than two fhillings in the pound of the prefent value of referved rents. At that rate, therefore, the real neat produce to the proprietors will amount to twenty millions, and the grofs or entire production to fixty millions. —Of this fixty millions in grofs, only one-fixth part pays the tax out of the pockets of the land proprietors; and the remaining five-fixths is paid by the confumers; to wit, labourers, mechanics, manufacturers, and merchants.—Thus, out of the two millions land-tax, part of the ten millions general tax, the landed property, in the firft inftance, pays but the thirtieth part of the whole; the remaining twenty nine thirtieths falling upon commerce and agriculture; or rather upon induftry and ingenuity, even when the land-tax is at the higheft that has ever yet been affeffed.

APPENDIX [C.]

SECRET DEPARTMENT.

Confultation, Wednefday, 15th December, 1779.

READ again the Governor General's propofition for a reply to Mr. Purling's letter, entered in the laft confultation.

Mr. Wheeler.—Although I have little or no concern in the tranfactions, that have reduced the Nabob of Oude to the neceffity of reprefenting his prefent diftrefs to this board, and highly difapprove of the principles on which they were governed; I fubmit to the neceffity of concurring in the prefent motion.

Mr. Francis.—If indifpenfable neceffity alone had been pleaded in defence of the meafure propofed in the governor's motion, I fhould have contented myfelf with enquiring how far the plea might in fact be well founded. It fuppofes an extremity, to which no general reafon can be oppofed. If fuch a cafe exifts at prefent, we may lament the fteps that have reduced our government to a fituation, in which we are compelled to renounce the principles of juftice and good faith, or to incur the hazard of ruin. But we muft yield to facts, by which the claims of right are too often fuperfeded. I muft defire it to be underftood, that it is on this ground alone, I acquiefce in the fubftance of this motion. Many things are
said

APPENDIX [C.]

said in support of it, to which I do not assent. Some of them, I think, are very unfit to be urged to the Nabob.

I have not been long enough in the habits of dominion, to see any thing offensive or alarming in the demand made by an independent prince, to be relieved from the burthen of maintaining a foreign army, which, it is notorious, have devoured his revenues and his country, under colour of defending it.

On what principles do we profess to act towards our neighbours and allies, when a demand apparently so reasonable, is construed into a grievous injury or offence? He tells us, he is no longer able to pay our troops, and desires they may be withdrawn.—It is said, that the principle on which his objections are made, is repugnant with his engagement with the Company. I wish to see his engagement stated, if it exists. With respect to the regular brigade, the treaty of Fyzabad fixes the subsidy he is to pay for it, while it is stationed with him; and the Court of Directors, in their letter of the 15th of December, 1775, approve of their keeping a brigade in the service of the Soubah of Oude, provided it be done with the free consent of the Soubah; but by no means without it.—Concerning this part of the army, however, there is at present no dispute, since the Vizier does not desire to have it recalled. His demand goes solely to the temporary brigade, and independent battalions under Major Hannay and Captain Osborne. The former, he says, is not only quite useless to the government, but is the cause of much loss, both in the revenues and the customs; the latter, he asserts, bring nothing but confusion to the affairs of government, and are entirely their own masters.

If this representation were not strictly true, as I am convinced it is, it would not affect the right and justice of his demand.—The question is, Have we a right to keep an army in his country against his will, and whether he be able to pay them or not? The Governor says, " It is our part, and not his, to judge and determine in what manner, and at what time, these troops shall be reduced or withdrawn." I believe there is no precedent of a treaty of subsidy formed on such a principle. The state that could submit to it, must by the same act renounce its own political existence. In the instance before us, the fact is, that when the temporary brigade was formed out of the Vizier's troops, he was expressly assured by the Governor General, " that the expence of it should remain a fixed charge to him, for so long a time as he should require

the

the corps for his service."—The observations which the court of Directors themselves have made on this part of the transaction, are so exactly in point, and describe the present case with so much precision, that I shall insert their own words, as much better and stronger, than any thing I could say on the subject.

"If by this proposition it is intended to leave the Vizier at liberty to discharge the troops at his pleasure, we think such a stipulation dangerous, and likely to operate to our very great inconvenience; and if more be meant than is expressed, and you intend to exert your influence, first to induce the Vizier to acquiesce in your proposal, and afterwards to compel him to keep the troops in his pay during your pleasure, your intentions are unjust, and a correspondent conduct would reflect great dishonour on the Company."

The motion supposes, not only a necessity of our compelling him to keep those troops in his pay, but that we ourselves should be the collectors of the revenue which is to pay them, which, as things are now managed, is nearly equivalent to putting the country under military contribution. Thus one necessity produces another, and will continue to do so, as long as the Indian states possess any thing that can tempt our avarice, or gratify our ambition, or until we ourselves are taught by experience, that there is some self-wisdom in doing justice to others.

The system which has created our present necessities† does not belong to me, though I am compelled to participate in the measure which they have rendered unavoidable.

Governor General.—I scarce know in what light to regard this minute. It consists solely of objections to the question, except the conclusion, which is an acquiescence in it. If the measures which I have recommended be unjust, if it be contrary to the orders of the Court of Directors, and to the principles of public faith, no consideration should compel us to persevere in it; but other expedients should be suggested, if any others can be devised, or we ought implicitly to yield to the Nabob's demand, especially if it be, as Mr. Francis states it, "apparently so reasonable, and supported by right and justice."

To the assertion, that the system which has created our present necessities does not belong to Mr. Francis, I must beg leave to reply, that it belongs to the administration of this

† Alluding to the Marratta war.

government

government, which formed the exifting treaty with the Nabob Afoph-ul-Dowla, and created a new military eftablifhment for the defence of thofe parts of his dominions, which were interdicted to our troops by the pofitive orders of the Company. Neither Mr. Barwell nor myfelf were efficient parts of that adminiftration. Mr. Francis was; and therefore, in my underftanding of it, the fyftem which has created our prefent neceffities does fpecially, and, with relation to the prefent board, exclufively, belong to him. The treaty which was concluded with the Nabob Sujah Dowla, placed him on the moft refpectable footing, as the fovereign of an independent ftate, and left all his rights untouched, with a provifion for their fecurity againft eventual encroachments upon them; and the duration of his alliance with the Company depended yet more upon the reciprocal and equal advantages which it held out to both parties, than on the formality of a written compact.—This treaty was broken at his death, and a new one, conftructed on far different principles, was made with his fon and fucceffor, by which the latter eventually and neceffarily became a vaffal of the Company, and their interefts bound by fuch ftrong and intricate ties, as muft render it dangerous at any time to feparate them, and fatal to both at fuch a time as this. It would lead me into too wide a difcuffion, to bring proofs of this, by a deduction of all the effects which have been fucceffively derived from this treaty; nor, in this place, is it neceffary. The treaty itfelf is in the hands of the public. Its confequences were forefeen from the commencement of it; and on this occafion, I fhall be content to rely on the general opinion of the world for its fanction of my own. With refpect to the troops appropriated to the defence of the new-acquired dominions of the Nabob of Oude, thefe were raifed at the exprefs folicitation of the prefent Nabob, and by a vote of the prefent adminiftration, in which I had not, as I have before declared, an effective voice, nor any other concern, but in the charge of their firft form, and nominal dependency. Their fubftance is ftill the fame. They were originally engrafted on our own conftitution, and became at once fo intimately united with it, as to implicate it in all the dangers incident to the defects of their firft formation. They have now no feparate or diftinct exiftence, and may be faid properly to confift of our whole military eftablifhment, with the exception only of our European infantry. They cannot be withdrawn without impofing on the Company the additional burthen of their expence, or difbanding of nine battalions of

difciplined

disciplined Sepoys, and three regiments of horse, at a time when our actual strength is confessedly unequal to all the possible exigencies of the extensive dominions, which depend on us for their protection†; and when we should not only lose their services, but must expect to see them become the most active and dangerous instruments in the hands of our enemies. In repeating Mr. Francis's assertion, I do not mean to deduce all the necessities which attend the present state of our connection with the Nabob of Oude, as effects from any system, but only the necessity of maintaining the influence and force which we possess in his country. The disorders of his state, and the dissipation of his revenues, are the effects of his own conduct, which have failed, not so much from the usual effects of incapacity, as from the detestable choice which he has made of the ministers of his power, and the participation of his confidence. I forbear to expatiate further on his character. It is sufficient that I am understood by the members of this board, who must know the truth of my allusions.

As no period was stipulated for the continuance of the temporary brigade, or of the troops which are to supply their place in his service, nor any mode prescribed for withdrawing them; the time and mode of withdrawing them must be guided by such rules, as the necessity and the common interests of both parties shall dictate. These, either he must prescribe, or ourselves, if we cannot agree upon them. In such a division, the strongest must decide. This consequence is inevitable; and I trust that in our decision, we shall be warranted by the strictest principles of justice, of public faith, and of the obligations required by the obligation in which we stand to the Nabob. If we abandon him, or, which would be equivalent to it, if we withdraw the actual defences of his dominions, his ruin must be the consequence, and ours may be drawn after it. No one will affirm, that he is capable of defending them by his own strength, or of providing resources for their defence from his own abilities.

I see many defects in our political system, and especially that part of it which appertains to the Nabob of Oude; but this government wants the present means of correcting them, nor dare I suggest them. Perhaps expedients may be found, for affording the Nabob a gradual relief from the burthen of

---

† And yet Mr. Hastings has invariably pursued plans of extending conquests, and wasting the Company's funds, by an increase of the military establishment, from about six hundred thousand pounds to about two millions of English pounds annually.

which

which he so heavily complains, and it shall be my endeavour to seek out, and to recommend, those means of relief. But these must be gradually applied, and their complete effect may be distant; and this I conceive is all that he can claim of right. At his solicitation, for the purpose of his convenience, and for the support of his interests, these troops were raised. He has no right to require us to disband them to our own hurt, and immediately. I, for my own part, do not attribute the demand to any conviction on the Nabob's mind, by the necessity of his affairs, but to the knowledge which his advisers have acquired of the weakness and divisions of our own government. This is a powerful motive with me, however inclined I might be, upon any other occasion, to yield to some part of his demands, to give them an absolute and unconditional refusal upon the present, and even to bring to punishment, if my influence can produce that effect, those incendiaries who have endeavoured to make themselves the instruments of division between us.

Mr. Francis.—I have acquiesced in the substance of the motion, on the grounds of immediate necessity; and I have combated some of the principles on which it is supported. This distinction is a clear one.

The system of measures to which the conclusion of my former minute alludes, is that general one which has created our present necessities, and which I have uniformly opposed; the Marratta war is a principal part of it.

The establishment of the temporary brigade in the Company's service, was voted about the middle of the year 1777, against the opinion of Sir John Clavering and myself. The corps commanded by Major Hannay and Captain Osborne, are of a still later date.

Whether those acts were a necessary and unavoidable consequence of our lending the Nabob a number of British officers to discipline his own troops, still continuing under his own authority, is a question on which enough has been said already. When the measure was proposed here, it had the concurrence of the Governor General's voice. With respect to the treaty of Fyzabad, I believe it to be the general opinion of the world, that it is a very advantageous one to the Company. The Governor General himself has hitherto declared it so in terms, and the Court of Directors have approved of it highly. In what manner it made the Nabob a vassal of this government, I cannot comprehend.

I have

I have nothing to do with the Vizier's private life or character. He may, or may not, be guilty of the vices imputed to him. The spirit of party is apt to paint all characters in extremes: but I do know, that in this respect, nothing could be more atrocious than the character of his brother Saudut Ally; yet it did not prevent his being perfectly well received in Calcutta. For my own part, I have no wish to be acquainted with either of them.

As to the defence of the Vizier's dominions, and the ruin which would ensue if our troops were withdrawn, I shall only say, that I know of no enemies he has, but those which his actual connections with us may have created.

Governor General.—I have said and repeated, that the establishment of the temporary brigade, was but a continuation of the former measure, though differently modified. As to the corps commanded by Major Hannay and Captain Osborne, it would be immaterial to me, whether they were retained or not. I have no wish to continue them; but when they are made the parts of such a demand, I will not separate them in the reply, which I advise to be made to him. They might be of the greatest utility. The Nabob renders them useless, and defeats the purposes of their appointment, and then proposes their abolition.

I well remember, that my assent was given to the general proposition for disbanding the licentious and expensive multitude, which composed the Nabob's army, and substituting a corps disciplined and commanded by British officers in its stead; but I had no share in the formation of this corps, nor did I approve of it. Many measures passed at that time, of which I did not approve, although I did not think it necessary, nor consistent with my public duty, to make an effectual opposition to them, and to impede the course of those affairs, which I was not allowed to conduct. The sense which I have now expressed of the treaty of Fyzabad, is such as I have always entertained of it. As I do not know the passage to which Mr. Francis alludes as a contradiction of this opinion, I cannot say whether it will or will not admit of that conclusion; although I will readily admit, and must admit, the advantages which the Company immediately derived from the treaty.

Mr. Francis was surely not aware of the injury which he did me, in ascribing to the spirit of party the character which I gave of Asoph-ul-Dowla. He himself knows it to be true. He has had as authentic means of knowing it as I
have;

have; and it is one of thofe notorieties which fuperfeded the neceffity of any evidence. Why his character fhould be contrafted with that of his brother Saudut Ally, I know not; the fubject did not require it; I was forced to the allufion which I made, by the imputation which appeared to me to be caft upon this government, of having caufed the evils which prevail in the government of the Nabob of Oude; which I could only anfwer by afcribing them to their real caufe, the character and conduct of the Nabob of Oude. Mr. Francis miftakes, if he fuppofes that I am hurt by any reflection that may be caft on Saudut Ally; or that I fhall ftand forth in his vindication: I have heard the fame imputations caft on Saudut Ally with fome others; which, becaufe they had relation to the peace of this town, I made a ftrict and formal enquiry into them, and found them to be totally falfe. Thefe charges may be true; but let them be admitted, What reference has his character to the prefent queftion? Were his vices, in a ten-fold degree, greater than they are, they have not affected nor influenced the difficulties to which our debates have alluded. Nor, whatever may be the character of his brother, fhall I ever draw any conclufion from it, by which the obligation of our engagements to him may be affected.

Mr. Francis.—The opinion of the Governor General, concerning the treaty of Fyzabad, is recorded on the 14th of September, 1775, in the following words:

" As, however, the treaty which has been concluded is very advantageous to the Company, it is my wifh that it may be confirmed by the honourable Court: but I take the liberty of recommending, that your orders may be fuch, as may tend to conciliate the mind of the Nabob, and to remove the apprehenfion of any future encroachments on his dominions."

Governor General.—I fhall let the opinion which Mr. Francis has quoted, pafs without a comment. I find it to be a part of a letter addreffed by me fingly, to the Court of Directors, and I do not believe that any perfon who reads it with a candid attention, will find it inconfiftent with my prefent opinion. I defire that the whole paragraph may be added, after the quotation made of it by Mr. Francis.—viz.

" You will receive, in our proceedings of the 6th of June, a copy of the new treaty which has been concluded with the Nabob Afoph-ul-Dowla. You are already acquainted with my my opinion, that our engagements with the late Vizier† were equally binding upon us with regard to his successor; and, consequently, that we could not with justice make any further demands upon him; and you will find by our consultations,

"That this was so strongly the idea of the Nabob Asophul-Dowla, that for some time he seemed resolved, rather to dispense with the assistance of our army, than to submit to new terms. Although, therefore, upon more mature consideration of his inability to maintain himself without our support, the necessity of his affairs has obliged him to acquiesce, I doubt not but he is at heart dissatisfied at the measures which have been taken; and the express limitation of the present engagement to his life, will naturally encourage an opinion, that upon his death we shall make still further demands. As, however, the treaty which has been concluded is very advantageous to the Company, it is my wish that it may be confirmed by your honourable Court; but I take the liberty of recommending, that your orders may be such as may tend to conciliate the mind of the Nabob, and to remove the apprehension of any future encroachments on his dominions. For these purposes, I submit the propriety of your giving peremptory instructions to your administration in Bengal, to be particularly attentive to support and befriend him; to maintain him in the possession of the Rohilla country, without making the demands upon him, to which you are intitled by the 7th article; and that, in case of his death, the present treaty shall be confirmed with his successor: and to make known these orders to the Nabob. I recommend this with the greater confidence, as it is so intirely consistent with the tenor of your former commands, and particularly the second paragraph of your instructions to the commissioners, of the 15th of September, 1769, wherein you direct them to make known to the powers in India, that it is by no means the intention of the Company to encroach upon their neighbours; but that they are determined to confine their views to the revenue of Bengal, and their present possessions‡." To maintain the Nabob in the possession, seems necessary indeed to enable him to make his stipulated payments to the Company; and I am persuaded, that the knowledge of our resolution to do so,

† Alluding to the treaty of Benares, in September, 1773.
‡ Yet, however generally and openly has Mr. Hastings disobeyed the very commands which he thus pointedly quotes and refers back, for their future government.

will

will alone be sufficient to effect the purpose, as no power of Hindostan will in that case venture to invade it."

Mr. Barwell.—I confess I do not understand how an acquiescence can be given to the Governor General's motion, and the principle on which it is made denied. Such an acquiescence doth, in fact, assert all that is advanced in the letter proposed to be written to our resident, and to be urged to the Nabob, to be false, and yet to authorise the falsity. The proposed letter asserts, that he stands engaged to our government to maintain the English armies, that have been formed for the protection of his dominions : and that it is our part, not his, to determine in what manner, and at what time, these shall be reduced or withdrawn ; that this right is in our government; and that the Nabob cannot dismiss any part of our troops without our leave, I affirm, upon the very principle on which we undertook a defence of his dominions, at his own request. A principle understood at that time by Mr. Francis, and acquiesced in by every other member of the Council. The subject was introduced to us by the following letter from Mr. Bristow.

Extract of a letter from Mr. Bristow, recorded in Consultation, the 29th of November, 1775.

" I addressed the honourable Board on the 6th instant; since which the Nabob having maturely weighed the bad consequences which will inevitably ensue, if order be not introduced into his army, he requests of me to apply to the honourable Board for their assistance in effecting this very important measure.

" The mode he particularly points out, is to beg the favour of the honourable Board to furnish him with English officers to fix battalions of Sepoys, as well as for the corps of artillery and cavalry in proportion ; which would at all times be a sufficient cheque on his other troops, and serve to strengthen his government. He has not mentioned his desire for any particular arrangement of this corps, which he submits entirely to the consideration of the Board, and engages to have the pay regularly discharged.

" The honourable Board are well able to judge of the expediency of this measure; I humbly conceive it would be greatly to the advantage of the Company, as a very considerable force would be hereby obtained ; for although this corps is to be paid by the Nabob, and maintained for the support of his government, yet it may be subordinate to the

honourable

honourable Board, whenever they pleafe to make it fo; at the. fame time, that order and regularity will be thus introduced, the Nabob will be difabled from forming projects to the detriment of the Company; and, in cafe of accidents, the fucceffion will be eafily fecured in the line the honourable Board may judge the moft. advifeable for the peace of Hindoftan, which, of all other points, is the moft material, as an ambitious and ill-difpofed prince in the poffeffion of thefe Soubas (collecting above three crores of rupees a year, and maintaining a hundred thoufand fighting men) might prove dangerous to the Company's exiftence."

Conformably to the foregoing letter, the Board's refolutions were difpatched to Mr. Briftow, as follow:

Extract of a letter to Mr. Briftow, in Confultation, the 29th of November, 1775.

" We have received your letter of the 7th inftant. At prefent we have only to fignify our approbation in general, of the fyftem you have propofed for curbing the refractory fpirit of the Nabob's troops, and introducing regularity in his army, by the appointment of Britifh officers. In a few days we fhall confider the fubject, and form fuch arrangements as may be neceffary for this purpofe, which we fhall immediately communicate to you, together with our fentiments upon the plan of 'regulations propofed by Murtiza Cawn, which we have ordered to be tranflated."

By this we adopted, what Mr. Briftow recommended, and. referved to ourfelves the future arrangements that might be propofed for fuch troops. The fubject was again taken up in confultation on the 14th December, 1775; and General Clavering, agreeably to this principle, delivered himfelf in the following words:

" I beg leave to offer my opinion, that the affiftance to be given to the Nabob of Oude, fhould be ftrictly confined to his requeft; that is to fay, to fix battalions of infantry, and to a proportion of cavalry and artillery agreeably to this requifition. I take the liberty to offer my idea on the formation of fuch a body of troops as he feems to require. That the infantry confift of 4,200 men, divided into fix battalions, each to confift of 700 men, and two battalions to form one regiment; the regiments to be commanded by captains, and the battalions lieutenants, aided by a cadet, as an adjutant and quarter-mafter; and that, as the Company now poffefs a great number of fupernumerary black officers, that a proper proportion

proportion of them be allowed to each battalion. I think that one company of artillery, confisting of one hundred men, will be sufficient for one regiment, and to be attached to it, commanded by a lieutenant. According to this plan, there will be required three captains to command the three regiments, six lieutenants to command the six battalions, and six cadets to be quarter-masters and adjutants, and three lieutenants for the artillery. The cavalry, I think, should confist of six regiments of six hundred men each, divided into six troops and three squadrons; this body will then confist of 3,600 men. I would recommend that each regiment be commanded by a captain, and each squadron by a lieutenant appointed to command two troops, which will then confist of one hundred men each; and that an ensign be appointed to act as adjutant and quarter-master to each regiment. The whole corps, amounting to 8,100 men, will be, I conceive, fully sufficient for the defence of the Douab and the Rohilla country for the prefent, and will be as many as the Nabob will find funds to pay. If any member of this board shall think that this corps is too great, or too little, it may be easily reduced or augmented by the same proportions."

"Agreed to the plan proposed by General Clavering, for regulating the troops of the Nabob Asoph-ul-Dowla, by the appointment of English officers to his army, and to recommend to him the reduction proposed by the Governor General." The recommendation of the Governor General is, that he be desired to dismiss a great part of the useless rabble which he now keeps in his pay; and still to shew this principle more strongly influencing the Board, General Clavering follows the resolution, by recommending in addition, that the Nabob be also advised to employ English officers upon the same system, to command his body-guard, and any increased number of forces that he may find it necessary to take into his service, beyond the proposed establishment. These resolutions are followed by another on the 18th of December, 1775, in these words, "Resolved also, that this Board reserves to itself the right of recalling the whole or any part of these officers allotted to the Nabob's service, whenever it may be thought necessary." When this measure took place, the governor of Oude was in the utmost distraction, owing to the causes that are enumerated in the representations received at that time. The question simply now is, whether we shall allow the Nabob to revert to a system which was attended with such pernicious effects, as to risque the overthrow of his government;

vernment; or, whether we shall adhere to the policy that influenced us to step forth, and to take charge of the military force of his country? The Nabob's ability to pay the English establishments I cannot question, while I have before me the letter of Mr. Bristow, which states his revenue at three crores of rupees, and the estimated demand upon him by the Company, as stated by our resident, amounts only to 136,12,188:12; and this sum is not a yearly rent charge, but includes articles that ought to have been paid by the Nabob, so long since as in the residency of Mr. Bristow at his court, viz.—The balance of the debt due to the Company, 20,60,688:19; the donation to the army, ten lacks; and the private debts contracted with the officers of his army in that period, 7,59,109. These, taken with the gross amount, would reduce the current demand of the year to 97,92,471:10 rupees.

I regard the forces paid by the Nabob of Oude as part of a large military establishment, totally independent upon the Company. Policy will neither allow us to reduce our own strength, nor to increase, independent of it, that of a prince who, with such a revenue as he possesses, might become a formidable enemy. As the distresses of the Soubah of Oude compelled him to put the military force of the country into the hands of our government, without any stipulation whatever, or any reservation of right in himself to resume it into his own hands, it would be a breach of the duty we owe to the nation, to yield up so great a portion of its real strength. I therefore most heartily concur in the Governor General's motion; and, without any reserve, adopt all the reasoning on which he made and defended it.

Mr. Francis.—Mr. Bristow's letter, I presume, contains the best reasons that occurred to him in support of the measure, and such as he thought most likely to recommend it to our approbation. But neither doth he any where suppose, that the Vizier was bound to maintain the corps under British officers as long as we thought proper, without reserving to himself the power of dismissing them; nor would any private opinion of our resident, communicated only to us, if in reality it had only amounted to the meaning ascribed to it by Mr. Barwell, constitute an obligation upon the Vizier. The question is, whether there does exist between the Vizier and this government any specific stipulation, by which he is bound to maintain the troops in question, as long as we think proper? If there does, I am totally unacquainted with it.

Governor

Governor General.—I muſt beg leave to add a word or two in anſwer to this laſt minute. When the board formally adopted the reaſoning† of Mr. Briſtow, it becomes their own, and I preſume they are bound by it. If it be true, which may be granted, that there is no ſpecific ſtipulation, by which the Nabob is bound to maintain the troops as long as we think proper—neither is there any ſpecific ſtipulation, by which we are bound to diſband them, or take their pay upon ourſelves, at any inſtant in which he ſhall think proper to demand it: and this I take to be the point immediately appertaining to the queſtion.

Approved the draught of a letter to Mr. Purling, and agreed, that it be wrote to him accordingly.

Agreed.—That the Governor General be requeſted to write a letter on this occaſion to the Vizier—the following draught of which is accordingly prepared and approved.

To the Nabob of Oude.

" I have received your Excellency's letter, informing me (recapitulate the contents of the letter) I have likewiſe ſeen a letter from your excellency to Mr. Purling, the reſident at your court, to the ſame effect.

" It is a cauſe of equal concern and ſurpriſe to me, that you ſhould object or heſitate to grant tuncaws for the charges of an eſtabliſhment which was formed at your own particular ſolicitation, for the defence of Rohilcund and the Douab, at a juncture when your ancient and natural enemies the Marrattas are actually in arms, and ready to enter your dominions upon the firſt opening which ſhall be given them; nothing in my opinion will deter them from it, but the preſence of a formidable and well-regulated body of troops to oppoſe them. The dangerous conſequences of their entering your country, and finding it in a defenceleſs condition, are too obvious and ſtriking for me to mention; yet this muſt certainly be the caſe, if the Company's forces allotted to its protection be withdrawn or diſbanded. You are not to imagine, becauſe you have enjoyed an uninterrupted ſeaſon of peace for ſome years paſt, that you have no enemies to interrupt you, and may therefore reſt in ſecurity, without the expence of maintaining the force. On the contrary, it is to their power that you owe this tranquility. And the neighbouring ſtates, whoſe annual incurſions and ravages in the territories of your

† Perhaps the plan without the reaſoning

late father of blessed memory were the cause of the Company's troops being first applied for, and stationed in your dominions, to repel them, will not fail to disturb you again, as soon as this bulwark is removed, and the nakedness of your country will invite them. Exclusive of this important consideration, I think it proper to inform your Excellency, that I understand a mutual obligation between us to have been implied in the formation and maintenance of this establishment. The Company are bound, on the one hand, to protect your dominions by its means; and you are bound, on the other, to defray the charges of it. While these terms are complied with on both sides, neither has a right to complain. But you could never have supposed, when you applied to us to appoint this force for your service, that the Company would be at the pains to raise and discipline so large a body of men, and to augment their establishment by the addition of such an extraordinary number of officers as were necessary to command them, if they were liable to be burthened with the sole weight and expence of this force, by a sudden resolution on your part to discharge them, without previous and timely notice given to us, and our consent received; and this too at such a distance from the Company's possessions, as the countries in which they are now stationed.

I am convinced, that a resolution so pernicious to the real interests of your government, so repugnant to the intimate connection which subsists between us, and so dangerous in the end, both to your possessions and the Company's, cannot have been suggested to you by any but secret enemies to your state; and that, on a mature consideration of the case, this advice will appear to you as insidious as it does to me. I therefore recommend to you in the strongest manner, not only to shun the evil councils of such false friends, but to dismiss them from your service and confidence, as unworthy of both. I beg you to consider, that it is equally my inclination and interest, to endeavour to provide for the support of your government, and the defence of your dominions against the power of invasion of a foreign enemy. For this purpose, General Coote has thought it adviseable to visit the different stations of the army in your country; and he will be constantly attentive to take means for your security, while your dependence is placed on the Company's alliance and assistance; but if you are determined to withdraw yourself from both,

and

and to diffolve the union which has fo long fubfifted between your family and this government, I expect that fufficient time and notice of your intention be given, to prevent our being involved in troubles, from the hafty execution of it. I cannot confent to your difmiffing the Company's troops at fuch a diftance from home, and at fuch a crifis; nor can I at prefent agree to recall them. As much time at leaft muft be given to difpofe of this force, when you fhall have no further occafion for their fervice, as was allowed for the raifing of it. I therefore requeft, that you will attend to the reprefentations of Mr. Purling, who has been ordered again to apply to you, in the name of this government, for tuncaws for the neceffary difburfements of the current year. And although your revenues have fuffered a diminution by the unfortunate failure of the harveft, yet I am perfuaded, that there will be fufficient, with œconomy and attention, to anfwer every fervice required from them; and that you will therefore chearfully comply with the demand which Mr. Purling is ordered to make. At all events, the defence of your country is the firft object to be attended to, and the regular payment of a well difciplined body of troops is indifpenfably neceffary for this end. Add to this, that your engagements to the Company are of fuch a nature, as to oblige me to require and infift on your granting tuncaws for the full amount of their demands upon you for the current year, and on your referving funds fufficient to anfwer them, even fhould the deficiency of your revenues compel you to leave your own troops unprovided for, or to difband a part of them, to enable you to effect it."

Agreed.—That a copy of thefe papers be tranfmitted to the Commander in Chief, with the following letter:

" To Lieutenant General Sir Eyre Coote, K. B. Commander in Chief, &c. &c.

" Sir,

" In a letter which we received from Mr. Purling, under date the 19th ult. we are informed of the Vizier's refufal to grant tuncaws for the expences of the Company's forces, allotted to the defence of his dominions in Rohilcund and the

Douab,

Douab, for this year. As we cannot, by any means, consent to this ill-timed and sudden dismission of that part of our establishment, we have written letters to the Nabob and Mr. Purling, of which we inclose copies for your information.— We request that you will add your personal influence to the arguments we have urged to the Nabob, and assist with your endeavours to give effect to the application which will be made to him by Mr. Purling.

                        " We are, with esteem, &c."

Fort William,
   15th Dec. 1779.

FINIS.

www.ingramcontent.com/pod-product-compliance
Lightning Source LLC
Chambersburg PA
CBHW032111230426
43672CB00009B/1699